THE
TRAVELING
SKIER

THE
TRAVELING
SKIER

★ 20 ★
★ FIVE-STAR ★
SKIING
VACATIONS
★
ANDREW SLOUGH

DOUBLEDAY

NEW YORK
LONDON
TORONTO
SYDNEY
AUCKLAND

PUBLISHED BY DOUBLEDAY

a division of Bantam Doubleday Dell Publishing Group, Inc.
666 Fifth Avenue, New York, New York 10103

DOUBLEDAY and the portrayal of an anchor with a dolphin
are trademarks of Doubleday,
a division of Bantam Doubleday Dell Publishing Group, Inc.

Library of Congress Cataloging-in-Publication Data

Slough, Andrew.
The traveling skier : 20 five-star skiing vacations / Andrew
Slough.
p.   cm. — (Traveling sportsman)
1. Skis and skiing—Guide-books. 2. Ski resorts—Guide-books.
I. Title. II. Series.
GV854.S588   1991
796.93—dc20   90-28368
CIP

ISBN 0-385-41133-2

BOOK DESIGN BY SIGNET M DESIGN, INC.
ILLUSTRATIONS BY DEBORAH READE

CONTENTS

CONTENTS

FOREWORD

I FIRST MET ANDY SLOUGH TWELVE YEARS AGO BY *phone.*

My publisher was having an apoplectic fit over a short piece on Sun Valley, Idaho, that my executive editor had assigned to Andy, a Sun Valley local and peripatetic young writer whose work—then largely regional in scope—we had admired.

Andy had written a hard-hitting piece that told of the on-again, off-again relationship between the mountain company and the town. It certainly wasn't a resort PR man's dream, but it was forceful, thoughtful writing, and it gave the Ski reader new insight on a resort that had long been placed reverentially on the pedestal of legends. It also prompted the people who ran the resort to call Ski's publisher to complain.

So the first time I actually spoke with Andy Slough it was with the intent of telling him not to write any more stories that destroyed the health and well-being of magazine publishers. But I was so impressed by his earnestness and candor that before hanging up I asked him to field three more articles for me.

Andy Slough is unique among ski writers. In a field rife with hyperbole, he is refreshingly honest. Andy's interests and insights also go beyond the mountains—to the towns and the people who populate them and provide the ski experience. His snoopings and wanderings are exhaustive, as you'll find in the dozens of tidbits that serve so aptly as spice and condiments for his yarns—from neat side trips and colorful mountain guides to ski schools and both cheap and top-dollar eats. In fact, it's Andy's ability to poke around a story's fringes—who else can tell you about places like No Grease Maurice's, Shady Lady, Levensky's Pizza, and Scissor Bill's?—that has for years endeared him to Ski's readers.

It certainly doesn't hurt that Andy is also a skier—a very good one—and that he writes from a skier's perspective. Let others gush about food, about health clubs, about the après-ski scene and drop a dozen trail names to impress while they're at it. Such is the stuff of directories, which this is not. And in the end, that's what's so downright charming about The Traveling Skier. *Its disparate and altogether exhilarating ski experiences will transport you to exotic places and rarefied altitudes. More important, it will introduce you to Andy Slough, whom you will come to consider a companion, compatriot, and good skiing friend.*

That Andy's journeys take us from Ashton, Idaho, to Switzerland's St. Moritz—the big, the small, the swank, the sweet, the well-mannered, the ill-mannered, the familiar and the exotic— happens to be a bonus.

In describing an especially memorable day of skiing in his wide-eyed and ingenuous way, Andy admits, "It's tough not to abuse superlatives." After reading this first book by one of the world's most gifted ski writers, I could not have said it better.

RICHARD NEEDHAM
EDITOR
Ski Magazine

INTRODUCTION

THE ASSIGNMENT WAS A WRITER'S DREAM. PICK twenty of the world's best ski adventures and write them up as you see fit. Forget the typical bed-and-breakfast review; from the beginning this book was intended to focus on the essence of skiing—those rare powder days that appear only once in many seasons. Or those moments of high adventure in Switzerland's Haute Route, the Soviet Union's Caucasus Mountains or New Zealand's Southern Alps. Closer to home, it offered a chance to explore the world-class runs of Steamboat, Sun Valley, Snowbird, and Whistler. It invited me to listen to Mozart in Salzburg, Austria, watch a Shakespearean play in Ashland, Oregon, and visit the Winter Carnival in Stowe.

If a problem existed in writing this book, it was which of the world's hundreds of ski areas would make the final cut. What criteria do you use? Vertical drop and skiable acres? Number of lifts, snow depths, and après entertainment? Or is it combinations of the above that produce incandescent memories of a resort? This last is closer to the truth. Admittedly one writer can only ski a small percentage of the world's great mountains, and those that remain unseen and unskied offer compelling reasons to book a flight or hit the road.

As a general note, skiing is weather-dependent, and though 9 feet of snow can fall in December, February and March are traditionally the most dependable months in the Northern Hemisphere. July and August are your best bets below the equator. Also, with the exception of the Soviet Union, credit cards are universally accepted by ski resort accommodations, and transportation from major airports to mountain resorts is usually painless. By using the information contained in the sidebars, you can easily reproduce any trip in this book. So the only question is, what's keeping you?

THE
TRAVELING
SKIER

CHAPTER 1

THE MYTHICAL ST. MORITZ

"AHEAD OF US YOU CAN SEE ST. MORITZ'S world-famous bobsled run," the taxi driver comments as he downshifts into second and the tachometer soars through the red line. The Mercedes sedan drifts toward a melting tunnel of blue ice as the coppery taste of fear flushes through my mouth. I try to relax and am a millisecond from assuming the position airlines recommend for crash landings when the car careens out of the hairpin and accelerates down the next straight.

"A month ago you could have run the bob. Now, of course, too much has melted," the driver observes as the Mercedes hurtles next to the hanging blue gutter at fifty miles an hour— on this twisting road, a suicidal rate that reduces budding trees, stained snowbanks, and rock retaining walls to a blur.

A month late or not, I already know what St. Moritz's world famous bob run looks, tastes, and feels like; know the rattle of the runners and the scrape of the sides on glare ice; recognize

1

the queasy lift of my stomach as the Mercedes enters a corner and the prickle of neck hair when it exits. My knees are braced against the front seat, my shoulder strap is cinched to the stop, and my heart has been getting an aerobic workout since the cab picked me up ten minutes ago at the Post-Platz in front of the Hotel Steffani.

Zurich is St. Moritz's nearest major airport and is serviced by Swissair with direct flights from New York, Los Angeles, Chicago and Boston. Reservations: (800) 221-4750. The Swiss rail system offers connections from Zurich to St. Moritz. The Swiss Rail Holiday Card is a great deal. It allows unlimited travel on Swiss trains, postal buses, and certain ferries for a specified amount of time (one week, two weeks, etc.). For more information: Swiss National Tourist Office, 250 Stockton Street, San Francisco, California 94108, tel. (415) 362-2260. Or in New York: 608 Fifth Avenue, New York, New York 10020, tel. (212) 757-5844.

★

If most articles on St. Moritz amount to bed-and-breakfast critiques that focus on where to eat, where to sleep, and where to watch the rich and famous air their Afghans, they also typically ignore the skiing in favor of horse racing, snow polo, snow golf, skating, and shopping. As a result, anyone reading about St. Moritz's "Champagne Climate" remembers only the strong Swiss franc, the celebrity balls, and the health spas.

"Champagne's expensive," they observe, turning to the next page. For that reason you rarely meet anyone who has actually skied in St. Moritz.

St. Moritz sits on the Italian border an hour north of the tropical Lake Como, 123 miles or roughly three hours by train from Zurich. Climbing a hillside above the isthmus between Lake Champfèr and Lake San Murezzan, the resort faces the 14,000-

St. Moritz offers a range of hotels for any budget. At the top of the list—and overlooking the lake and ice rink on Via Serlas—is the five-star **Badrutt's Palace**, tel. 2-11-01. Amenities: 350 beds, garden and park, numerous restaurants, dancing, sauna, indoor and outdoor swimming pools, squash, solarium, gymnasium, central to ski runs, bowling, hair dryers, pets. Terms: $136–$232 half pension per person per day.

Hotel Steffani is also centrally located on Via Somplaz, tel. 2-21-01. Amenities: 120 beds, indoor swimming pool, sauna, day nursery/playroom, garage, aerobics, whirlpools, solarium, gymnasium, central location to ski runs, rooms with balcony, hairdresser in hotel, pets permitted. Terms: $72–$88 per person, breakfast included.

Or, within a short walk of the baths is **Hotel Bernina**, tel. 3-60-22. Amenities: 55 beds, private bath, parking, restaurant, color TV, quiet location, central to ski runs, pets accepted. Terms: $48–$56 per person, breakfast included.

Information and central booking agency, Ch-7500, St. Moritz, Switzerland; tel. 3-31-47 (48).

★

foot Grison peaks—Palu, Bellavista, Bernina, and Roseg. In winter, while St. Moritz's narrow streets still lie in blue shadow, these towering faces flare pink and yellow in the rising sun. Walking in ski boots across Post-Platz to catch the bus that connects to the Silvaplana tram, I inhale the heady fumes of fresh croissants and Swiss coffee, the faint, rich aroma of Gruyère cheese, the cold cuts and fruit that characterize a typical Swiss breakfast. Though I ate at the Hotel Steffani, I am still tempted by the blueberry pastry and the Lindt hazelnut chocolate bar in the bakery window. Across the Platz, however, the bus is pulling to a stop and I must to run to catch it.

On a spring morning in St. Moritz, temperatures hang in the

twenties, and I catch the tram across the lake from Silvaplana to a ridge below Corvatsch's 11,319-foot summit. Here the sun fills the mountain restaurant, tempting me to linger over a hot chocolate *mit Schlag* before dropping into the shadowed runs below. With four resorts to ski in as many days, time is valuable, and for now I skip the chocolate, step into my skis, stretch out, and accelerate down the groomed piste. In the early morning, with the cool air pushing behind my goggles and the Grisons rising in my peripheral vision, I concentrate on carving long arcs in the hard glacial snow as the terrain unfolds endlessly below.

Corvatsch offers everything from immaculately groomed pistes to bone-crushing bumps to extreme chutes. "Let the skier beware" sums up the Swiss attitude toward litigation, and if you plan to test the limits, make sure your liability, life, and health insurance are paid up. You'll want to have a clear mind, since St. Moritz has superb off-piste skiing, much of it off Corvatsch's south backside into Sils-Maria, a small village above Lake Segl. If you have an unerring sense of direction you can probably navigate the series of open faces, ice falls, and chutes that lead to the valley. If not (and especially after a new snowfall), hire a ski instructor to show you the way. If the snowpack is stable, this offers some of the best powder and corn skiing in the area.

Facing Corvatsch on the opposite of Lake Champfèr, Nair is known for its intermediate terrain. Accessed by a network of lifts that service 4100 vertical feet and miles of groomed pistes, and with its southern exposure, Nair's snow turns to corn in the midmorning, and from then until early afternoon, you can ski the shadow lines, areas where the surface hangs in suspended animation—neither slush nor crust, but a delicate inversion between the two. The Swiss insist skiing is a total experience. Admittedly chasing vertical feet is part of their vacation, but just as important are immaculate hotels, haute cuisine, and shops that stock more than souvenirs. St. Moritz may not be Europe's cheapest ski resort, but the adage "you get what you pay for" is especially true here. Years afterward no one remembers what a week in the Engadine Valley cost, only the clean swimming pools and streets, the white table-cloths at breakfast, the trams and groomed pistes and mountain restaurants, and the views.

Along with Corvatsch and Nair ski areas, you should ski Diavolezza and Lagalb up the valley from Pontresina or Sils beyond Silvaplana. Though smaller than the St. Moritz resorts, both Diavolezza and Lagalb offer excellent terrain. Diavolezza mixes intimidating steeps with advanced intermediate pistes, while Lagalb is more of a true intermediate resort. Lagalb's mountain restaurant makes its own excellent fresh pasta daily, which you can try after a long off-piste run down into Italy near Fórcola di Livigno.

If too much publicity can be a bad thing, St. Moritz suffers from it. Even if they have never been here, skiers are convinced they know all about it. Because St. Moritz is so famous, they know it's too expensive. At $125 per night (breakfast included) at the Hotel Steffani, it is pricey, but that's four stars, and if all you need is a room and breakfast, there's the Corvatsch for $68.

Everyone also knows it's too crowded. But during the high season lift lines are short, and in the spring, nonexistent. Too touristy? Too socially frigid? The neighboring hot-blooded Italians would never allow it.

Few know that St. Moritz hosted the Winter Olympics in 1928 and then again in 1948, or that its spa is internationally recognized for its treatment of rheumatic diseases and circulation and kidney dysfunctions. Almost no one knows that Romansch, one of Switzerland's five official languages, is still spoken in the Engadine's tributary valleys. And fewer still are aware that St. Moritz has 250 miles of marked runs, sixty trams and chair lifts, nine mountain restaurants, four hundred ski instructors, and 100 miles of cross country tracks. But then everyone does know that Prince Charles skis here.

He doesn't.

Though written records date tourism in St. Moritz to the fourteenth century, when pilgrims came to drink from its ferruginous springs, archaeological evidence pushes human habitation in the area back three thousand years. By the mid-eighteenth century St. Moritz had built a reputation around the springs, which, according to the writer Heigelin, tasted "like the sharpest vinegar which goes to the head and is like champagne in the nose." (Recent analysis reveal that the water's iron and carbonic acid help anemia.) Baths were subsequently built near the springs, which were thereafter known as St. Moritz Bad. Hotels soon followed, and by 1859 a newspaper reported that a total of 450 travelers had visited the resort in a single year. By 1910 that number had grown to 10,000, which today would amount to an average weekend.

While in St. Moritz you should take advantage of its mineral springs. Treatments include mineral baths ($17.50), free drinking cures, peat baths ($28) and packs, the Kneipp Cure ($6.50–$20.00), and physical therapy ($17.50–$32.00). For more information: Tourist office, Ch-7500, St. Moritz, Switzerland; tel. 3-31-47.

★

Along with Nair, Corvatsch, Lagalb, and Diavolezza, St. Moritz also offers heli-skiing in the Albigna Range—a rugged basalt-and-ice monolith that rises 20 miles southeast of the city center.

That's why my taxi driver is testing even the liberal Swiss speed limits to get to the Bell Ranger on time.

Spring helicopter skiing in southern Switzerland embodies a guaranteed Icarus complex—that sense of limitless freedom and spontaneous joy that tempted the son of Daedalus into his high-altitude go-round with the sun. Hanging from a four-hundred-horsepower rotor and hurtling at 100 miles per hour around rock outcroppings, I savor omnipotence and vulnerability—exhilaration and repentance.

Heli-skiing is great fun—in fact, too much fun—and fragmented lines about man and god and the madness that separates one from the other appear in the clean mountain air. The rising sun is casting long shadows across the snow fields, and for an instant I wish the pilot would haul back on the stick, pour the high octane to the turbine, and let this baby climb. For an unfettered moment I wish the towering peaks above would slowly recede to ripples in the green plane of Western Europe, while the morning's soft gold light fades to deep purple and the sun grows in stark relief against the infinity of space.

Like Icarus, that last image carries it a heartbeat too far. Belted into the backseat, I feel the airframe vibrate as the rotor cat scratches for a purchase in the thin air. Not that the Ranger creates any cause for alarm. It's all power and dependability— a miracle of modern engineering that's best used for lifting skiers onto isolated ridges. Topping out over the Engadine Range and Lake Silvaplana, the world is framed in black rock, glaciers, and rotten lake ice. Between one and the other are long, sinuous runs that Peter Leutwyler admits are, unfortunately, off-limits. Leutwyler owns and is one of three Bergführers for the guide service "A Special Way of Skiing."

For information and prices contact: Peter Leutwyler, St. Moritz Experience, 7512 Champfèr, St. Moritz, Switzerland; tel 3-77-14 or 3-29-52.

"Switzerland is different from your Rockies," he says, ducking slightly to study the surrounding peaks. "It is smaller and more densely populated. It is impossible to simply ski where we please. We have many runs scattered across four major ranges, but our license is very specific about landing and pickup points."

Leutwyler explains that with a confederation dating back to the thirteenth century, Switzerland is both singularly democratic and passionately independent, and the image of a helicopter on final approach scattering even a single Schweizer's Sunday picnic scratches across the social grain. This place-for-every-recreation-and-a-recreation-for-every-place attitude is simply one thread in a rich social tapestry that has made Switzerland the richest country per capita in Europe.

The Ranger settles onto a southwest-facing saddle below Mt. Cantone's summit; hesitates just long enough to unload skis, packs, and poles; then lifts, rotates, and descends toward the distant toe of the glacier. With the throb of its rotor echoing against the valley's vertical rock walls, Peter adjusts his pack and slowly pushes off.

I wish I could claim perfection shadowed those first turns. I wish that first run were all carving skis and toothy grins in an unnamed couloir. But we are half an hour early onto that west face, and for most of that first run we ski boilerplate. Not that the run doesn't spawn its own unique images of sliding wall-to-wall down frozen gun barrels, of the deserted Albigna Hut, or of spectacular 360-degree horizons and Leutwyler's powerful edge sets as he steps from one ski to the other. But in all truth the run is more visual than visceral, and as we load into the helicopter for another run, we anticipate perfection. If it exists for a skier, it will exist here.

Minutes later the Ranger flares above a smooth, steep slope that descends in sinuous hollows and rolling hummocks to a distant frozen reservoir. At ten A.M. the Val Albigna is hazy from moisture precipitating off the southeast faces. Even as we step into our skis, a faint blue aura shimmers above the highest peaks, signaling a rapid metamorphosis from boilerplate to silk.

During those first turns, we may be skiing in Switzerland, but our edges still speak English. Corn snow! Central Rockies or Southern Grisons, the feel of a ski carving across its satiny surface translates perfectly. Corn! Married to the sunline, which even now is casting our shadows toward the valley floor, for this morning at least, it is our raison d'être. Forget that spring holds sway on the valley floor. Forget the birds singing in the larch pines. Forget St. Moritz's shops, the restaurants, the hotels, and the beautiful people sunning in sidewalk cafes. For the next two hours the corn is as good as it gets.

A seductive face drops into a round bowl that leads in turn to a vertical drop through black rocks. We skirt yawning crevasses and ice-blue cliffs, dodge basalt outcroppings and awakening lichens, carve figure eights and hold high-speed tucks across the flats, link endless turns for the sheer thrill of pushing on an edge, and when we finally reach the helicopter, wish out loud that we could fix the sun in the sky.

Peter pours a dry white wine into gold cups, and I wonder if the mythical horses that pull Apollo's flaming chariot ever pause in their race across the heavens. On a warm spring day do they ever stop to water or nibble new grass? And if they do, does the corn snow also hesitate in its cyclical journey from snowflake to stream and back again? Standing beneath the glacier's sheer blue toe and staring up at our rapidly disappearing tracks, we toast the conditions. Then, following Peter's example, I sacrifice the last sip to the snow.

To reach Saas-Fee and the start of the Haute Route, you

must catch the Glacier Express in the early morning. Running from St. Moritz to Zermatt in just under eight hours, the Express offers a preview of the Haute Route's year-round winter as it crosses 291 bridges, runs through 91 tunnels, and climbs a vertical mile from the lowest valley to the highest pass.

Running from St. Moritz to Zermatt, **The Glacier Express** offers one of the world's most spectacular train rides. Lasting roughly seven and a half hours, the Express passes through the Grisons, Central Switzerland, and the Valais. Dining car, snack cart, and souvenirs available. For information: Swiss National Tourist Office, in New York, San Francisco, and St. Moritz.

During the day the Express passes beneath ice blue glaciers and 40-foot avalanche deposition filled with shattered trees and building-sized boulders. It rushes by belled Simmental cows grazing in green meadows, flowering fruit trees, and lakeside parks, and descending into Andermatt it arrives in Brig in the midafternoon. Packing my skis and bags, I ask a blue suited-Swiss Rail conductor where to find the train to Saas-Fee.

"Saas-Fee?" he says glancing at his watch. "That would be a postal bus. The last one for three hours is about to leave. You must hurry!" And so I gallop through the station like an overloaded mule, down the stairs, and out onto the main street, yelling for the yellow-and-red bus as it pulls out. The driver hits the brakes, then descends to help me with my baggage.

Thanking him, I stagger down the aisle looking for a seat. The bus is almost full, and the effort has winded me. My face is speckled with sweat, and I drop into a seat near the back and nod to the dubious Swiss grandmother across the aisle.

For brochures, hotel listings, restaurants, and flights contact the Swiss National Tourist Office: 250 Stockton Street, San Francisco, California 94108, tel. (415) 362-2260. Or in New York: 608 Fifth Avenue, New York, New York 10020, tel. (212) 757-5944. Or in St. Moritz: Ch-7500, St. Moritz Switzerland, tel. 3-31-47.

REST AND RECUPERATION

When weather or muscles give out, St. Moritz offers first-class shopping along the **Via dal Bagn** in the central city. Also the **Moritz Health Spa** (tel. 3-30-62) will do wonders for aching muscles and jet-lag lethargy. Once revitalized you can try the bobsled run (tel. 3-41-10) One run costs SF130: photo, drink, and certificate included. Or similarly the **Cresta** (tel. 3-31-17), first five rides SF400. Curling (tel. 3-45-88) is SF15 per person, and hang gliding (tel. 3-24-16) with a certified instructor is SF190 including photo, drink, and certificate. Indoor swimming can be found at (tel. 3-60-25), admission SF5. There's ice skating (tel. 3-50-30)—entrance fee and skates for SF9.

St. Moritz also has the **Engadine Museum** (tel. 3-43-33) featuring local history and fauna for an admission of SF4. Try a horse-drawn sleigh ride from St. Moritz-Bad to Meierei and return for SF75. Or horseback riding (tel. 3-57-33) for an hour dressage in groups SF30 or tennis and squash (tel. 3-15-00) for SF23 to SF47 per hour.

CHAPTER 2

CHALLENGING THE HAUTE ROUTE

DRAGGING MY SKIS OFF THE POSTAL BUS IN Saas-Fee, Switzerland, my first glimpse of the Fee Glacier makes me pause in wonder. Five hundred meters away, a blue, black, and white wall erupts 8600 vertical feet to a knife-edge ridge formed by the Täschhorn, Dom, and Lenzspitze summits. Scored by avalanches, falling rocks, and cascading streams, the Fee Glacier tells me more about the Haute Route than any guidebook or topographical map. If this is only the first hurdle, what will the Haute Route's next 80 miles contain?

"Entschuldigen Sie, bitte," I apologize to a young climber in knee-length wool climbing pants. *"Wo ist die Hôtel Walliser-hof?"*

"The Walliserhof? I believe it is just off this main street," he replies in nearly unaccented English.

"Danke," I reply, shoulder my backpack and skis and start along the busy street. No cars are allowed in this village of three thousand, and in late March two colorful armies appear

13

to be passing on the road to a nearby front. Those headed east have obviously been seasoned by the trek, while those headed toward the Fee Glacier are anxious to test themselves. A majority carry frameless packs with shining ice axes, rusted crampons, and red, blue, and purple ropes. Hundreds of skis flow between the bright storefronts, and the tramp of mountaineering boots adds a steady beat to the melody of German, Italian, and French voices.

Geneva-Cointrin Airport is serviced by direct flights on Swissair from New York and connections through Zurich from Los Angeles, Chicago, and Boston. Swissair recently completed a comprehensive alliance with Scandinavian Air System (SAS) that will cover hotels, in-flight catering, aircraft maintenance, and staff training as well transferring passengers into reciprocal routes. For reservations: (800) 221-4750.

The Swiss rail system offers connections from Geneva-Cointrin Airport to Visp, where a postal bus connects from the station to Saas-Fee. The Swiss Rail Holiday Card is a great deal. It allows unlimited travel on Swiss trains, postal buses, and certain ferries for a specified amount of time (one week, two weeks, etc.). For more information: Swiss National Tourist Office, 250 Stockton Street, San Francisco, California 94108, tel. (415) 362-2260. In New York: 608 Fifth Avenue, New York, New York 10020, tel. (212) 757-5944.

It takes roughly ten days to ski hut to hut across the Haute Route. It is a hard if temporary life, and though the majority of those who fill Saas-Fee's main street are in their late twenties to early forties, the sun, cold, and physical effort has aged them. Week-old beards, peeling sunburns, and raccoon eyes speak eloquently of victory by those coming off the Haute

Route. And just as eloquent, the slow, deliberate step of badly blistered feet and the thousand-yard stares address the penalty.

Rising 5600 vertical feet from the west end of the village, Saas-Fee Ski Area offers a Metro Alpin funicular, two trams, three cable cars, and twenty other T-bars and chairs. Combining gentle groomed pistes with steep bump runs and rolling powder fields, the ski area offers excellent variety and incredible views. Add Saas-Fee's fine hotels, varied restaurants, and typical Swiss standard of service, and you might reconsider starting this 80-mile hike to Chamonix.

A majority of those who arrive in Saas-Fee underestimate the Haute Route. From the numbers who attempt this trek, many assume that this "High Road" is little more than a pleasant hike at 10,000 feet—a chance to work on a tan, ski some late-morning corn snow, and shoot a few rolls of Fujichrome to show the folks back home. What they cannot plan on is the impact of weather—an oversight many soon regret.

The High Road is well named. Though sketchy records exist of ski mountaineering in the Bernese Oberland as early as 1850, it was not until January of 1903 that six Chamonaird alpinists pioneered the route from Chamonix to Zermatt. Until then primitive equipment and inefficient ski technique discouraged a winter attempt. With the twentieth-century improvement of both, however, what had once been the exclusive summer domain of climbers, goatherders, and chamois hunters began to be explored by the first guides and their clients. In 1904 the Frenchman Hugo Mylius accompanied by three Swiss guides made the first ski ascent of Mont Blanc. And in the following years Monte Rosa, the Finsteraarhorn, and the Bernese Oberland were skied. It was not until April of 1910, however, that the final section from Saas-Fee to Zermatt over the Adler Pass was pioneered, linking what has become the classic trek.

In the time since, uncounted thousands have skied the

Haute Route. The year 1988 alone saw roughly thirteen thousand, with the numbers increasing at nearly 10 percent annually. During the past decade, the High Road has become a highway with accompanying problems of overcrowded huts and inexperienced skiers. Much of this increase is due to an improvement in ski mountaineering gear, the expense of traditional alpine resorts, and the spectacular beauty of the Alps. For many the Haute Route represents a once-in-a-lifetime

Known as the "Pearl of the Alps," with twenty-five hundred beds in hotels and B-and-Bs, sixty restaurants, three discos and 50 miles of marked runs, Saas-Fee offers some of the best skiing in Switzerland. The majority of the hotels are centrally located. Since cars are not allowed in the village, the hotels dispatch small taxis to pick up bags at the bus station. Before starting out on the Haute Route, plan on acclimating here for two days.

The **Hotel Walliserhof,** tel. 57-20-21, is centrally located and offers fine views of the Fee Glacier and surrounding summits. Amenities: 114 beds, swimming pool, sauna, TV, telephone, public restaurant, central location, discotheque. Terms: $190–$244 double, half pension, midseason.

Hotel Saaserhof, tel. 57-15-51. Amenities: 100 beds, sauna, radios, phones, TV, central location, public restaurant, bar. Terms $139–$180 double, half pension, midseason.

Hotel Gletschergarten, tel. 57-21-25. Amenities: 40 beds, public restaurant, centrally located, grill. Terms $84–$110 double, half pension, midseason.

For more information: Saas-Fee Tourist Office, Ch-3906, Saas-Fee, Switzerland, tel. 57-14-57. Or, Swiss National Tourist Office, 608 Fifth Avenue, New York 10620, tel. (212) 757-5944.

★

chance to challenge untracked snowfields, living glaciers, and high-altitude passes.

In late March, before climbing to the Britannia Hut and the Haute Route's first leg across the Adler Pass, our guide Aldo Lomatter suggests we first spend a day skiing together. Swiss guides are reputed to be the best in the world, and requirements for inclusion into this elite group eliminate all but the strongest. After stringent physical and comprehensive tests, Lomatter spent two years in apprenticeship, then two more as an associate guide before he was allowed to lead clients. Besides being in excellent shape, he was the first to ski the 14,700-foot Täschhorn summit. He is also an accomplished climber, speaks four languages, and despite his clients' diverse range of ability, exhibits a quiet confidence.

Though it's possible to ski the Haute Route without a guide (and in fact many people do), if you are not an experienced alpinist a guide is essential. A guide not only knows the route (and alternatives) but can reserve space in huts, hotels, and restaurants, lead you to the best snow, and advise you on where to rent equipment (packs, skins, and if necessary boots and skis). He will also be able to answer questions about local history, culture, and fauna. The guide packs the ropes, compass, altimeter, maps, and is also trained in first aid. Each major ski area along the route has local guide offices. For our purposes, it would be best to start at Saas-Fee or Chamonix. For further information: Society of Guides, c/o Saas-Fee Tourist Office, Ch-3906, Saas-Fee, Switzerland, tel. 57-18-60.

★

Our group is composed of two Italians, a German, a Swiss, two other Americans, and myself. After an early breakfast at the Walliserhof, we catch the tram to the 9000-foot Felskinn Station, from where we ski down to a double chair that rises to the top of a moderately bumped, 1,000-vertical-foot pitch.

Now is the time to relax, stay in control, and at all costs, don't fall. At this point details make a big difference. If a guide doubts your skiing ability or suspects your conditioning, he won't accept the responsibility. During the next ten days a fall at the wrong time can result in severe injury or worse, and thus an average group will be split between experts and advanced intermediates. To attempt the Haute Route you should be able

to ski conditions ranging from ice to deep powder, breakable crust, and steep faces. In our group everyone skis well, and Lomatter makes plans to cross the Adler into Zermatt.

"We'll make a final decision there," he tells our assembled group at dinner.

The following afternoon we catch the tram to Felskinn. From there we travel along a service road to the Britannia Hut, which sits out of bounds above the ski area. A rising wind and lowering clouds signal an approaching storm, and we stand our skis in a protected snowbank and shed our packs.

Compared to some huts along the Route, the spacious two-story stone Britannia Hut is a luxury hotel. Under most circumstances the downstairs dining room and upstairs bunk rooms can handle the spring crowds, but tonight the intensifying storm has forced teams that are camping out to seek shelter;

and now packs, foul-weather gear, and bodies jam its dimly lit hallways, bunks, and dining room. Built in the twenties to accommodate 120 skiers, tonight over 200 are crowded between its thick stone walls. Under ideal conditions a reservation (which is made by the guide) would insure a bunk, a hot meal, and information about the Route. Tonight it's chaos, and yet in spite of the line for dinner and crowded beds, we are grateful for the refuge.

"So, who would you turn away?" Lomatter says in reply to a complaint about too few beds for too many people. He advises us to secure a bunk and blankets first, then worry about something to eat. Even novices quickly realize that at this altitude life is reduced to essentials: a warm place to sleep, a full stomach, boots that fit, and dry socks.

At one time supplies for an entire winter were carried up on the backs of the hut keeper and hired laborers. Today what used to require an entire summer now takes a helicopter an hour.

"It is no longer possible to supply these huts by porters," Lomatter tells our crowded dinner table. "In a season ten thousand people will stay here. The size of these huts limits how many can ski the Haute Route."

Evenings in the huts run toward recalling past climbs, organizing and repairing equipment, and speculation about the weather. Some read, some play chess, but most turn in early. Tonight one person sleeps touching the next, sixty bodies to a room, twenty to the hall, and uncounted others downstairs. While the storm howls outside, the air grows stale, and the snoring of people unaccustomed to sleeping at high altitude serves as a reminder that rest is as important as food and water. When sleep finally does come, it is broken by people moving around the room, whispered conversations, and the rising wind.

In order to reach Zermatt before the snow turns to slush, you must depart at 5 A.M. In the cold bunk room a flashlight flickers across your face, and you turn, find your sweater in the dark, and fumble to pull it on. Around you people are slipping into extreme gear, organizing packs, and buckling boots. After a hurried breakfast of bread, jam, and tea, I shoulder my pack and with a first faint light showing through the swirling clouds, step into the blowing snow.

The majority who ski the Haute Route use alpine equipment: plastic boots, steel-edge skis, and hinged mountaineering bindings. Recently however the numbers attempting it on free-heel Nordic mountaineering gear have increased—a trend the guides view with trepidation.

"If the weather and snow conditions are perfect, you can ski the Haute on telemark equipment," Lomatter tells us that morning. "But there are places where you cannot fall or even slip. And if you have ice, wind, and poor visibility—" he shakes his head, "—why take chances?"

With the blowing snow restricting visibility to 20 feet, we ski a short, powdery face. Two of our group immediately go head over heels.

"Well, you see, now the worst part of the day is over," Lomatter says, eliciting smiles as they brush themselves off.

The grade flattens, and we attach synthetic sealskins to our skis and start to climb. Though it is the highest pass in Europe, the Adler appears to be little more than a depression between equal 13,700-foot Rimpfischhorn and Strahlhorn summits. During that first hour our group is in high spirits, and one or two skate ahead to take photos. Five hours later the wind has subsided, the clouds have disappeared, and by late morning the heat has settled onto the Allalin Glacier.

We have just started up a sheer face below the pass when Dan, one of the other Americans, steps out of line and refuses to go any farther. "I've had it," he says, sweating profusely and gasping for air. "My feet are blistered, these boots hurt like hell. . . . I can't go on."

"You must not stop," the guide quietly advises him. "It takes more energy to get started again than to continue at a slower pace. You can see the top from here. It is not far, and I will help you." Lomatter picks up his pack and ties it to his own. "It will be easier now," he says and takes a hesitant step toward the pass.

Dan glances uphill, mutters an unintelligible threat, and manages to start moving again. The grade grows steeper, and he soon starts to sag. "I've had it. . . ." Too tired to talk, he can only lean heavily on his poles and shake his head in refusal.

Lomatter, however is just as adamant. "The group is only as fast as its slowest member," he says, calmly pointing to a distant line of clouds. "The weather is going to change. In half an hour it will start to snow. Then you will lose the track." He does not add that, without the track, it is only a matter of time before Dan stumbles into a crevasse or skis off a cliff. "For the sake of the others you must keep moving," Lomatter says, lowering his voice.

Pain is one thing, humiliation is another. Dan looks at the rest of us, grits his teeth, and slides one ski in front of the other.

"It is only a little way until we start downhill," Lomatter says as encouragement.

On top a cold wind is pouring across the pass. Studying the Monte Rosa massif, we start to cool off. After studying the 2 inches of snow deposited by the night's storm, I start linking turns toward the transition.

"HOY! STOP!" Lomatter shouts down to me. "No closer to the edge!"

Aldo could only guess that a combination of sun, cold, and wind had scoured the Zermatt side down to blue glacial ice that would resist all but crampons, ice axes, and ropes. Four more turns and I would have lost the edge and started to slide. From there I could not have self-arrested before the cliff below.

There have been ten fatalities this season. A dry, cold midwinter followed by a series of wet storms created a treacherous snowpack, and now large releases scar the steep gullies. Two weeks before my arrival in Saas-Fee, four Frenchmen died in an avalanche. The others were lost in crevasses, in falls, and from exposure. But then death has always haunted this High

Road. Aside from the huts, the only sign of humanity are solitary wooden crosses anchored to pinnacles above the track. Some represent a herder's devout act of faith, but others mark accidents, and each time we pass one, I am reminded that among these high Alps, death is a violent sojourner separated from life by a few seconds.

Lomatter fixes a rope, and we belay down the Adler Pass's icy face then ski down the Findelen Glacier to the frozen Stelli-See and finally to Sunnegga, where we catch the Sunnegga underground metro down to Zermatt. It is late afternoon when we reach the Hotel Continental. Though it has been a long day, it has not been a killer, and I wonder how Lomatter will grade our efforts.

There's a reason Zermatt is a sister city to Snowbird, Utah. It has great snow, great skiing, and excellent accommodations. Zermatt guides, hotels, and restaurants all have an international reputation. For information: Zermatt Tourist Office, Ch-3920, Zermatt, Switzerland, tel. 66-11-81.

My room has a fine view of the Matterhorn, which Edward Whymper first climbed in July of 1865. In the century and a quarter since, the Matterhorn has become known as something of a walkup, an exhilarating hike to 14,690 feet. One story claims that a Zermatt guide once led a Simmental cow to the top of the Matterhorn. Besides the cow, a monkey, a bear, and a man in a wheelchair are also reputed to have summited. Bizarre records aside, the Matterhorn is far and away Switzerland's most famous landmark—as recognizable as our own Statue of Liberty. In this country of five million its profile dominates ads for watches, cars, butter, jam, chocolate, and cheese. Over the years the Matterhorn has been reduced to a visual cliché, and this familiarity has bred a certain contempt.

During a normal summer from thirty-five hundred to five thousand climbers will attempt to reach the summit. Of that number less than a third will succeed. Some will lack conditioning, others experience. The majority, however, will be defeated by the weather.

In the time since Whymper climbed the Matterhorn, Zermatt has changed from a small herding village into what is arguably Europe's most famous resort. This evening, with unbroken clouds and approaching dark, the mountain presents a grim northeast face to the village. In Zermatt there is no escaping the Matterhorn. The first spring storms appear over its summit, glaciers guard its north face, and when the temperature rises and snow falls, avalanches rumble into the valley below.

In Zermatt's Alpine Museum, black-and-white photographs show guides smiling on the summit. Closer to the mountain, however, the climber's graveyard chronicles past tragedies with the simple *Am Matterhorn*. Sobered by both, I study Zermatt's shops, where engraved Swiss Army knives, T-shirts, posters, and a hundred other useful and patently worthless souvenirs that bear the famous outline compete for yen, francs, and dollars. I buy a knife but decline the engraving and quickly return to the Continental, where I learn that Dan has decided not to continue with the group up to the Schönbiel Hut.

"My feet are full of blisters," he admits with only a trace of remorse.

"We will spend the night at Schönbiel and start in the early morning," Lomatter says. The following morning the group catches a series of trams from Zermatt to the Klein-Matterhorn. There are two ways to ski the Haute Route. Weather permitting, the purist will not leave the High Road from Saas-Fee to Chamonix. A realist, however, will take advantage of the numerous lifts that intersect the Route. Saas-Fee and Zermatt offer superb lift-assisted skiing. Among them dozens of trams, chairs, and T-bars access miles of groomed slopes.

With the Matterhorn towering above, we spend the morning skiing Trockener Steg, the Plateau Rosa, and the Theodule Glacier before descending through Schwarz-See to Staffel and lunch. By 2 P.M. we are climbing a 2500-foot glacial moraine that leads to the Schönbiel Hut.

To prepare for the Haute Route, I jogged, rode my bicycle, and Nordic-skied. With the added burden of a pack, skis, and boots, the Haute Route's climbs are strenuous. People who live at sea level often experience shortness of breath, cramps, an inability to sleep, blisters, and nausea.

Perched above an enormous glacial moraine, the three-story stone Schönbiel Hut sits beneath the north faces of the Matterhorn and Dent d'Hérens. Lomatter hands me a pair of binoculars, and I study two climbers who are halfway up the Matterhorn's technical Z'Mutt-Bach Ridge. Sitting on a stone wall, I watch the evening shadows search across the Matterhorn Glacier and recall the final chapter in Whymper's climb. Following a short celebration on the summit, the team started to downclimb the technical section above the Shoulder. Seconds later Douglas Hadow slipped and tumbled into Michel Croz, knocking him off his feet. Fighting to save themselves, the two dragged the Reverend Charles Hudson (one of the best amateur climbers in Europe) and the Lord Francis Douglas (brother to the Marquis of Queensberry and also an experienced alpinist) off their feet. Whymper and Taugwalder (a second guide) braced for the shock, but the manila rope broke, and the four subsequently fell 4,000 feet down the north face.

A cold wind gusts down the valley, and I wonder what Whymper must have thought when he later contemplated the victory and the subsequent tragedy.

The following morning I am holding a flashlight in my teeth and chopping short swing turns down a steep, icy face that leads from the Schönbiel Hut to the Z'Mutt Glacier. It is 4:30 A.M., and our group is one of the first out of Schönbiel, skiing toward the glacial floor before turning up the east face of the 11,000-foot Col de Valpelline. Alternately crowned by iridescent blue glacial ice, brooding under dark rock faces, and hidden in swirling fog, this morning's Haute Route has a harsh, inhospitable beauty, and I sweat and pole and try to vary my stride to avoid blisters.

Dawn grows at our back, and by the time the sun rises over the distant Adler Pass the grade is starting to flatten out. In front the Haut Glacier de Tsa de Tsan drops into Italy, and we follow its long, gentle grade between rock faces, past Mont-Brûlé, back into Switzerland, and up a gradual grade toward the Col de l'Évêque. Lomatter sets a steady pace; we pass other trekkers headed east toward Zermatt, and by late morning the sun has disappeared behind a lowering cloud layer.

"We must move more quickly," Lomatter says during a rest stop. "If we are to reach Cabane des Vignettes before the storm hits, speed is essential." One foot in front of the other, a pole plant, the other foot slides forward: the switchbacks continue upward.

Four hours later we are navigating in a whiteout. A storm is whipping snow into our faces, which reduces visibility to the pair of skis immediately ahead. It is impossible to see cliff faces or crevasses, which are frequent on this glacier, and the only difference between uphill and downhill is the sudden cessation of effort. Without Aldo's compass and altimeter we would be lost. Bivouacking without tents or sleeping bags is out of the question, and so we continue, head down, one foot in front of the other, matching Aldo's now-unrelenting pace.

It is late afternoon before we reach the Col de Chermontane—a broad glacial plane that leads to the steep face below Cabane des Vignettes. The wind is howling around the stone hut, and we tiredly make our way through the crowded dining room. After fourteen hours without a break, I'm looking forward to a hot meal, a warm bunk, and eight hours of sleep, and have just dropped my pack in the corridor outside the crowded dormitory when Lomatter steps around me.

"A man has suffered a heart attack," he whispers. Aldo's expression says it is bad. "He is older, perhaps fifty. . . . A doctor downstairs believes if he does not reach a hospital, he will die. A helicopter cannot land in this storm. . . ." Moments later we watch a guide lead a loaded basket down the Col des Vignettes toward Arolla below.

"It is a mistake to think the Haute Route is easy," Aldo remarks at dinner. "Sure, if you are young and strong with the right weather, then you can ski it without difficulty. But it is never easy, and the biggest mistake people make is to underestimate it."

That night the wind shakes the shuttered windows, and at dawn a heavy snowfall has cut visibility to 20 feet. "The forecast is not good," Lomatter admits. The storm is expected to continue for three days, and with no chance of continuing, our itinerary begins to fall apart. The rest of the group had budgeted ten days for the trip, and with the storm expected to last half that, we must decide whether to wait in the hut or abandon the trek.

Tracing the Haute Route on a topo map, you will see that the huts are not only a day's hike from each other, but within a few hours of the towns Saas-Fee, Zermatt, Arolla, Verbier, Bourg-Saint-Pierre, and Chamonix. In the twenties, when many of the huts were built, access for supply was important. Just as important, however, was sanctuary from the huge North Atlantic storms that periodically slam into the Alps. When a meter of snow falls in two days, travel among these exposed peaks is impossible. In that case your only option is to ski down.

Faced with a long wait, most of our group reluctantly returns to families, jobs, and deadlines. Aside from the training, planning, and expense, by now I have come more than halfway, and quitting is not an option. The hardest part is behind me, and so I call home, juggle my schedule, and wait. Lomatter returns to Saas-Fee and I start across Switzerland, first to Interlaken, then to Wengen, Berne, and the Lac Léman resort of Montreux, where I wait for the weather to clear.

Sitting on a lakeside bench in Montreux and watching the Windsurfers cut beyond the moored yachts, I cannot stop

If you get blown off course, Geneva is within two hours by train of the **Valais** (of which Zermatt and Verbier are a part). With its walled old town, World Health Organization, Red Cross, United Nations, museums and excellent hotels, shopping and dining and setting on the lake, it is one of Europe's most beautiful cities.

If you have time on your return to Geneva, spend a night in **Montreux**, "The Pearl of Lac Léman." It's blessed with a wonderful climate, a lakeside ambiance, world-class hotels, shops, and the **Castle of Chillon**. Montreux is a stop on the train back to Geneva Airport, and its lakeside **Quai des Fleurs** botanical walk should not be missed. For more information contact Swiss Tourist offices in New York, tel. (212) 757-5944, and San Francisco, tel. (415) 362-2260.

thinking about the Haute Route. While the Valais floor is marked by greening vineyards and flowering apple, cherry, and peach trees, life among the distant peaks is confined to lichens clinging to spare earth and black Taki birds following the sinuous track in search of scraps abandoned by the trekkers.

It takes five days for the storm to dissipate. Six days after skiing out of Arolla, I hire a Verbier guide, Jean-Louis Coquoz. Because I am his only client, the fee is somewhat expensive, but if I finish the Haute Route it will be worth it. On the first sunny day we climb up out of Arolla and over the Pas de Chèvres to the Cabane des Dix. In spite of having to belay off a rock face, we make excellent time. From Arolla it takes three hours to cross the glistening white plane of Cheilon Glacier to Cabane des Dix. Jean-Louis tells me his plan is to overnight at Cabane des Dix before skiing southwest over the Col de Cheilon, the Col du Mont-Rouge, and the Col de Lire to the Cabane de Chanrion. If the weather holds, from there we will turn due

west across the Col de Sonadon, across the south flank of the
Grand-Combin, and eventually down into Bourg-Saint-Pierre.
Catching a bus, we will descend to Champex then climb to the
Cabane du Trient on the Mont Blanc massif, cross into France,
and finally ski down into Chamonix.

Coquoz was born and raised in Verbier and knows each of
the guides seated around the Cabane des Dix's smoky dining
room—if not personally then by reputation. The Society of
Mountain Guides is an elite group, and its members share a
mutual respect. Chain-smoking cigarettes, the weathered
thirty-four-year-old father of four says he teaches skiing in the
winter, guides during the spring, and works construction in the
summer. Even so he finds it difficult to make ends meet.

"No guide looks forward to retirement," he admits, lighting
a Gitane. "The best an old guide can hope for is a hut of his
own. You can sell lift tickets or load trams. If you are lucky, you
save enough for a small bar . . . but it is very difficult."

The following morning Jean-Louis is studying the leaden
western horizon. "Soon it will start to snow," he says. "It would
be very dangerous to attempt to reach Chanrion. Our best
chance is to turn toward Verbier. When the storm passes we
will cross to Champex and up to Cabane du Trient."

Shouldering our packs, we turn north from Cabane des Dix
on a long downhill traverse around the frozen Dix reservoir
where just above a curving concrete dam we start uphill. To
the south Mont Blanc de Cheilon is spotlighted by a break in
the overcast. For a minute it lifts like a sparkling white battle-
ment then disappears beneath a lowering cloud layer. A rising
wind carries the smell of blooming vineyards, orchards, and
rich earth. Two ptarmigan flush from a rocky outcropping, and
we surprise a herd of chamois that trot across an exposed face.

The overcast continues to lower, and we are close to the
Rosa Blanche summit when the first snowflakes slide off our
parkas. In half an hour we are enveloped by a whiteout. Using
Jean-Louis's altimeter, compass, and knowledge of the terrain,
we cross the frozen waste of the Grand Désert and climb the

Col de Moming. The cloud layer lifts, and we hurriedly ski down to Cabane du Mont-Fort, which marks the outer boundary of Verbier's massive ski area. The season has been over for three weeks, and without crevasses or avalanches to worry about, we pound down through the soft moguls that drop to the resort outskirts.

I am barely checked into a private pension before the storm pounds down with a vengeance. Sleet streaks the windows, puddles begin to fill the streets, the ground grows soggy. I wait. A day passes, then another. On the third day I find Jean-Louis sitting in the downstairs bar.

"Perhaps we will travel to Argentière," he says without enthusiasm. "At least if it clears we can catch the tram and perhaps cross to Cabane du Trient."

Anything is better than sitting, and so Jean-Louis and I catch a bus to Martigny and from there take the train to Argentière. In France, however, the story is the same. Heavy snows continue on the high passes as we take the last room in a sagging, musty hotel. It bears a certain resemblance to the huts, and studying a broken window, we flip for the lumpy cot. I lose and at breakfast the following morning, push has come to shove. For two days sleet has poured in through broken roof tiles, and now we watch a dark stain spread down the floral wallpaper.

"So, Jean-Louis, what's the forecast?" I ask him.

"For the next three days, more of the same," he replies.

"And after that?"

"After that . . ." he says, lighting the morning's fifth cigarette, ". . . who can predict the weather? A meter of snow has fallen, and the lift operators say there are high winds in the Col du Chardonnet. You must ask yourself, is it so important to finish this last section that you would risk your life?"

"It is very important," I admit, trying to hide my disappointment. Life-and-death considerations aside, I had hoped our luck would change. "It's only 20 kilometers . . . There must be a way," I persist.

"None. Twenty or only two . . . it is impossible," he says,

taking a deep drag. "For the next five days, it is suicide." He shakes his head and slowly rises to catch the morning train back to Verbier. "Against this," he gestures with his cigarette toward the sleet-streaked window, "what can you do? You cannot climb in a whiteout, you cannot hike in waist-deep snow. Only crazy people defy the weather. . . ." He shrugs helplessly. "It is unfortunate, but you were just one of many who were beaten by the weather."

In the end we are unable to cross the Mont Blanc massif. The storm proves to be the largest in two decades. During the following weeks nearly 6 feet of snow falls on the high passes, creating a severe avalanche cycle. If you must submit to weather, there are worse places than Switzerland. After three more days I could not delay any longer and returned to Geneva where I caught a Swissair flight home.

At that time I figured the Haute Route was a failure; but in hindsight, the High Road isn't like climbing the Matterhorn, with no second best to reaching the summit. Two passes or twenty, when faced with mountain weather, keeping score doesn't make much sense. The Europeans figured this out years ago, and now if they're blown off, at least they've got a nice tan and some slides to show the folks back home.

REST AND RECUPERATION

On the Haute Route evenings are spent in the huts. Thus a good book such as Edward Whymper's *Scrambles Amongst the Alps*, which can be purchased in Saas-Fee or Zermatt bookstores, will help pass the time. The majority of Swiss speak English, and conversations cover a range of topics but focus mainly on the weather and past expeditions. On off days caused by weather or a desire to linger on one section of the route, equipment is checked, journals are updated, photos are taken. If you have time and decide to ski down to Zermatt, Arolla, Verbier, or one of the other villages, options increase dramatically. In Zermatt do not miss the **Alpine**

Museum behind the post office (tel. 67-41-00), which chronicles past climbs of local peaks, including the Matterhorn, as well as local history and fauna. Also the **climbers' graveyard** provides a sobering insight into Zermatt's past triumphs and tragedies. Zermatt also has a **fitness center** in the Hotel Christiania (tel. 67-19-07), dancing at the Bristol, Zermatterhof, and Christiania as well as swimming, bowling, and helicopter rides.

Verbier has an ultra-modern **sports center** in the middle of the city which offers squash, tennis, ice hockey, ice skating, and swimming. Verbier is also a center for paragliding, has fifty restaurants, four nightclubs, and shopping. (tel. 67-62-22).

CHAPTER 3

SNOWY DAYS IN SUN VALLEY

AT 8:45 A.M. WHEN I ROUND THE NORTH FACE Hut where the hardcores are waiting for Bald Mountain's Challenger quad to open it is snowing an inch an hour. Fourteen inches have fallen during the night, and the storm shows no signs of abating. Though most Ketchum locals are grateful for the 14 inches, few dare hope for more. And yet, with little to do besides champ at the bit, rumors begin to generate spontaneously.

"We're supposed to get 2 feet out of this storm," someone in a fluorescent green mountain parka advises the crowd around him. If he had lived in the Wood River Valley for more than two months, he would realize that a 2-foot dump is such a rare meteorological phenomenon that as soon as the forecasters commit to that number there is an equally good chance blue skies will appear within the hour.

With fifteen minutes before the lift opens, roughly 250 powder hounds have gathered on the flats in front of the Warm

Springs Bridge. Rich Fabiano has been waiting for half an hour.

Though I've known Rich for twenty years, I don't share his mania for punctuality. Two minutes or two hours, to Rich late is late, and if it was possible to tap his foot while locked in a ski boot, binding, and a 207 cm Pre giant slalom, his left tip would now be silently slapping the snow.

By excusing myself, waving at Rich, nodding and smiling vacantly in response to the glares, I manage to cut the line. "Glad you made it," he nods in greeting, brushing the snow off his jacket. "More trouble with your truck?"

At that moment the chair begins to load. If you can believe the shack clock, it is ten minutes early—an unexpected gift from management to the rabid pack salivating in the heavy snowfall. Seconds later the first group of four clears Warm Springs Creek. Visibility is down to 50 feet, it's twenty-three degrees, snow is falling at an inch an hour—all signs point to another brilliant day in paradise.

"We're twenty," Rich says, counting the loaded chairs in front of us. Figuring four per chair, eighty skiers are ahead of us. Realistically it doesn't make that much difference. With Bald Mountain's 1300 acres and sixty-four runs, we're virtually guaranteed two hours of untracked powder. Figuring four runs an hour at an average 1500 vertical feet, that's 12,000 feet—or about what you can expect from a day of heli-skiing.

It is January 10th—unofficially winter slack—a two-week respite from the Christmas crowds who choked Flying Squirrel, jammed the North Face Hut, and ran amok at Ketchum's retailers. In spite of the lines at Atkinson's Market, the Pioneer Saloon, and now the Challenger quad on a powder morning, you won't catch anyone complaining. Far from it; for if Sun Valley once cultivated a reputation as the winter playground of the stars, Utah and Colorado's consistent snow, high-speed lifts, and easy access nearly marketed this isolated Idaho resort out of business. In fact, after the droughts of '85, '86, and '87 caused a decline in skier numbers, locals now underwrite a boosterism that makes the Voice of America seem tepid by comparison.

As a result, Sun Valley has been rediscovered. An acre lot that once sold for $3,000 now sells for $75,000, Highway 75 is overloaded with rush-hour traffic, and the county is studying creative ways to finance a sewage treatment plant.

But then locals have always understood that life in Sun Valley requires certain sacrifices.

If Sun Valley's history hadn't been documented by ten thousand photos and a hundred times that many published words, it would have made bestselling fiction. With the discovery of high-grade galena ore near the headwaters of the Wood River, the valley was inundated with the miners, hookers, and freighters who built Ketchum and Hailey. In a boom-bust cycle duplicated throughout the American West, the mines closed, the towns withered, and until the coming of the resort, Ketchum served as a railhead for the large flocks of sheep that summered across the Boulder, Smokey, and Pioneer foothills.

To encourage travel on the Union Pacific Railroad's northern line, Averell Harriman dreamed of building an isolated ski resort. During the winter of 1935–36 he commissioned Austrian Count Felix Schaffgotsch to search for what he hoped would become the St. Moritz of the Rockies. After months of following dead-end leads, and on the verge of giving up, Schaffgotsch followed a final rumor into the Wood River Valley. A week later he wired Harriman that he had discovered a perfect combination of sun, snow, and calm days. History records that the winter of '36 represented the peak of a ten-year snow cycle. Locals now realize that if the resort had been built twenty miles farther north, it wouldn't need the snowmaking or cloud seeding to fill in the early-winter blanks.

To increase rider numbers, Harriman stipulated that the resort should be isolated. And today, from Ketchum's sole stoplight, you can travel a hundred miles to the east or west and, except for the occasional mine, find only snow-covered ridge-

lines, frozen streams, and dormant forests. The nearest major
city is Twin Falls, which is ninety miles south through unbroken sagebrush and black lava flows. Sun Valley is eighteen
hours by car from San Francisco and six hours by air from New
York.

---

orizon Air (tel. 800-547-9308) and Sky West (tel. 800-
453-9417) service Hailey's Friedman Airport from Salt
Lake City/Boise and L.A./Las Vegas/Boise respectively.
Sun Valley Stages offers connecting buses to United Airlines flights into Boise ($30 and three hours).

★

If the logistics of getting here appear formidable, unfortunately Sun Valley's isolation is becoming less of a deterrent.
Among the most recent draws is a detachable quad that climbs
3140 feet in eight and a half minutes. And then there's Bald
Mountain's diversity—its vertical drop, superb terrain, and surrounding vistas—where if you have the thighs, lungs, and
heart for it, 60,000 vertical feet makes a long but not unusual
day.

To ski 60K in a single day you must stick to the Challenger
quad, and to ride the Challenger you must maintain a certain
faith in American technology. The ground speed of this detachable chair is so astonishing that despite having ridden it a hundred times before, I still can't shake the feeling that I'm about
to be catapulted across the summit flats into Lookout Bowl as
it races toward the upper bull wheel. Smiles fade and all eyes
face front as the chair disengages from the cable and rapidly
decelerates to a slow walk.

"So, what's the call?" Rich says as we skate across the summit.

Studying the myriad tracks that point toward the bowls, I
venture, "Warm Springs top to bottom?"

As a rule ski writers shamelessly abuse superlatives. Raw

ice becomes "packed powder," impassable moguls become "forgiving bumps," and half-star hotels exude "a certain country charm." Thus I'm reluctant to claim those first turns were the decade's best. In front of us four sets of tracks dropped into Warm Springs, but two immediately ended in craters where their owners were struggling to retrieve their skis.

Simple good manners dictate we stop and inquire after their health. But considering the conditions, stopping would also be extremely dumb, and since they're on their feet anyway, Rich and I steal their line down Upper Warm Springs. Unbelievably the second two are inspecting Warm Spring's Face from the "I-80" cat track. Without stopping Rich and I dive past them, down the steep face into the center gully where the snow eddies past our knees. With six other skiers now chasing us, we float past International to the right side of Mid Warm Springs and away from the Greyhawk quad.

Admittedly this is a rare day. Surrounded by what geologists refer to as high alpine desert, Sun Valley is not known as a soft-snow resort. In fact, reaching for the next turn as the sweat runs beneath my jacket, I would guess that during the past sixteen years there have been fewer than 100 twelve-inch–plus dumps.

Sixteen years! Could it be that long since I coaxed an overloaded van down Ketchum's deserted Main Street? My plan was to say six months before moving on to career, hearth, and family. January, however, turned into June, I was seduced by Sun Valley's summer, and blithely rationalizing that firsthand experience is as valuable as a formal education, I traded graduate school for a September spent drifting elk-hair caddis flies over the Wood River's native rainbows. Today, I have no regrets.

With the visibility down to a single line next to the trees, I must apologize for not describing the scenery. Looking east into the swirling flakes, Ketchum gives way to the Trail Creek Ridge, the Pioneers, and the Devils Bedstead. Visible to the south on Highway 75, Hailey and Bellevue serve as Ketchum's bedroom communities. To the north you can see the Boulder

Mountains tinted gray, rose, and yellow; they shrink to the Galena Ridgeline, which in turn divides the Wood River from the spectacular Sawtooth Valley, Redfish Lake, the headwaters of the Salmon River and jagged Sawtooth Mountains. In spite of the surrounding scenery, however, Baldy is the big gun.

In fact, if you were to pay a dozen area managers to design the perfect mountain, they would be hard-pressed to better this 3100-foot peak. From its summit four main ridges—Lookout, International, College, and Ridge—radiate out roughly toward the major compass points. These ridges lead to sixty-four designated runs that descend through north-facing forests, open south slopes, and huge east-facing bowls that, in turn, funnel back to Sun Valley's sixteen chairs. Divided into six doubles, seven triples, and three quads, these chairs access 1300 skiable acres of which 20 percent is covered by snowmaking.

My problem with Bald Mountain is I have skied her extremes. Soft and hard, sun and storm, groomed and bumped, trees and wide bowls, I might not remember the lows, but I doubt I'll forget the highs. Before coming to Ketchum, I would have claimed I was an advanced intermediate or even expert with the emphasis on the latter. Now, sixteen years later, I have learned that my expertise varies with the conditions. Groomed steeps are fantastic, corn is paradise, and powder needs no superlatives. Breakable crust, however, still throws me onto my tails. Icy bumps cause me to go catatonic. Tight trees make me snow-plow cautious, and whenever I attempt air, my lower back seizes up.

With the snow filling the hollows, Rich and I link turns past where the Limelight double used to be. It took less than a season for the quads to kill Limelight. Its demise can be found in the math problem: If the Challenger climbs 3100 feet in ten minutes and Limelight climbs 1900 feet in fifteen minutes, then how many more vertical feet can Johnny ski in a single hour if it takes him five minutes to ski Warm Springs top to bottom? Answer: Enough that skiers stopped riding the Limelight double, and Sun Valley Company uprooted it in the summer of '90. As a bonus, however, Limelight has been widened and groomed, producing one of the best runs on the mountain.

Reaching the Challenger, we join a short line and are soon launched at the summit. So far the storm shows no signs of letting up, and with our goggles fogging we lift into the trees and consider the necessities. If man cannot live indefinitely on knee-deep powder and quad lifts, where would I stay?

If I wanted a strong dose of local history, I'd check into the Sun Valley Lodge. When Union Pacific workmen built this three-story complex in the summer of 1936, they used rough sawn lumber to form the walls. The hardening concrete took the Douglas firs' heavy grain, which to this day gives the Lodge its rustic appearance. Hemingway finished *For Whom the Bell Tolls* here, and at one time or another most of Hollywood's movers and shakers danced in the Duchin Room, table-hopped in the Lodge dining room, and swam in its heated out-door pools. With bus service to Ketchum, Bald and Dollar mountains and a central mall, the Lodge is one of the Valley's win/win deals.

An obvious side effect of skiing the Challenger is you quickly amass vertical. At ten minutes to the top and half that back to the base, Rich and I ski International out to the area boundary. Here the storm wanes between the massive spruces and, sucking my knees up, I plummet down the steep fall line back to Warm Springs. From there we cut down Upper Greyhawk to Cozy and Hemingway, which were extended 1000 vertical feet farther up the hill in the summer of '90 and drop down the long perfect pitch back to the Challenger.

Numerous north-face variations follow. Upper River, Ridge, Blue Grouse, Cut Off, Rock Garden, Olympic, and Holiday, are all added to January 10's portfolio. We ski the intermediate College to River Run South Slopes, where by dodging the sage-brush and easing onto the cat tracks to avoid the subsurface shale, we merge into Mid River Run and ski into the Exhibition triple, which connects to the Christmas quad.

It is a quarter past twelve. By now the major bowls—Christ-

At the top of the list of accommodations is the **Sun Valley Lodge/Inn**, Sun Valley Mall, Sun Valley, Idaho 83353, tel. (800) 786-8259. Located a mile east of Ketchum and surrounded by numerous shops and mature landscaping, the Lodge is a local time capsule full of photos chronicling the area's past fifty-four years. Amenities: 380 rooms, heated pools, full resort, restaurants, shopping, lounges, ice skating, game room, bowling, movie theater, sleigh rides, shuttles to mountain. Terms: $115–$275.

If walking across the street to the Challenger quad is a major consideration, reserve a room in the **Warm Springs Resort** at Sun Valley, 319 Skiway Drive, Ketchum, Idaho 83340, tel. (800) 635-4404, (208) 726-8274. Amenities: Hot tub, ski-in ski-out, TV, toilets, close to restaurants, shopping, shuttle. Terms: two bedrooms or double room, $90, condo $295.

On the River Run side, just west of Ketchum's downtown commercial zone, try the **River Street Inn**, 100 River West, Ketchum, Idaho 83340, tel. (208) 726-3611. Amenities: bed-and-breakfast inn, suites, homemade breakfasts, walk to shops and restaurants, overlooks Trail Creek and is a short walk to lift, gracious hostess. Terms: $95–$150.

The **Ketchum Korral**, 310 South Main, Ketchum, Idaho 83340, tel. (208) 726-3510, is a bit more rustic. Amenities: kitchens, fireplaces, free ice, Jacuzzi, cabins, laundry. (Hemingway slept here.) Terms: $47–$125.

In central Ketchum: The **Christiania Lodge**, 651 Sun Valley Road, Ketchum, Idaho 83340, tel. (800) 535-3241. Amenities: thirty-eight rooms, hot tub, some fireplaces, kitchenettes, family rates. Terms: $58–$85.

In Elkhorn: **Elkhorn Resort**, Box 6009, Sun Valley, Idaho 83353, tel. (800) 635-9356. Amenities: 132 rooms, Jacuzzis, sauna, steam room, five restaurants, six lounges, sleigh rides, Nordic tracks, lift access to Dollar Mountain, shuttle to Bald Mountain. Terms: $58–$378.

★

mas, Lookout, Easter, Mayday, Farout, and Lefty's—are tracked up. Taking the quad to the summit, we contemplate the Lookout Restaurant's flat profile. A brownie would prevent early afternoon flameout, but between the major bowls are myriads of lesser lines, and skipping the brownie we circle left around the quad to the Christmas Ridge boundary rope.

How many times have Rich and I skied Christmas? Over the years, hundreds, and now I stop to watch him. In the past sixteen years Rich's skiing has improved markedly. Somewhere between a hundred thousand and a hundred million vertical feet he lost the skid on his left turn, the exaggerated pole plant to initiate the right. Now his knees pump through the bumps and his upper body is quiet as he reaches for each successive turn. Pushing from edge to edge, he arcs through the shredded powder, his Pre skis accelerating then slowing as he weights and unweights until the storm closes behind him.

I start after him, the snow alternately swirling around my shins, rising over my knees, and breaking across my thighs until I drop onto the Roundhouse-to-Bowls cat track and traverse to the Mayday. Rich is waiting with local architect and old friend Ned Hamlin, and we pole forward and drop into a chair. Compared to the new quads, the Mayday feels as if someone left the parking brake on. Can it be only a year since this was a fire-breathing, 400-horsepower Yan triple?

"The Weather Service claims this storm is going to last through the night," Ned says as the chair climbs through the torrential flakes. "We may get as much as 2 feet."

"Where'd you hear that?" Rich asks, squeezing the water out of his gloves.

"Dan Hawley."

"And you believe him?" I reply. Since Dan skis one hundred days a season, he would regard a 2-foot storm as equivalent to winning the Publisher's Clearinghouse Sweepstakes.

"He said they're predicting 2 feet," Ned comments as we unload from Mayday and follow the cat track down to Farout

Louie Mallane's **Louie's**, 726-7775, is another local institution—a home-style Italian restaurant that serves great
pizza. Jeff and Shiela Key's **Soupcon**, 726-5034, offers a
creative American and European menu. I like Jim Funk's
Desperados, 726-3068, for Mexican and Peter and Stacey
Weisz's excellent **Peter's**, 726-9515, for their service, Chinese Chicken Salad, game and Austrian specialties.
Creekside, 726-8200, has great après entertainment as
well as a romantic view of Warm Springs Creek running
beneath the dining room windows. There's **Barsotti's
Mountain Cafe**, 726-3388, for views and après socializ-
ing. There's the **Christiania**, 726-3388, for its piano bar;
China Pepper, 726-0959, for pricy Chinese; **Perry's**, 726-
7703, and the **Buffalo Cafe**, 726-9795, for a local's lunch.
The Coffee Grinder, 726-8048, for coffee and rolls; the
Western, 726-3396, for breakfast. In Sun Valley the **Lodge
Dining Room**, 622-2150, for white-glove service; the **Ore
House**, 622-4363, for steaks and the **Konditorei**, 622-
2235, for breakfast and lunch. Across the ridge in Elkhorn
there's **Jesse's**, 622-4533, and in Hailey Lloyd and Nancy
Gurney's **Gurneys**, 788-3697.

★

Bowl. With no trees to define the open slope's rise and fall, we
ski as much by feel as sight, the buried moguls pushing
against our skis, the troughs suddenly sinking away. And for
an incautious moment I wonder if the Weather Service might
be right and regret not stopping for lunch.

Wood River Valley history is littered with dead restaurants.
As long as the snow fell, No Grease Maurice made a fortune
selling hot dogs on Main Street, but after the first drought,
Chez Maurice folded. Time judges all, and Ketchum's oldest
are still some of its best. The beauty of Duffy Witmer's Pioneer
is that its ambiance speaks of Ketchum in the heady thirties—

those promising Depression years when Union Pacific's construction crews blew into town. Duffy started by bartending at the Pio, and the restaurant now mirrors his various fall passions. Mounted elk, birds and trout, side-by-side shotguns, and fly rods fill the walls, and his prime rib, steaks, and trout are the best in Idaho.

If the snow holds up for another two hours, January 10 will set a bench mark for future winters. It will be remembered as one of those days when conditions transcended the useful range of language. Mists moving between the trees lend a timelessness to Farout. This could be '73 or some other pre-Mayday lift winter when you'd spend forty minutes riding lifts to ski ten. It was one reason the snow lasted all day. Now the massive trunks pass like specters in the fog, my thighs burn, I try to drive with my shoulders and go down, the fall punctuated by a soft whump, and white.

Unloading off the Seattle Ridge triple and looking northwest toward the summit, we have a choice of three marked runs. Two are named for past Olympians, Christin's (Cooper) Silver, Gretchen's (Frazer) Gold, with the third, Southern Comfort, resulting from a contest that traded a season's pass for the best name.

There is also a fourth. Not as popular as the other three, but far more dramatic. The Fire Trail. A steep bump-and-glade gully that drops to an isolated cat track, it has been skied today but not often, and Rich and I are quickly swallowed by the trees.

By now I'm too tired to truly attack the Fire Trail. Instead I search for the easy line, the smallest moguls, and most forgiving trees, until I finally run out of gas and pull to one side and stand with my legs burning, my goggles fogging, and my breath coming short and choppy.

Legend records that skiing arrived in Central Idaho with the opening of Union Pacific Lodge during Christmas of 1936. It was the year it didn't snow until New Year's Eve. Long before that auspicious date, 1880 to be exact, locals were exploring the surrounding hills on 8-foot wooden skis, canvas bindings, and stout steering poles. Smiling from century-old sepia photographs, it doesn't appear as if they missed the lifts that much. But then skiers have always been an adaptable bunch. Looking up into the torrential snowfall, I'm starting to think that Dan Hawley and the Boise Weather Service may be right. And sucking in my stomach and getting a purchase on my wind, I drop to the first bump, unweight and drop to the next, the terrain materializing out of a gray fog of falling flakes.

REST AND RECUPERATION

If you want to take a break from Alpine skiing, the Wood River Valley offers an extensive network of cross-country tracks, some free and maintained by the **Blaine County Recreation District**, others for a fee just east of the Lodge in Sun Valley (622-2251) and at **Galena Lodge** (726-4010) 25 miles north of Ketchum on Highway 75; or further in the Sawtooth Valley, the **Busterback Ranch** (774-3544) with overnight accommodations.

Besides studying politics or reading the Wood River Journal and Mountain Express, Ketchum offers more conventional entertainments. If Jackson Hole and Taos are the gallery capitals of western resorts, Ketchum—Sun Valley would place a close third. More than two dozen galleries manage to cover the artistic spectrum, and along with numerous openings offer a refreshing alternative to the local fixation with houses built for speculation, powder skiing, and elk hunting.

As far as I'm concerned two out of three aren't bad, but if I had my druthers I'd rather go country swing dancing at **Country's** in Elkhorn. Or rock and roll to the Heaters at **Slavey's** on Main Street. I wish Rude Bruce and the Vile Tones were still around and hope the Vuarnettes stay together. Once a winter Rick Kessler's **Magic Lantern** features a film festival, and each day at 5:00 P.M. Sun Valley's **Opera House** runs *It Happened in Sun Valley,* with Sonja Henie. Joe Cannon plays at Sun Valley's **Ram Bar,** and Mike Murphy can be seen at **Creekside.** Dinner sleigh rides can be booked from the **Sun Valley Inn** out to Trail Creek Cabin; Sawtooth Sleighs (622-5019) also offer rides out North Fork canyon for $48 per person—steak, lobster, wine, etc. included.

You can ice skate at the **Sun Valley ice rink** or watch a weekly semipro hockey game with the **Sun Valley Suns.** Bowling is also available in the **Lodge Basement** or in Bellevue 15 miles south.

Don, Mark, Chip, and the boys at **Sun Summit** (726-0707) on Warm Springs Road will tune the magic back into your skis. Ketchum's **Community Library** on Spruce Avenue has a wonderful regional history department; the library is just up the street from the **Ore Wagon Museum.** You can take a glider ride with **Sun Valley Soaring** (788-3054). Or if you want some of the best helicopter skiing in the Northwest, **Sun Valley Helicopter Ski Guides** (622-3108). Depending on the month, the **Sun Valley Center for the Arts** presents plays and concerts and periodically the local art galleries feature **gallery walks** combining food, heady conversation, and art. KART, Ketchum's free bus service, allows you to leave your car parked.

CHAPTER 4

THE PLEASURES OF TELLURIDE

THE PACKAGE WAS WRAPPED IN PLAIN BROWN paper—an obvious effort to throw the postal inspectors off the scent. By the time I freed it from my post office box, one corner had ripped open and was leaking confetti onto the floor. Retreating to my truck where I could inspect it in private, I discovered one party hat, one roller party horn with a feather on the end, and two double handfuls of confetti that spilled across the front seat.

"You are invited to *Powder Magazine*'s 15th Anniversary Party," it began, and then proceeded to list the writers, photographers, editors, and manufacturers who were planning to attend. The invited read like a who's who in American ski journalism—Chris Noble, Rod Walker, Neil Stebbins, Gary Brettnacher, Gordon Wiltsie, Don Patton, David Moe, Bob Woodward, Jan Reynolds, Casey Sheahan, Ron Dahlquist, Peter Sholton, Tim Petrick, Lito Tija Flores, Greg Stump, and near the bottom, my name with a question mark.

"In exchange, you will be asked to contribute a short anthology," it mentioned in closing.

There was never any question about my RSVP. This would be the social event of the season—a chance to slam the best writing in the business, rip off photographic angles, steal ideas, trade insults, and play mind games all in the name of good fellowship and honest criticism.

The designated site of this love feast was Telluride. Never having skied Telluride, I had read about it. I knew it sat in a high Colorado box canyon. I knew it had an awesome front face, and I knew its main street had been frozen circa 1880s, when miners scaled the surrounding cliff faces to discover all that glinted was gold. And I knew to get there from anywhere else required a road trip to hell.

Continental Express (tel. 800-525-0280) offers nonstop flights to Telluride Regional Airport from Denver. Mesa Airlines (tel. 800-MESA-AIR) offers direct flights from Denver, Phoenix, and Albuquerque. Stateswest Airlines (tel. 800-247-3866) flies daily into Telluride from Phoenix. United Express (tel. 800-525-1143) connects to Montrose and Grand Junction from Denver. And America West (tel. 800-247-5692) flies into Grand Junction and Durango out of Phoenix.

This remote Colorado resort rarely makes the nation's top ten. Based on such values as Grooming and Lodging, Telluride gets buried by Vail, Aspen, and Steamboat. It doesn't stack up in Onslope Service, where Deer Valley employees carry your skis to the slopes and Beaver Creek hands out free hot chocolate and cookies. It doesn't place in the Snowmaking, Family Fun, or Gourmet Food categories. In fact, the more you study the surveys, the more depressing it gets. Telluride doesn't do well in Mountain Food, and it doesn't even show up in Resorts That Offer Daytime Diversions Other Than Skiing. So why would a skier ever want to come here? Good question. Unless you consider Most Challenging Terrain and Wait in Lift Line surveys, where Telluride suddenly explodes into the top three. No lift lines, big terrain, and the same storm pattern that regularly boosts Taos into the top four. What more could a skier ask for?

Well, a little easier access. But then location, location, and location have always been Telluride's boon and bane. Unless you fly, this box canyon is off the map. In fact, it's not near anything, unless you count Montrose, Ouray, or Durango on Colorado State Highway 550 as somewhere. That's why you never hear about stars settling here. No Demi or Bruce or Clint to put this place on the map. It's too high, too isolated, and (here's the worst part) too rustic, too authentic with its weathered brick façades, bed-and-breakfasts, and honest-to-God moguls on the shadowed faces above.

Flying into Telluride is one of those rare experiences, every traveler worth his bonus miles should experience. With the Dash 8 propjet skimming above the glistening San Miguel River and the hillside cliff faces flickering off the right wing, everyone takes an extra purchase on their belt and stops breathing until the runway miraculously appears beneath the wheels.

Downtown Telluride is short on cedar condos and long on weathered brick mercantile. Victorian plays well here. In '64 Telluride was designated a national historic landmark, spurring the preservation of two-story classics shaded by gingerbread eaves, shiplap siding, and ornate front porches. Tourism now dwarfs the past output of the Tomboy Mine, and in an effort to perpetuate the past, locals have restored, repainted, and in many cases copied that Victorian style.

Telluride offers guests free mountain tours. Lasting roughly an hour and requiring advanced beginner or better proficiency, the tours meet at the top of the Coonskin lift. From the summit

With over sixty hotels, condominiums, and bed-and-breakfasts, Telluride and the Mountain Village Resort offer ski-in and ski-out convenience. Located in Telluride and within a block of the lifts is the new **Ice House Lodge**, 310 South Fir, Telluride, Colorado 81435. Res: (303) 728-6300. Amenities: Hot tub, Jacuzzi, sauna, private baths, cable TV, maid service, phones, and continental breakfast. Terms: seven nights skiing, six days lodging, $629 per person. Restrictions: no pets.

For a condominium on the river and within a block of the lifts try the **Manitou Riverhouses**, 333 South Fir, Telluride, Colorado 81435. Res: (303) 728-4011. Amenities: Hot tub, Jacuzzi, sauna, fireplaces, kitchens, cable TV, maid service, phones, and parking. Terms: $532 for seven nights skiing, six days lodging. Restrictions: no pets.

Or in the downtown area and within two blocks of the lifts try the **New Sheridan Hotel**, 231 West Colorado, Telluride, Colorado 81435. Res: (303) 728-4351. Amenities: Private bath, cable TV, maid service, phones. Terms: seven nights skiing, six days lodging for $289. Restrictions: no pets.

A great bed-and-breakfast within a block of the lifts is **San Sophia**, 330 West Pacific, Telluride, Colorado 81435. Res: (303) 728-3001. Amenities: Hot tub, fireplace, kitchen, private bath, cable TV, maid service, phones, parking, and full breakfast. Terms: seven nights lodging, six days skiing for $611 during the regular season. Restrictions: no pets.

For prices, brochures, and reservations contact: Telluride Central Reservations, P.O. Box 1009, Telluride, Colorado 81435, tel. (800) 525-3455. Or inside Colorado call (303) 728-4431.

★

the run includes several stops to cover local history, mountain facilities, and future expansion. By rights this free tour should come under the elusive heading of Onslope Service. There are others, of course. Catching the base chair before it slams into the back of your knees is thoughtful but not extraordinary care. By now the classic "Have a good run" is an automatic audible. There is Telluride's "Early Season Warm-Up," which offers a 25 percent savings on lift tickets from November 22 to December 15.

Riding the number eight chair up the Telluride Face, I get my first look at Colorado's San Juans. Surrounded by the Uncompahgre National Forest and inundated by 300 inches of snow per year, the towering north-south ridges run to the horizon. With 3155 vertical feet serviced by six double chairs, two triples, and one quad, Telluride's 735 skiable acres are divided among 14 percent beginner, 54 percent intermediate, and 32 percent advanced. In this case "advanced" is a relative term, for studying the monster bumps on Plunge beneath the number eight chair, I realize that at most resorts this run would be declared off-limits (or at least named Off-Limits).

Along with a definable intimidation, the Plunge offers an eagle's view of Telluride. Magazine "how to" pieces advise not to look at your tips, but on Telluride's face it's about impossible not to. Here you don't really look at your tips, you look through them at the dirt streets below where bent 4 × 4 pickup trucks, rusted-out Volvos, and the free city buses circulate through Telluride's square blocks. It's only with some effort that you study the first set of bumps and try to decide whether to go right or left.

If Telluride is light on Onslope Service, it needn't apologize for its terrain. Big bumps on Spiral, Stairs, and Mammoth, or groomed intermediate trails such as See Forever, Butterfly, or Smuggler; or untracked crud and shaded glades where powder lies undisturbed beneath the lowering spruce on Happy Thought above the Gorrono Basin—in the space of two runs Telluride can make you feel like a hero or a clown.

Not so odd when you figure heroes, clowns, and outlaws built Telluride. It wasn't until 1875 (late by Western standards) that prospectors put up a bunch of tents and called it Columbia. Columbia was a pretty common name in the Old West, and since the element tellurium is often found with gold and silver, the name Telluride naturally followed.

Along with Welsh and Italian miners, cowboys, Indians, and women of easy virtue were drawn to this canyon by dreams of overnight wealth. Telluride was also visited by Butch Cassidy, who robbed the local bank, and William Jennings Bryan, who, in his turn-of-the-century presidential campaign, thundered against the "Cross of Gold" at the New Sheridan Hotel on Colorado Avenue. Jack Dempsey once washed dishes here, and mine owner Bulkeley Wells narrowly missed being blown up by a bomb during union violence. The mines witnessed boom, bust, and cave-ins, and today Telluride depends on brightly plumed skiers in front-buckle boots and black Vuarnet glasses who take the right at Ridgway and wind up the canyon.

Skiers who are drawn to the "Face" tend toward Zen in both dress and style. Here massive knee action is matched by a certain idiomatic color scheme. Little wonder that the USSA Junior National Freestyle Championship originated in Telluride or that the U.S. Men's Pro Tour stops here. As in the past when locals let their picks, revolvers and dynamite do their talking, today long skis and fast feet are quotable.

That doesn't mean mirrored goggles and hunter neon orange jumpsuits are prohibited on this mountain, but you see them mostly on Butterfly or Misty Maiden—pleasant intermediate runs where you can strut your stuff without fear of crossing your tips and getting launched at the distant Meadows Base Facility.

Coinciding with the *Powder* party, Telluride is hosting the "King of the Hill" competition—a giant slalom, mogul, fresh powder *mano a mano* where the winner is judged on elapsed time and a certain alpine joie de vivre.

Unloading above Jaws, I catch the connecting number nine

chair to the 11,890-foot summit where the competitors are already skating away from the start of the giant slalom course.

See Forever is a wide intermediate run, and I carry decent speed next to the dark Doug fir down to the number three chair. With a tradition of hard-rock miners tunneling to the earth's core, it should come as little surprise that Telluride uses numbers in place of names for its lifts. None of that cutesy "Sky High Express" stuff here. It's number one, number two, and number three, which sounds more like grocery list. It's a small criticism and quickly forgotten when you hit Palmyra and Polar Queen off the number five lift.

It is early afternoon when I follow a group of fellow writers into the trees off Bushwacker. It is a tight, unforgiving slot and I traverse around the tight spots and shiver before the promise of picking bark out of my teeth.

Stopping to stare across into a steep, out-of-bounds chute, a friend tells us that two days before, an avalanche swept off the Gold Hill Ridgeline. With tracks leading into the fracture, it didn't take the Ski Patrol long to figure out that someone kicked it off. The victim is a kid on vacation who gambled and lost. Now a supply helicopter beats away from the 30-foot deposition where sixty volunteers are probing for the remains. No one wants to dwell on it, for we have all taken chances and the only difference is timing—the right place and wrong time.

For après stars in your eyes try **Leimgruber's von Telluride German Bierstube**, 728-4663. Serves breakfast, lunch, and après views of the mountain. The **Excelsior Cafe**, 728-4250, serves a world-class breakfast, lunch, pastries, and espressos. Try **China Cellar**, 728-4680, for Cantonese and Szechuan. The **Floradora Saloon**, 728-3888, for Western American; and **Sofias**, 728-4882, for Mexican and Southwest specialties.

Though the sun departs Telluride proper by midafternoon, Telluride's eastern ridgeline catches the day's last rays. Sitting in the condo's hot tub, it's clear *Powder* parties are hard work. In half an hour I'm expected for the ritual dark beer at Leimgrubers followed by dinner at the Floradora Saloon. It's a tough job, and I drag myself away from the frothy water and stumble upstairs to dress in the closet.

In the surveys Telluride is noticeably absent in the après department. Then, too, so are Bend and Jackson Hole. The point is you shouldn't believe everything you read. If, however, you arrive in Telluride expecting to bust bumps all day and rodeo all night, you may be partly disappointed. The mountain won't let you down, but local entertainment does run to pleasant conversation, country swing, and the occasional special event—Christmas Week, January's Pro Tour and Governor's Cup, and the Butch Cassidy Nordic Chase.

And just when I'm convinced how boot heel–common Telluride's nights can be, I hear a disturbance in one corner and turn to see a figure fighting to remove a surgical glove from his head. For a moment no one reacts as the glove expands to 18 inches. Inside an embryonic face is screaming for help.

Someone starts to move, there's a bang, and a dusting of talcum powder fills the air.

Morning comes early. Too early. I'm not sure what happened after the Sheridan. I do know I made it home at 1 A.M. The following morning I find myself skiing Spiral. Today are the King of the Hill finals—the mogul and deep-powder finals. The moguls will run on Stairs, an aptly named north-facing run the grooming crews abandoned to the bumps. Today they are big, arrhythmic cardiac arresters. Rather than risk a major crash, I see spectators packing their skis down the left side. With the light lying obliquely across the top of the bumps, the big dogs begin to run in the tall grass.

Following the bumps, the competition shifts to the powder run. For the past two weeks Telluride has kept the double-black-diamond Dynamo Bowl roped off. Now visions of big-money powder shots—blue sky, deep snow, and skier after skier throwing crystal contrails up against the jagged horizons—fill my creative eye. Later, as sky divers spiral down to a huge birthday cake lit with road flares, the awards are announced.

One detail remained in *Powder*'s fifteenth anniversary. The Powder Prom—the fragrant corsage, evening gown, cummerbund blowout. I dress my best in a white undershirt, letterman jacket, black shoes, white socks, and stained Levi's with the belt loops razored off. Slicking my hair back, I figure to fit in. And do. I win Best Greaser.

REST AND RECUPERATION

If your knees and back need a rest from Telluride's front face, you can trade your alpine ticket for a two-hour Nordic clinic, a day of rentals and track fees. Or if you want to go heli-skiing in the San Juans or take a scenic flight ($40 per person for a twenty-minute flight), call **Telluride Helitrax** (728-4904). There's shopping along

Colorado Avenue, where you should stop at the **Potter's Wheel** (728-4912), which features handcrafted Colorado pottery. Have a drink at the **Floradora Saloon** on West Colorado (728-3888). One mile west of Telluride at **Alpine Snowmobiles**, (728-4690), you can rent a snowmobile for $60/half day. And you can photograph the old Victorians, visit the art galleries, or go ice skating.

CHAPTER 5

STEAMBOAT SPRINGS: SMALL TOWN, BIG MOUNTAIN

A PHOTOGRAPH TAKEN IN STEAMBOAT SPRINGS, Colorado, shows a couple on horseback plowing through waist-deep powder snow. Deep tracks lead back to a weathered barn that, in turn, is backdropped by the ski runs on 10,388-foot Storm Peak. If it wasn't for the skis slung across their saddles, they could be headed out to cut a Christmas tree or round up stray cattle or chase mustangs or any of the other scenes tobacco companies use to suggest socially acceptable places to smoke.

Admittedly this skis-across-the-saddle business is the kind of thing Madison Avenue earns big dough for and yet, in this particular case, it works. On the strength of its Cowboy Downhill alone, Steamboat Springs is probably the only U.S. resort that's comfortable with the rodeo salute—a two-fingered wave rodeo queen contestants use on the Fourth of July as they hurtle around the arena. Now if you have to ask what a Cowboy Downhill is, you obviously haven't seen a bunch of rodeo stars dressed in chaps, Levi's, and ski boots risk all in a lemming start—winner take all—tuck for the finish.

No doubt about it: Steamboat Springs has a valid claim to the heart of the American West. Take Highway 40 through Northern Colorado and you'll understand why, for this is cow, antelope, and elk country dominated by the Rocky Mountains, the Routt National Forest, and the meandering Yampa River. Here big horses and bigger horizons stand shoulder-to-shoulder with big-hearted Western hospitality, and if you smirk at that description, you probably haven't stopped for chicken fried steak in Walden or seen the sun set from Highway 40 near Craig. Little wonder Steamboat's known as "Ski Town U.S.A."

But Steamboat is far from a dusty frontier fort surrounded by herds of elk, bison, and steers. If you're looking for a rustic eddy that time overlooked, you best keep searching, for Steamboat is far from a Wolverton Mountain with lifts. Still, compared to cows, organized skiing is a relative latecomer to the Yampa Valley. On January 12, 1963, Storm Mountain opened with one short lift, a small A-frame lodge, and one skier. From those humble beginnings the area expanded to twenty lifts and twenty-five hundred skiable acres. Because the ski resort started roughly twenty-five years after the nation's oldest resorts, it has had to play catch-up and during the past decade has invested over $30 million in improvements.

The result is a marked contrast between the old town and Gondola Base areas. If old town Steamboat has the red brick and cedar shingle façades of a national historic site, the separate ski resort feels new. Its style is contemporary: its lifts sparkle and groomers beat everything but black-bump runs into submission. You can take a clinic from ex-Olympian Billy Kidd, go cat skiing with Jupiter Jones, learn to drive on ice, or take a ride in a hot-air balloon. Among the 10,300-plus-foot summits of Mt. Werner and Storm and Sunshine peaks, skiers have a choice of 20 lifts, 101 named trails, 2500 skiable acres, 3600 vertical feet, a 200-person ski school, and a season that runs from Thanksgiving to the ninth of April. If those statistics aren't attractive enough, a lopsided 54 percent of Steamboat's runs are rated intermediate, a paltry 15 percent are reserved for beginners, with the remainder abandoned to those experts who find a visceral thrill dodging through aspen groves or skiing Buick-sized bumps.

Steamboat Powder Cats, P.O. Box 2468, Steamboat Springs, Colorado 80477, tel. (303) 879-5188. Cat skiing off Buffalo Pass in Routt National Forest using Thiokol Sprite. Capacity twelve, guides, continental breakfast, lunch. Rates: $125 per person. Groups of six or more rate a 10 percent discount.

Here you'd be wise to knee your horse in the ribs and take a cinch on your saddle's girth strap for the Steamboat Ski Corporation was recently purchased by Kamori Kanko Company Ltd. of Sapporo City, Japan. Surprising but true and though exact figures on how much the Kamori Kanko Company paid have not been released, you can bet Steamboat didn't come cheap.

Depending on the roads, Steamboat is roughly an hour and a half drive from Laramie, Wyoming. From 6 miles away on Rabbit Ears Pass, you can see the lights of Steamboat's Gondola Base hotels and the dimmer lights of the old town's main street. Above, on Thunderhead Peak, a fleet of groomer cats is erasing the combined impact of ten million edge sets. From this first impression it appears as if Steamboat has turned its isolation into an asset, a place where frustrated cowboys and cowgirls still can settle into a temporary home on the range to chase some of the driest snow in North America.

Except you're in a distinct minority if you arrive from Laramie. No one except Laramie locals or car caravans from Iowa arrive from Laramie. For that matter, few skiers drive from Denver unless, of course, they live there. With daily flights on American Airlines from New York, Newark, Chicago, Dallas, and Los Angeles, as well as three flights a week on Northwest Airlines from Minneapolis/St. Paul and three a week from Phoenix on America West, there's little need for any of that "Wagon's Ho!" pioneering spirit. Most skiers take advantage of the almost eighty thousand inbound seats per season which, if they only ski five days, account for half of Steamboat's 900,000 skier days.

Steamboat is serviced by American Airlines from Chicago, Dallas/Ft. Worth, and Los Angeles. Weekly from New York, Newark, and San Francisco; reservations: (800) 433-7300. America West from Phoenix, reservations: (800) 247-5692. Continental Express connecting service from Denver, reservations: (800) 525-0280. Northwest Airlines three times weekly from Minneapolis/St. Paul, reservations: (800) 225-2525.

Steamboat's express bus runs daily from Denver's Stapleton Airport to Steamboat, tel (303) 879-0740. Express shuttle available from Yampa Regional Airport, tel. (303) 879-0740.

Rental Cars from Denver's Stapleton Airport and Yampa Regional Airport. Avis, tel. (800) 331-1212. Budget, tel. (800) 527-0700. Hertz, tel. (800) 654-3131.

One of Steamboat's major draws is the Steamboat Sheraton Hotel. Located in Ski Time Square and rising five stories above the Christie II and Christie III base lifts, a major advantage of the Sheraton (and in fact all of the hotels at the Christie and Gondola Base) is its ski-in ski-out access to the mountain. No shuttle buses, no long walks to the lifts or search for a parking place here. If you drive, you park your car and forget about it for the week. If not, there are free buses to the old town, while the Gondola Base (with its shops and restaurants) is a short walk out the back door.

Within a snowball's throw of the lifts is **Sheraton Steamboat Resort**, P.O. Box 774808, Steamboat Springs, Colorado 80477, tel. (800) 325-3535. Amenities: pool, whirlpool, Jacuzzi, ski-in ski-out, parking, retail outlets, and restaurants on premises. Terms: double $109–$139. A seven-night/six-day ski pass costs $556 per adult.

The **Inn at Steamboat**, 3070 Columbine Drive, Steamboat Springs, Colorado 80477, tel: (303) 879-2600. Amenities: pool, TV, phones, maid service, quarter mile from lifts, shuttle. Terms: $84 double. Seven-night/6-day passes, $468.

Harbor Hotel, 703 Lincoln Avenue, Steamboat Springs, Colorado 80477, tel: (303) 879-1522, 3 miles from area, access to shuttle. Amenities: whirlpool, Jacuzzi, continental breakfast, restaurant on premises. Terms: double $65–$85. Seven-nights/six-day passes, $412–$472.

Nordic Lodge Motel, 1036 Lincoln Avenue, Steamboat Springs, Colorado 80477, tel: (303) 879-0531. Amenities: whirlpool, Jacuzzi, continental breakfast, parking, pets allowed, 3 miles from area, shuttle. Terms: double $50–$62. Seven-nights/six-day passes, $349–$391.

All hotels listed can be booked through central reservations, tel. (800) 922-2722.

If the Sheraton is full, you'll probably be directed down the street to the Sheraton Thunderhead Lodge. Despite its romantic name, you can forget about sagging brass beds and bear-claw baths down the hall. Between the Lodge and Hotel there are two pools, five spas, men and women's saunas and steam rooms, and various tinkling piano bars where tanned couples sip white wine and trade notes about what they bought and where they skied.

After the flight or drive, all you'll want to do is flip the TV on and go facedown on the Lodge's queen-size bed, but this may be your only Saturday night in town. So the first question is, where and what to eat? With over fifty restaurants to choose from, you can go for the common or rare—and that's not a veiled reference to Colorado's aged beef.

The Sheraton has Cipriani's (879-2220) for Northern Italian and Remington's (879-2220) for theme buffets—oriental, seafood, pasta, and southwestern. There's Hazies (879-6111 ext. 465) on Thunderhead, which offers mind-blowing views to go with its nouvelle continental cuisine. For Italian there's Giovanni's Ristorante (879-4141) with Brooklyn-style Italian, and Mazzola's (879-2405) for traditional Italian at reasonable prices. French is served at L'Apogee (879-1919), which features veal, lamb, game, and seafood complemented by an extensive wine cellar. Try the Inferno (879-5111) for ribs, or beef at the Old West Steakhouse (879-1411) and at the Ore House at the Pine Grove Restaurant (879-1190). The Steamboat Yacht Club (879-4774) occupies a renovated fish hatchery, opens onto the Yampa River and faces the 90-meter jump. Along with watching Nordic jumpers and the Yampa River, diners have a choice of seafood, steaks, and daily specials.

Because it's close to the Lodge and because the desk clerk recommends it, try Dos Amigos (879-4270). Here you'll be more than a little grateful to the busy waitress who takes a minute to make small talk. At Dos Amigos, the down-home service suits the excellent Mexican food.

After paying the bill, drift past the retail shops that mix ski gear, T-shirts, and souvenir trinkets with classy boutiques and rock-and-roll bars. One of the more popular, the Tugboat, combines steamed windows and teeth-rattling rock and roll. Inside you'll find a band dressed in New York punk and western yoked shirts slashing away at guitars, drums, and synthesizers. Despite a packed dance floor, there's not a whole lot of cheek-to-cheek romance evident here. It's all flying boots and skintight Levi's, sparkling western hats, belts with silver buckles, and tight knots of dewy girls smiling at single guys. Five middle-aged women in fur coats enter the packed room. Grimacing at a wailing guitar solo, they huddle to vote on whether to stay or go, then beat a hasty retreat.

Breakfast has never been a skier's meal. By the time you order, wait for the food, eat, pay, and then run back to your room for your boots, goggles and gloves, it's 10 A.M., the lifts have been running for an hour, and the runs are starting to bump up. A quick cup of coffee is bad for the nerves and worse for your stomach. Though Steamboat's lifts start to load at 9 A.M., the Silver Bullet gondola will let you on at 8:15 for the Breakfast Express at BK's (Billy Kidd's) Corral. On a powder day this has to be the best line move in the Rockies. Imagine having a 2000-foot advantage on the competition when the flag drops. As the lower lifts start to load, you're on your way down Rudi's Run toward the Storm Peak triple. That gives you two free runs before the first base wave hits.

The Storm Peak chair climbs 2000 vertical feet to the 10,388-foot summit of the same name. Before ten o'clock you can have Storm Peak to yourself and, for a few runs at least, can let your skis run without fear of someone blundering into your line. (Later in the day this lift gets a lot of pressure.) Once on top turn toward Buddy's Run. Named after Buddy Werner, the now-legendary Olympian who was killed by an avalanche while filming in Europe, this broad intermediate trail serves as a perfect warm-up. Buddy Werner was one of two Americans to win the Inferno, a sixty-year-old citizens' downhill in Murren, Switzerland. As a result the Swiss still remember him with great respect and fondness. He also raced in Badgastein, Austria, where he fell 100 feet short of winning a downhill. The Austrians think Buddy's being born an American was a mistake. From the way he skied, he obviously had an Austrian soul.

A youthful death is tragic, but if you have to have something dedicated to your memory, a Colorado ski run is far preferable to a statue in the park. At least there's emotion in a ski run just as there's a life in a ski, and though a fair number of the people who turn down Buddy's Run won't know who he was, those who ski it pay silent homage to his memory.

Each night Steamboat's cats produce groomed corduroy. With cats knocking down the bumps and a summer blasting crew eliminating any subsurface obstacles, Steamboat serves as a prototype for a twenty-first-century resort. In the future skiers will demand more, not less service—more consistent grooming, faster lifts, additional runs, and better snowmaking, lodging, restaurants, and shopping. A little history won't hurt either. A chance to make a connection with the past, to imagine a bunkhouse full of cowboys dealing cards, staring at the wooded Storm Mountain and waiting for spring.

Though everyone loves a slalom ski's responsiveness, this morning Tornado is better suited to a giant slalom. You would expect Storm Peak's Cyclone, Tornado, Twister, and Hurricane to be massive bump runs. Though jumping from edge to edge down their groomed fall lines is great fun, these runs are neither tornadoes nor hurricanes. That's not saying they wouldn't be if they were allowed to grow moguls. Their pitch is conducive to bump building, and given a few days' vacation from the cats, they'd soon look like the aftermath of dredge mining.

In the Thunder Head cafeteria, I find Rickie Mewborn, who was a U.S. Nordic team jumper and now works as a Steamboat ski instructor, sitting with Larry Pierce, an international photographer, and Dr. Dave Wilkinson, Steamboat's emergency-room physician. Stepping into our skis, we head down Huffman's short face to Sundown triple, and Priest Creek double lifts that rise to Sunshine Peak's 10,385-foot summit. Mewborn, Pierce, and Wilkinson are all strong skiers, and on top Dr. Dave leads the way down Three O'Clock. Ten turns into this deceptive-sounding run tells me the cats haven't visited here in weeks—if ever. On Three O'Clock nature supervises the grooming by dumping an estimated 27 feet of snow per season. Today big bump leads to big bump with only short, deep transitions between. It makes no difference to Mewborn, who skis with a smooth, silent, almost distracted grace. The good doctor is more scientific in his approach, invariably picking the best line and sticking with it until it disappears into the aspens or ends on a cat track. Pierce points out that there are intermediate ways down. Tomahawk for example is a pleasant blue run that follows the area boundary back to the Sunshine triple. Add Quickdraw, Flintlock, and Highnoon, and intermediates can spend the entire day on this south face.

If you only ski groomed runs and ego snow, you're ultimately only able to ski groomed runs and ego snow, and so the trio takes another run down Three O'Clock, Pierce chasing Mewborn and Doctor Dave through the bumps until Mewborn hits a cat track and pops a breathtaking 360 that seems to freeze

time until he sticks the landing and is gone, banging from edge to edge as he races off to meet a private lesson.

Catching the Elkhead quad out of Priest Creek, they take Vagabond's intermediate ridge, then discover it's blocked by a crowd listening to Billy Kidd's daily clinic. Kidd is Steamboat's director of skiing, and though he learned to ski in Stowe, Vermont, and subsequently won a silver medal at the '64 Innsbruck Olympics, his signature is a white Stetson—the same style good guys wear in old westerns. Judging Kidd by his help with the Jimmy Huega Express, or his work as head ski coach for the International Special Olympics, or his position as an advisor for the President's Council on Physical Fitness and Sports, or his commentary for CBS, or his column for *Skiing magazine*, or any of the companies he represents, or his race camps, or even his skiing, you can't help but conclude that this transplanted Woodchuck is one of skiing's good guys.

Ski School, two-hour lesson, $24; all day, $34; ski week (5 two-hour lessons, BBQ, NASTAR, pin), $102.

   Billy Kidd Race Camps, 2305 Mt. Werner Circle, Steamboat Springs, Colorado 80487, tel. (303) 879-6111 ext. 284. December–March, six-day lifts included, $550.

If you watched Kidd win the Innsbruck silver, it's a thrill to take his clinic. Along with a hundred other skiers, you can see how he gets on and off his edges, what he does with his hands, hips, and ankles. During this informal lesson he describes the mechanics of a turn and the importance of the end game, then starts down Vagabond. The crowd takes off in hot pursuit, hoping the great one himself will pick one of them as an example of what he means by a carved turn.

If you mark years by the places you travel, real time passes at a blinding pace. The memories, of course, are brilliant, but the week passes so quickly it seems the days are little longer than a strobe flash, framing seconds in twenty-four hours. In that time you may catch a small storm and ski Steamboat's trademark aspen groves.

Ultimately if Steamboat is isolated, it's that very isolation that's attractive. If the couple in range dusters recently moved here from Chicago or the weathered brick building was finished last year—the ravages of time aside—both bear a believable authenticity. Steamboat still has a small-town, big-mountain feel—a rarity in these days when the reverse if often true. Surrounded by a million acres of empty range, national forest, and Rocky Mountains, here you ski into lifts, have runs to yourself, and don't need to jump through fire to get a table. And taking the Tower 3 traverse to the top of Vertigo, you see the cats have worked their magic, and hoping that the forecast for new snow is true, you push on one edge, step to the other, and drop toward Ski Time Square.

REST AND RECUPERATION

Along with the shops, galleries, restaurants, and nightclubs one would expect to find in Ski Town U.S.A. you can also find the **Ford/Michelin Ice Driving School**, tel. (303) 879-6104. Directed by French rally driver Jean-Paul Luc and equipped with its own cars and ice course, the school teaches the theory and practice of driving on ice- and snow-covered roads.

Swimming, saunas, fitness centers, and après entertainment are also available at the Sheraton. In mid-January Steamboat holds the **Cowboy Downhill** with slalom race, hostess lasso, horse saddling, and a final sprint to the finish. You can ride a wagon load of hay out to a wild elk herd, take moonlight sleigh rides, fly in a hot-air balloon, or hit the water slide (tel. 303-879-0470).

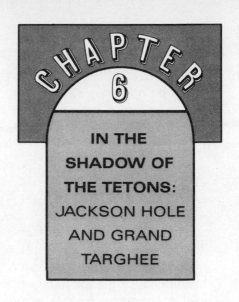

IN THE SHADOW OF THE TETONS: JACKSON HOLE AND GRAND TARGHEE

OR THE PAST THIRTY-SIX HOURS THE NATIONAL Weather Service has been predicting 2 feet for Grand Targhee Ski Area. Named for the last warrior chief of the Blackfoot Indians, Targhee sits on the Wyoming/Idaho state line just outside Grand Teton National Park. If the adjoining Snake River Plain seems to have little in common with the Grand Teton's 13,766-foot summit here, roughly 90 miles northeast of Idaho Falls, it is partly responsible for the area's deep winter snow. Between Wyoming's western border and Oregon's Cascade Mountains, little more than sage and scrub pine serve to impede the Pacific lows. These storms conserve moisture for an all-out assault on the Grand's jagged west slope. During an average winter 600 inches of snow will fall on Targhee, and though Jackson on the east slope receives a little less, 600 inches equals 6 inches a night for one hundred consecutive nights. If you encounter three days of blue skies, bet on an 18-inch dump the fourth day. If you book a week, watch out.

Rising like a ghostly gray mirage to the east of Driggs, the Tetons are always the first to show the effects of a gathering storm. And now they slowly disappear beneath the lowering cloud layer; the first flakes whirl across the road, and from then on it's a race against the building storm. Out on State Highway 33, which runs between Newdale and Tetonia, I see a bumper sticker that says, "Where the hell is Driggs, Idaho?" Most ski resort locals would pay big money for that kind of anonymity. Driggians might have to think twice; dependent on potatoes, cattle, and sheep, Driggs has weathered more than its share of economic drought, and that's not a veiled reference to the Teton Dam collapse that flooded Rexburg.

In all honesty Driggs is something less than quaint, or breathtaking, or immaculately preserved, or any of the other useful euphemisms used to plate ski towns with a romantic if false patina. From the local Spud Drive In to the Teton Teepee, to Joe's Place, Salsa de Border, and O'Roarkes, Driggs is a no-nonsense burg where turbo Mercedes, lynx coats, and other conspicuous displays of consumption still draw quizzical stares.

"Hell . . . probably missed the turn to Jackson," locals muse in front of the tiny post office.

In other words, you won't feel comfortable rave dancing in Driggs, Idaho. For après entertainment you've got a choice of Country Swing at Targhee's Trap Bar or a Budweiser at Mike's Eats. Gold chains, white suits, and disco fever will only get hooted out of this cow town. Best stick to a good steak, green salad with ranch, and an Idaho spud at the British Rail before retiring back to your motel room to watch the flakes drift out of the black Idaho night.

Morning in Driggs often arrives to the grate of highway plows. During the night the world metamorphoses into white mounds—big mounds for trucks, small mounds for sedans, conical mounds for pine trees. To ski Targhee on a powder day you need full assault gear—Gore Tex everything, turbo fan goggles, and soft giant slaloms. Then you'll need to dig your car out, chain up, and somehow get to Highway 33. If you're lucky the motel owner will have a snow blower, a path will miraculously open, and you'll be able to get started up the canyon. And if you're very lucky, your prayers for the highway crew will be answered, the road to Targhee will be plowed, and at 9 A.M. you'll abandon your car in the base lot and wade toward the Bannock chair.

Rising 2200 vertical feet to the summit, the Bannock chair is one of Targhee's two major lifts. The other is the Blackfoot double, which rises 1200 vertical feet to the top of Floyd's Fantasy. On clear days Targhee offers spectacular views of the 13,770-foot Grand Teton, 12,804-foot Middle Teton, and 12,514-foot South Teton west faces. If there's a downside to Targhee's numerous storms, it's missing this view. The poor visibility, however, is a fair trade as you pole through the knee-deep powder toward Chief Joseph Bowl. Here, along the area's north boundary, which faces the 12,605-foot Mount Moran, the grade increases, the speed comes up, and your skis float across the fall line. The key is to relax, unweight, and let your skis rise as the snow washes over your knees, and the trees pass like shadowy wraiths in the gray mists.

Seventy percent of Targhee's open glades and gentle bowls are rated intermediate. Ten percent is devoted to beginners, with the remaining twenty set aside for those experts who seek satisfaction in steep trees and deep powder. Off the Bannock chair, Sitting Bull Ridge accesses the expert runs of Good Medicine, The Ugly, and Bad Medicine, which offer a mix of trees, steeps, and buried bumps that drop into Chief Joseph Bowl, and a quick return Shoshone lift.

Trappers Jim Bridger and Joe Meeks are credited with exploring the Yellowstone and Teton watersheds, but the western drought of '87 was responsible for the arrival of Targhee's present owners. A lack of snow in Sun Valley caused Boston architect Mory Bergmeyer and his wife Carol to switch their reservations to Targhee. The previous owner was looking to sell and, in the Bergmeyers' words, "We saw a gem waiting to be polished."

This polishing image spooked locals, who preferred Targhee's affordable if tarnished authenticity to the glitzy, expensive alternative—a jet-in destination for the Fortune 500. And yet, saddled by its own isolation, shadowed by Jackson Hole Ski Area, and sited one and a half hours from Idaho Falls (which is not particularly known as a skier base), Grand Targhee had a reputation for great snow and little else. Targhee did have the snow, however, and the Bergmeyers set to work improving the lodging, restaurants, and lift capacity the resort needed to turn a profit. To pay for three proposed new lifts on

Replacing the old cafeteria and downstairs Trap Bar, the new Targhee Lodge will offer three restaurants, a ski-in ski-out bar, a movie loft, three specialty shops, a pro shop, rentals and repairs, a general store, and an activity center. Targhee's **Sioux, Targhee,** and **Teewinot lodges** were fortunately spared the conflagration, and entering the winter of '90–'91 this self-contained village also includes a swimming pool, sauna and hot tub, a day-care center, and two new snowcats that will operate on Peaked Peak; tel. (800) 443-8146.

Targhee appeals to families. Big Scout, Big Horn, and Little Big Horn are fall line beginner runs. Children twelve and under ski free when accompanied by an adult who is staying in one of Targhee's rooms. Targhee also rents a child's equipment package.

Down the road from Targhee try the **Teton Teepee**, Alta, Wyoming 83422, tel. (307) 353-8176. Amenities: ski packages, restaurant, entertainment, hot tub, resembles a large teepee, great fun. Terms: call for specific rates.

★

Peaked Peak and to house the number of skiers needed to pay for them, a complicated land swap with the Forest Service was arranged. In exchange for prime eagle habitat along the Snake River, the Bergmeyers would get an adjacent ridge near Targhee for a condominium development. Opposing the plan were locals who insisted on an environmental impact statement. Then Targhee's main lodge burned to the ground. When the smoke cleared the Bergmeyers shook their heads, rolled up their sleeves, and started in on the new lodge, which opened in November of 1990.

Located 90 minutes down Highway 22 across the 8429-foot Teton Pass, Jackson Hole, Wyoming, once served as a pretty fair symbol of the American West. Crowding the southern border of Grand Teton National Park, and within an hour drive of Yellowstone National Park, Jackson was about as western as anyone wanted to get. Up until the mid '60s grizzlies still panhandled along Yellowstone's roads, a gravel path led up to Old Faithful's steamy vent, and elk horns, bear traps, and rusted big-bore rifles filled downtown coffee shops.

Those symbols of the American West still form the foundation for Jackson Hole's booming tourist industry. Mounted elk heads, huge traps, and rolling block rifles are still pretty common fare in stores, restaurants, and even the banks. There is the Jackson Hole Museum, which displays Indian artifacts, the Wildlife Museum, the Colter Bay Indian Arts Museum, and Wildlife of the American West Art Museum.

But the city of Jackson Hole has lost its rough edges. It's been cleaned up, remodeled, painted, and organized. The food can be out of this world, the transportation system works, and the motel beds won't give you backaches. You can buy a new saddle, a silver belt buckle, an octagon-barrel 30-30, a graphite fly rod, and a new 4 × 4 truck. Even if the board sidewalks are filled with L.A. dudes in pearl-snap shirts, pre-washed bootcut Levi's, and $100 Stetsons, Jackson Hole isn't about to apologize for success.

Cow towns and Indian reservations have always appealed to

Alpenhof Lodge, Box 288, Teton Village, Wyoming 83205, tel. (800) 732-2311. Amenities: 41 rooms, swimming pool, lounge and restaurant on premises, cable TV, sauna, hot tub, ski lockers, ski to slope. Terms: $60–$135 midseason double.

The **Inn at Jackson Hole**, Box 328, Teton Village, Wyoming 83205, tel. (800) 842-7666. Amenities: 83 rooms, swimming pool, sauna, restaurant and lounge on premises, cable TV, fireplace in room, ski to slope. Terms: $115 double midseason.

The Sojourner Inn, Box 348, Teton Village, Wyoming 83205, tel (307) 733-3657. Amenities: 98 rooms, swimming pool, sauna, hot tub, TV, restaurant and lounge on premises, telephones, game room. Terms: $96–$135 midseason double.

tourists, and if someone stopped a bullet in a card game or went down in a scalping spree, it all ended up on the historical plaques that followed. In fact, the vanishing West has been chronicled to death, and today the last thing anyone wants to hear about is what a tragedy it was when someone invented barbed wire, built a railroad, or portrayed a broken-down cowboy as Ulysses on horseback.

Though Jackson saw its share of Indians and cattle, it was never dependent on either. The town traces its origins back to 1807, when John Colter split from the Lewis and Clark expedition to explore a vast geyser basin that became known as Colter's Hell. From 1810 to 1840 Jackson Hole served as crossroads for French-Canadian trappers who named the adjacent peaks *Les Trois Tetons,* or The Three Beasts. During that period the trappers held annual rendezvous near the present town site to trade, shoot, fight, and catch up on the news. Between 1871 and 1878 what would become Yellowstone Park was explored by the Hayden expeditions. As a result, in 1872 (eighteen years before Wyoming became a state), Congress set aside the park "For the Benefit of the People." Since the 1890s Jackson has been a stepchild of Yellowstone, a rough welcome mat for the adventurous few who rode the train to Victor, Idaho, before braving the Teton Pass to tour the park.

A century afterward there are a disproportionate number of women in western skirts, tooled leather boots, starched Dale Evans blouses, and string ties managing art galleries filled with Art d'Teton. If sex sells, in Jackson Hole at least, the Grand Tetons sell a whole lot better. With more than 2.5 million visitors a year, it's impossible to overcharge for oils of wizened trappers leading pack trains into the Tetons, or grizzly bears rearing before the Tetons, or bald eagles circling above the Tetons, or royal elk fighting in front of the Tetons. Whether Jackson's Cache Street or L.A.'s Rodeo Drive, you see enough of it, and it starts to remind you of paintings of kids with huge eyes or Elvis on velvet—a commentary on the times and a way to match the couch.

With summer crowds contributing the bulk of Jackson's tourist bonanza, the town has thirty-two motels, inns, and resorts. Preferences are limited only by budget. For information: Jackson Hole Visitors Council, Box 982, Dept. 8, Jackson Hole, Wyoming 83025, tel. (800) 782-0011 ext. 8.

From the volumes of work published on this southern portal to the Tetons and Yellowstone National Park, you would think that the Teton Village is a classy-sounding suburb of Jackson Hole, that its lifts are a two-step away from the Shady Lady Saloon, that you can ski into a chair on the busiest day of the week, and that a missed edge set will land you in a downtown gallery. If that's the case you've got the right city but the wrong resort. Jackson Hole Ski Resort sits 12 miles to the northwest. Snow King, however, rises out of the city center.

In the years since 1948, when Jackson local Neil Rafferty hitched a pickup-powered rope tow up to what is now Exhibition run, Snow King has added two double chair lifts that service five hundred acres. You can now alternate open fall lines with a run out Leeks Canyon to Highway 89.

At a distance Snow King seems to belong to another era. From downtown Jackson its front face is a hanging tapestry of wooded glades, moguls, dizzying drops, and dancing marionettes. Because the King is a locals' mountain, it is shaped by expert skiers. Thus the bumps on Bearcat, Belly Roll, and Upper Exhibition can serve as either a challenge or a lesson.

This mountain skis bigger than its 1571 vertical feet. As the Snow King Double digs for altitude, Jackson and the Teton Valley stretch away to the north. On top this view is equaled only by the consistent pitch on Grizzly, Elk, and, Cougar—animals that frequent this northwest section of Wyoming and runs that offer a spectrum of conditions, bumps, crud, groomed and, when it snows, Central Rockies powder.

At Snow King you will find the **Great American Ski School**. Founded and directed by Bill Briggs, who was the first man to ski the precipitous Grand Teton, a single hour-and-a-half lesson costs $18; three and a half hours cost $32. Costs decline to $13 and $22 for four lessons. Snow King Ski Area, Jackson, Wyoming 83001, tel. (307) 733-5200 or (800) 522-KING.

By any standard Snow King is a bargain: a full-day lift is $20, a half-day is $14, and children under 14 ski for $14. **Snow King Resort**, Box Ski, Jackson, Wyoming 83001, tel. (800) 522-KING. Amenities: 204 rooms, swimming pool, sauna, hot tub, cable TV, lounge and restaurant on premises, pets okay, ski lockers, nonsmoking rooms. Terms: $100–$120 per night double occupancy.

Compared to the huge summer crowds, in winter Jackson is deserted. Vacancy signs mark West Broadway, Cache, and Pearl streets. Restaurant waiting lists are short, store shelves are full, and the START public buses are empty. If you squint slightly at the white lights on the town square's Elk-horn arches, Jackson might still just be a bend in a Wyoming road where travelers can find a room, a decent steak, and a cold soda.

The history of Jackson Hole Ski Area is tied inextricably to Paul McCollister, a California businessman who came to the Teton Valley in 1942 to hunt elk. What followed was a series of summer and winter vacations during which McCollister grew to love Jackson's fishing, skiing, and hunting. It's not known if McCollister ever got an elk. A more important result of that hunting trip, however, was the highest vertical and some of the best terrain in the United States. In '57 he sold his business and moved to Jackson. A few years later he was approached by a group of businessmen interested in building a ski resort.

Jackson offers more than steak and beans in its fifty restaurants. You can feast on Italian at **Anthony's** 733-3462, then spend a diverting couple of hours riding a saddle stool and watching couples swing dance to a live band at the **Cowboy Bar**, 733-2207. Or try the **Blue Lion**, 733-3912, and the **Teton Pines**, 733-1005, for continental cuisine. Fondue is good at the **Sojourner Inn's Fondue Pot**, 733-3657. Try the **Alpenhof**, 733-3462, for German, the **Lame Duck**, 733-4311, for Chinese and sushi and **Stieglers**, 733-1071, for Austrian. Lastly if you're looking for beef, try the **Mangy Moose**, 733-4913, at the ski area or the **Steak Pub**, 733-6977.

★

It's difficult to fault the view from Jackson Hole's Rendezvous Summit. To the north the Tetons offer their sunlit south faces to skiers stepping into their bindings. From here you can ski Rendezvous Bowl's Gros Ventre, a mildly bumped black run that drops to Laramie Bowl and the Upper Sublette Ridge quad chair. A second choice off the top is the infamous Corbet's Couloir, a near-vertical chute that requires a 10-foot leap of faith before you make the first turn. You don't, repeat do not, want to blow Corbet's entry. Standing below, I watched a tiny figure in red go for greatness. He seemed to be in control until just before the landing; then he rocked back, buried his tails, and rocketed out from the face. He next touched earth with his head, and the time after that on his feet in a nasty head foot endo down to the Downhill Traverse.

Avoiding what little temptation Corbet's might offer, I follow Gros Ventre, where the snow is cold and forgiving and the bumps rise and fall in harmony to the steep fall line's base beat. Catching the Sublette quad back to the top, I take the Hanging Rock traverse to Jackson's famous Hobacks. During the best of times the Hobacks' open faces offer a thousand-plus vertical feet of deep powder—during the worst, a thousand vertical feet of sun-softened corn. There's also Bivouac, a steep, bumped tree run that drops into Cheyenne Bowl. From here you can traverse back to the Thunder double chair, which climbs 1500 vertical feet in eight minutes, and then catch Gros Ventre as it sweeps through past the Cirque and Amphitheater.

For years Jackson Hole and Grand Targhee had a reputation for great snow and uncrowded slopes. Most of those missing skier days could be blamed on the transportation. Until 1986 Jackson was heavily dependent on charter flights. At that time Harry Baxter, Jackson's director of marketing, went to work on scheduled flights. Deregulation slowed the process, but eventually a ten-year contract was signed with American Airlines for direct flights out of Chicago. Delta, Continental, and United quickly followed, and today Delta offers daily flights from Salt Lake City, and United, Continental, and United Express have direct flights from Denver.

With 50 percent of its terrain rated expert, and a thigh-killing 4139 vertical, Jackson Hole is known as a technical mountain. Normally this adjective describes blue ice, tight trails, and off-camber runs. Jackson, however, is the exception. You can forget the ice and off-camber runs, but even with excellent snow, this mountain is intimidating. Black runs dominate Rendezvous Mountain and beginner/intermediates should know there is no cushy way off the top—no green traverse looping through the black diamond bumps. This is one reason Jackson charges $2 above its day ticket for each tram ride. If you're skiing the Hobacks, Lower Sublette Ridge, or the north or south Colter Ridges, which drop from the South Pass Traverse to the Union Pass Traverse, the tram offers the quickest return to the summit. Not everyone, however, can ski Rendezvous' upper runs or the Hobacks, and so the extra $2 offers quick access to the upper lifts without penalizing skiers who won't—or can't—use it.

Like Taos, Jackson Hole adds a yellow warning to the basic green, blue, and black ratings. Anyone capable of skiing the Alta Chutes that fall precipitously into Laramie Bowl can size them up from the Sublette quad chair. The same cannot be said for Paint Brush, Tower Three Chute, or Expert Chutes, Jackson's other yellow runs accessed off the Thunder double. More than any resort, Jackson resembles a maze, a groomed run leading to crud to a sheer moguled labyrinth that suddenly dives into the trees. To avoid these yellow runs, intermediates should commit a trail map to memory.

The majority of Jackson's intermediate terrain is serviced by the Eagle's Rest, the Apres Vous and Teewinot double chairs, and the Casper Bowl triple. Here, below Casper Bowl and Apres Vous Mountain's 8481-foot summit, the grade flattens out, the moguls disappear, and runs like Gros Ventre, Sundance Gully, Moran, and Werner offer wide-groomed fall lines. After a morning playing among Rendezvous' black diamonds, these broad blue avenues will rebuild your confidence.

Because Jackson has promoted its western origins, you would expect red bandannas, ten-gallon hats, and pointy-toed boots to be de rigueur attire. To an extent that is true, and if you're so moved, who's to know if the authentic-looking character moseying past the storefronts is a bona fide cowboy or a Chicago pork-futures dealer?

In the Tetons days swing between bright sun and dark snow-falls, and when you finally catch a flight out the next in a series of low-pressure systems has already begun to darken the jagged western ridge. Belted into Delta and seated next to the window, as the jet begins to roll, you have to admire those early tourists who labored across this same Teton Pass. Then it was a wagon and a team of experienced mules, and as the iron wheels banged down the rough shale road, one of the company might have complained that a century before the trappers had this all to themselves. Now the hotels and makeshift restaurants had reduced it to paradise lost. And the other passengers bore it for awhile, before suggesting he put a lid on it and enjoy the view.

On most mornings you'll find a crowd waiting for the **Jackson Hole Tram**, which takes twelve minutes to climb 4139 feet from the Teton Village to Rendezvous Mountain's 10,450-foot summit. Jackson Hole claims the highest vertical in the continental U.S. — which, when combined with its single quad, triple, five doubles, and sixty-two maintained runs more than compensate for the $28 day rate plus $2 for the tram.

★

REST AND RECUPERATION

Winter in Jackson Hole is not solely limited to skiing. Here you can go snowmobiling in both parks and tour the **National Elk Refuge,** where nine thousand elk winter. There are guided snowshoe tours in **Grand Teton National Park** (733-2880) and heli-skiing in the Snake River Range with **High Mountains Helicopter Skiing** (307-733-3274). Snowcat skiing at **Targhee** (800-443-8146). You can ski Jackson Hole's **Casper Bowl** with past Olympian and ski school director Pepi Stiegler (800-443-6931; local, 733-2292) or explore **Teton Pass**'s untracked meadows with Bill Briggs, the king of back-country skiing (733-5781). If you can ski 150,000 vertical feet in a single week, Jackson Hole Ski Area will give you a pin and certificate to commemorate your determination as part of its "I Skied the Big One."

In Jackson you can find Indian jewelry, Norwegian sweaters, Texas boots, French skis, or Jackson Hole real estate for those wealthy few who can afford to lock up their own corner of Wyoming paradise. Names like **Raindance Traders** (733-1081), **Wyoming Outfitters** (733-3877), and **Corral West Ranchwear** (733-0247) give you an idea of the merchandise to be found beneath the mounted elk heads.

The local **Dancer's Workshop** offers lessons in progressive western swing (733-6398). There's night skiing on **Snow King**, which has a Ski Ball January 27 (733-6433). And if you entertain fantasies about being the world's best powder skier, there's the **Powder 8s** run in Cody Bowl from February 10 to 11 (733-2292).

CHAPTER 7

SKIING THE SOVIET UNION

THE YOUNG RUSSIAN SLIPPED BETWEEN THE ELevator doors in the decaying Sport Hotel, glanced at my skis, and inquired, "Hey man, where you from?"

Galina Pavlovra had warned me about Moscow's black marketers, but I assumed they frequented Arbot Street, Gum Department Store, and the alleys around Red Square. After an eighteen-hour flight on SAS from Seattle to Sheremetyevo, I figured he wanted to trade pins, and replied, "U.S.A."

"Ah, U.S.A., good . . ." Then in a low voice he said, "Look, you change money? I give you eight rubles one dollar!"

Eight per dollar was twelve times the official rate! In spite of stiff penalties for illegal currency trading, his offer was almost too good to refuse. Less than two hours in Moscow, and I'm already off balance. Getting hit on by an eighteen-year-old black marketer in a shaking elevator is a long way from riding a detachable quad in the U.S.A.—perhaps too far—but who would have thought it would start like this? Due to the cost of

SAS offers daily flights from New York, Chicago, Seattle, and Los Angeles that connect with SAS's Flight 730 which departs Tuesday through Saturday from Copenhagen to Moscow; reservations: (800) 221-2350, ask for tour desk. SAS Viking Vacations (800-344-9099) and Bennett Tours (800) 221-2420 offer packages to the Russian resourt of Gudauri. Pan Am (800) 221-1111 also offers round-trip, nonstop flights New York to Moscow on Tuesday, Thursday, Friday, and Saturday.

If you book a tour, the operators will make in-country flight reservations. For me, Sovintersport handled these arrangements, which worked flawlessly.

If you plan to book your own travel, flights within the Soviet Union are all on Aeroflot. Planes are typically full and reservations are difficult, if not impossible, to change, so stick to your itinerary.

equipment, travel, lodging and lifts, alpine skiing is a patently bourgeois sport, and thus it wouldn't have surprised me if the Russian rank and file regarded sliding downhill as frivolously anti-Communist.

In fact, until just recently there was little, if any, hard information about Soviet ski areas. I knew the Russians had a ski team, and that was all I knew.

Even my friends were skeptical. "They don't actually ski in Russia . . . do they?" they typically inquired.

"Of course," I replied, unable to name even a single resort. And yet, whether Russians skied or not was a moot point until perestroika and glasnost. If Gorbachev's intent was to modernize Soviet heavy industry, tourism was the first to benefit. Almost immediately visa restrictions fell, travel increased, and skiing in the Soviet Union became a possibility.

Still, I didn't know where, or how much it would cost, or how

I would get into the country, until Ken Asvitt mentioned that he knew a ski instructor who lived in Elbrus. In 1986 Ken had climbed to 21,000 feet on Pik Communism with Vladimir Lukyaev, a high-altitude guide who was born in Elbrus. Ken gave me Vladimir's Moscow address, where I wrote to offer him a job as my guide and interpreter. "I will cover all expenses and pay you whatever you consider a fair wage," I said in closing.

Six weeks later I had given up hope when a telegram appeared from Alptour, a Soviet climbing society. "Can organize your stay Chimbulak, Elbrus, Dombai . . ." it started in a businesslike voice from the great abyss. Involved with a film project in Switzerland. Vladimir had forwarded my letter to a reputable agency.

Sovintersport can arrange trips to most Soviet ski resorts, including guides, flights, ground transfers, lift tickets, and hotels. Minimum group sizes of five are requested. Communications between the United States and Soviet Union take time, so start the process six months in advance. Also it is best to send a specific time frame and preferred destinations. All transactions are in dollars and do not include flights to Moscow. Sovintersport, USSR, Moscow 121069, Bolshoi Rzhevskii Pereulok 5.

That's how I found myself dealing with a black marketer. Back home I would have ignored the young hustler, but after forty years of cold war and two hours in Moscow, I hated to be typed as a Capitalist Running Dog (even by a black marketer), and so instead I was idiotically polite.

"Thank you, I'm sorry, no change money," I said.

"Okay, understand, I give very, very good rate . . . ten rubles, one dollar," he persisted, not rudely but astonished by his good fortune. To corner a veritable millionaire in an elevator and not somehow profit was inconceivable.

"No? Okay, lock boxes? Best quality?"

Where did he learn to speak English so well? "No, thank you, no lock boxes . . ." I said, not unkindly. At most he could only afford to trade ten dollars (eighty rubles, or about half what an engineer in Moscow will make in a month). The Soviet Union functions on two currencies. First there are official rubles—which, other than rent, food, and clothes (when the shops have them) will buy very little. And then there are the black market dollars, Swiss francs, marks, kroner, etc.—which, though illegal for Russians to possess, can be traded for luxuries: western clothes, cosmetics, toothpaste, shampoo, cigarettes, coffee, scotch, vodka, etc.

"Matrushka dolls?" He was getting desperate. "You give me room number, I bring."

The Soviet Union has chronic shortages in cigarettes, coffee, chocolate, gum, cosmetics, film, cassettes, etc. The Soviets are proud people, and some discretion must be used to avoid having a gift seem like a handout, but any of the above will be well received. Also western magazines are appreciated. Vodka, the national drink, is difficult to obtain, and it might be wise to buy as much as you can carry in the duty-free.

At dinner that night, I described the incident to Galina Pavlovra, my interpreter. "I see," she said, glancing away from the floor show where a dozen dancers were doing the rumba. Despite the recorded Cuban rhythms, low-cut flowered tops, and leggy dresses, their graceful arms and slender necks betrayed a classical background. Could they be washouts from the Bolshoi, simply superb if not brilliant, now reduced to baring their shoulders in dinner shows to pay the rent?

"And when he offered to exchange money . . . what did you do?" Galina interrupted my musings.

"Traded ten dollars," I replied to gauge her reaction.

"No!" she whispered, setting her fork down. "This is impossible! How could you know he was not working for the police? You must promise me you will not do these things!"

Russia. Pushkin, Tolstoy, Dostoyevski, Pasternak, and Solzhenitsyn. The Czars, Revolution, Lenin, and Stalin. Sputnik, Cuba, SALT, Afghanistan, and perestroika. The writers I have admired and the politics of fear combined in a monolithic system that most resembles Orwell's 1984—a social black hole from which no color emerges. Or at least these were my impressions before I cleared Sheremetyevo customs where Galina was waiting for me.

To ski in Russia you must have an invitation in order to secure a visa. In most cases that invitation is handled by a domestic tour company or Soviet Intourist. Make your reservations first, then apply for a visa using your confirmation. Visa applications are available at the Soviet embassies in New York, tel. (212) 861-4900, or San Francisco, tel. (415) 922-6642. Within the Soviet Union, Intourist, 630 Fifth Avenue, New York, N.Y. 10103, tel. (212) 757-3884, handles reservations for flights and the transfer from Mineral Vody to Elbrus. The Intourist Hotel Otrar in Alma-Ata is clean, the food is varied, and the staff efficient.

Dressed in red pants, a purple sweater, black boots, a gray beret, and holding a sign with my name on it, she does not look much like a citizen of the Evil Empire. In fact, for the next two weeks she will be invaluable, giving me not only literal interpretations, but the sense and emotion of what people say.

On the ride in from Moscow past gray blocks of apartments, crowds at bus stops, statues of Karl Marx, diesel trucks, and muddy streets, she displays an impressive grasp of U.S. history, politics, and literature. She speaks fluent English but confesses her French is better. She has read Western Europe's important eighteenth-, nineteenth-, and twentieth-century writers and can discuss their work intelligently. "And are you acquainted with our writers?" she asks.

"Acquainted yes, but unfortunately I have not made a study of Russian literature," I admit, a confession she accepts without comment.

Two days later, after a five-hour Aeroflot flight to Alma-Ata, we are met outside the Hotel Otrar by Valentine Rekhert who works for the local tourist office. Valentine has rented a car to take us to Chimbulak, which sits in a wide bowl in the Trans-Ili Ala-Tau Mountains, 20 miles up a narrow canyon above Alma-Ata.

Crosscurrents International Institute is a nonprofit, tax-exempt organization that tries to promote international understanding between people from different nations. To accomplish this, Crosscurrents organizes various trips to the Soviet Union. In '89 it offered ski trips to Tashkent and Dombai. Crosscurrents International Institute, 16 Enid Avenue, Dayton, Ohio 45429, tel. (513) 434-1909.

On the ride up the narrow canyon he tells me that Alma-Ata means "Father Apple" and straddles an ancient silk route near the Chinese border. This city of five hundred thousand is also the capital of the Kazakhstan Republic. The native Kazakh people are descended from nomadic Saka shepherds who were in turn conquered by Genghis Khan's Golden Horde in the thirteenth century. Now, in late March, dormant apple and apricot orchards surround the city and fountains; statues of Lenin and the Kazakhstan State University face the broad, rose-lined streets.

What Valentine does not point out is that most skiers ride the bus as far as the Medeo skating center then walk the last 4 miles up 12 percent grades to the Chimbulak Hotel. Passing lines of sweating Russians carrying their skis, boots, and army backpacks, I suddenly feel very bourgeois. If Valentine, Galina,

or Janich, our driver, share this impression, they don't mention it, and with the clutch smoking we stop below the lifts.

Valentine suggests we meet Angelique Vasilevskaja, Chimbulak's general manager. Owned by a national trade union, Chimbulak serves as a training base for the Soviet national team. Over tea in Angelique's office, I discover that Chimbulak averages 250 skiers per day and that the skiing, room, and board costs 325 rubles for ten days. Even at official exchange rates it is not expensive by western standards, but 325 rubles represents two months' wages to a Russian.

"Chimbulak has enormous potential for expansion," Shaken Suleev, Vice Chairman of the Kazakh Sports Committee, would point out later, adding that two triples are planned for 1990, which would access an enormous back bowl and effectively double Chimbulak's terrain.

"For the first time we are able to sign construction contracts with foreign firms without Moscow's prior approval," Shaken says with some excitement. Under these changes, a tentative agreement has been signed for a new resort to be built 75 kilometers from Alma-Ata. Called Tau-Turgen, with sixty scheduled lifts and a 175-million ruble investment, it will be a cooperative effort between the Kazakhs, French, and Yugoslavians. It will also be the largest ski area in Russia serviced by direct flights from western Europe into Alma-Ata.

"It has been a very warm winter . . . you must excuse our snow," Angelique says as we start toward the base lifts.

With a nod to the lift attendant, who studies my skis, boots, and jacket, I catch the base T-bar, which rises up a long, rutted track. Though Chimbulak's three chairs climb to a high north-facing saddle, a downhill race is scheduled for the coming weekend, and today the chairs are closed to keep skiers off the course.

Grooming is virtually nonexistent, and with half the normal base, the troughs go down to bedrock. If Chimbulak's lifts are old, if it lacks snowmaking and grooming, I didn't come to Russia to ski Colorado. When I later mention the differences to Galina, she listens intently, then says, "Far better this than nothing."

Reaching the top of the base T-bar, I traverse across a heavily moguled north face to a second T that rises up an intersecting ridge to a high knoll. From here you can see the city of Alma-Ata as well as an enormous out-of-bounds bowl known as Little Switzerland. Poised for a first turn in the Soviet Union, I start down the face, extend, check, and start to link turns. During my first run I set edges on rocks, change rhythms, and search for forgiving lines. Halfway through a second run, a young guy in red blows by me on the right, followed by a second hot skier with fabulous knee action in blue. Picking up the pace, I manage to catch them in the T-bar line.

"Pre-viet," I say touching the one in red with my pole. "Do you speak English?"

"English? Nyet!" he shakes his head.

"I speak English," a man in his mid-twenties with a dark tan says behind me. "My name is Sergei Perduss; the one in red is Vladimir Cushin, his friend is Alexi. They are coaches for the ski team that trains here. You are British?"

"No, American," I say introducing myself.

"Ah, American," he repeats with some surprise which, when translated, produces a similar reaction from Vladimir and Alexi. "And why have you come to Chimbulak?" he asks.

"To ski," I say. It turns out that Sergei is a Ski Saver (patrolman) and, accompanied by Vladimir and Alexi, we slip under a rope onto a downhill course. We are immediately accosted by a toothless woman who screams at us until Sergei tells me to give her a stick of gum.

"Her job is to protect the course," Sergei tells me, shaking his head. "And she thinks you're trying to break, uh . . ."—He searches for a word—". . . the laws."

On the next run I am introduced to Misha Muramov, a Soviet pop singer who is using a camcorder to film the team practice. Misha's song "Apples In the Snow," is number four on the Soviet charts, and in excellent English he says, "I heard an American was skiing here. So, I think maybe you are the first. If you have not made plans, I insist you join us for lunch."

Stories about Soviet shortages are not exaggerated. Galina tells me that for years soap, toothpaste, and other essentials have been in short supply, and thus I am surprised by the bounty that greets us at the hotel. Horse ribs (a Kazakh delicacy), salads, soup, two kinds of bread, vodka, and cognac fill a central table. The shortages make this a rare occasion, but it is also characteristic of Kazakh's selfless hospitality, and between toasts to the U.S.A. and the Soviet Union and Misha's singing, lunch spans two and a half hours.

With an afternoon fog reducing visibility in Chimbulak, Valentine suggests we see Alma-Tau, Alma-Ata's companion ski resort. Taking a winding road through villages set in vast hillside orchards, we arrive at dusk. Alma-Tau has been closed for hours, but General Manager Sasha Matvienko starts the tow lift. Though the snow is slushy, I ski Alma-Tau's three cable lifts, six major runs, and thousand vertical feet with a wild Soviet truck driver who keeps shouting "ANDRE! ANDRE! THEES WAY!"

It is past 10 P.M. when I arrive back at the Hotel Otrar, bid Galina good night, and wander into the dining room, where I order a bottle of mineral water. A four-piece band is playing to a capacity crowd, and I settle back to watch the dancers.

"Tovarich," a towering man seated near me inquires in Russian. "Why are you drinking alone on Soviet Service Workers' Day?"

Anton speaks passable English and, along with fellow black marketers Semyon and Pyotr, has been drinking vodka and cola since early that afternoon. Seated with them are two striking Kazakh women.

"You are an American!" Anton repeats with some wonder. "An American! So, why are you here?"

"I have come to ski!" I say, an answer that immediately earns an invitation to join them. Between the day's numerous toasts I have had far too much vodka, but when Anton raises his glass to "America!" simple good manners insist I reciprocate with "Alma-Ata!"

It is past midnight, and I am dancing with Anton's date, the lovely Tanya Ilovaiskaya. "I am sorry, I only spik Russian," she says as someone stumbles into us.

"We need more room to dance!" Pyotr shouts in Russian then kicks over a full dinner table. The crowd surges back, someone spills a water glass full of vodka on Tanya's black dress, and Pyotr begins to trade thundering rights with a stocky Kazakh. The militia suddenly appears, and everyone becomes fast friends. Pyotr throws his arm around the Kazakh, the lead guitarist cuts in with a hot lick, and couples start to dance, leaving the soldiers to stare confusedly at the broken crockery.

It is past 2 A.M. when I put Anton, Tanya, and the rest into a cab and bid them good night. From there I drift down to the hard-currency bar in the basement. I have heard the bartender works for the KGB, but the West German medical technicians who are staying in the hotel insist he's okay. Even so he speaks English, German, and French too fluently, and I order a five-ruble scotch and skip the tip.

For the next three days I ski with Alexi, Vladimir, and Misha during the day and explore Alma-Ata at night. During my stay I discover the city's après life consists of a local circus, scattered restaurants, and dancing at the Hotel Otrar.

Galina insists I see Alma-Ata's five-million-ruble public baths, and so on my last morning I step into the Kazakh Sauna, where I find Anton, Pyotr, and Semyon lying on a hundred square feet of heated white marble. Surrounding a 30-foot central court, the marble slabs are heated to twenty, forty, and sixty degrees centigrade, and I spend half an hour on the twenty-degree slab then move to forty degrees. Here, in a golden-tiled alcove that could have been lifted intact from *1001 Arabian Nights*, I sweat profusely, the moisture running in rivulets off my chest. Anton rolls onto his side and uncorks a thermos. From it he fills a chipped porcelain cup then holds it out to me. *"Chai?"* he inquires.

"Spasibo," I reply, empty the cup of hot tea, and hand it back to him.

"Horosho," he says, fills it again, and offers it to Pyotr. "Drink first, then we go to sixty degrees centigrade," he tells me, refilling the cup and handing it to Semyon. "The last stage is very hot, you will see."

I turn on my back and stare at the vaulted ceiling. At that moment Semyon puts his fingers to his lips and whispers, "KGB," as two powerfully muscled men step into the sauna. Late twenties, six feet tall, and a solid 195 pounds, they strut like pro running backs across the tile floor to our slab. Conversation subsides, and I keep my eyes down, my mouth shut, and listen.

It is obvious Anton, Pyotr, and Semyon are being watched.

Framed by gold mosaic walls and sweat, time passes slowly. We move to the sixty-degree slab. The stud horses follow. We sweat and wait. After half an hour the agents finally tire of the game, rise, and with a final word to Anton leave us.

"What did he say?" I whisper.

Anton shrugs and runs a hand through his dripping hair. "It is nothing. . . ." he says. When I persist he admits, "It is nothing, he warned us that too much heat is bad for you."

Galina and I catch a two-hour flight to Mineralniye Vody, where the driver, Anatole, is waiting with a van to take us to Elbrus. From Mineralniye Vody we drive through rolling farmland before entering the Baksan Valley. Legend claims that Jason and the Argonauts searched along the Baksan River for the golden fleece. The road changes from pavement to rough cobbles and dirt. For miles we are unable to make more than a few kilometers per hour, and it is past nine when we reach Prielbrusye.

Translated roughly to "Before Elbrus," Prielbrusye is a small village scattered among three major tourist hotels: Cheget, Itkol, and Azau. With Cheget and Elbrus ski areas rising up opposite sides of the glaciated valley, Prielbrusye is the Soviet equivalent of Colorado's Summit County. By combining ten lifts that access a respective 3,500 and 6,000 vertical feet, what

Cheget, Itkol, and Azau are within walking distance of **Cheget Ski Area**. By western standards the rooms are small, but most have a shower and toilet. Dining is communal, with a prix fixe menu. The three meals a day are filling but tend toward potatoes, root vegetables, meat, tea, and dessert. Since American digestive tracts lock up in the absence of grains and fruit, a bran cereal or laxative is recommended.

these two areas lack in uphill capacity they compensate for with nearly unlimited terrain. With no snowmaking, haphazard grooming, and two small mountain restaurants, by western standards the resort is rough but serviceable.

The following morning I meet Sasha Cama in front of the crowded Elbrus tram. Sasha is a native Balkar as well as an Elbrus ski patrolman and climbing guide. He doesn't speak English but, like the majority of Russians, he does smoke, and I give him a pack of Marlboros, which he offers to friends as we rise toward the Old Prospect Station. With smoke filling the packed tram, Sasha gives them background on his mute friend.

"Americanski?" two or three repeat in amazed voices.

From the cracked Plexiglas windows and repaired sheet metal, the Old Prospect tram has seen better winters (which seems to be true of most Soviet lifts). From the Prospect we transfer to a second tram, which rises 1800 vertical feet to the Mir Station. From here we ride a single chair 1300 vertical feet to a cluster of weathered Quonset huts that serve as mountain condos. Following Sasha's lead, I shoulder my skis and start to hike in the knee-deep snow. Our goal is Preuit, a three-story, dirigible-shaped mountain refuge that is used by climbers attempting Elbrus.

Rising to 18,000 feet at the head of the Baksan Valley, Elbrus's twin volcanic peaks are the highest in Europe. The eastern peak was climbed on July 10, 1829, by Balkar native Killar Kashirov, while the western summit was climbed forty years later by a trio of English climbers led by local guides. Located on Elbrus's southeast flank, in summer Preuit is crowded with climbers and skiers. In mid-March, however, verglas coats the mountain, the climbing is extremely hazardous, and thus the refuge is deserted.

"So, Sasha, would it be possible to climb Elbrus?" I ask the patrolman, using my fingers to imitate a man walking up the southeast face.

"Nyet," Sasha replies, then adds something about the verglas in Russian.

"Perhaps on the south face." I make hand motions.

"Nyet," he insists, pointing up to the blue ice and shaking his head. We take a quick look around then cut through the breakable crust 1500 vertical feet back to the Quonset huts. I am ready to ski, but Sasha insists we have tea in his friend Boris's hut. Inside the walls are covered with ski photos and pinups of popular Russian singers, and we drink tea and talk about equipment.

Sasha leads me down a smooth south face which in turn leads back to the main moguls and back to Mir. With new snow Elbrus would be a paradise—big, steep—and with Donguz-Orun and Nakaratu erupting to 14,600 feet across the narrow valley, as spectacular as any resort in the world. The day progresses, and I get a local's view of Elbrus as Sasha leads me down steep faces, narrow gullies, huge moguls, and a skiff of out-of-bounds powder.

As a patrolman, Sasha can cut lift lines. Though his red uniform commands a certain respect, I hesitate to follow him up the jammed concrete stairway to the platform. When he gets halfway up, he turns and signals for me to follow. Reluctantly I follow him, wondering how the Soviets regard this unproletarian behavior. I don't wait long to find out. A 6 foot 3 inch, barrel-chested comrade suddenly steps into my path. Taking my skis, camera, boots, and jacket in with a single disgusted glance, I don't need to speak Russian to know what's on his mind.

"I've been waiting for an hour," I hear him say. "So what in hell's name do you think you're doing?"

To which my only defense is a nod and a question. "Do you speak English?" I ask him.

The following morning Anatole, our driver, tells Galina that Comanche has come from Moscow to see me. "Comanche?" I inquire.

"Tole says his name is Vladimir Lukyaev," she replies.

Ken Asvitt's guide! Minutes later I meet Vladimir at the Cheget base lift. Dressed in a new ski suit and carrying new Volkl skis and Dynafit boots, Vladimir tells me he has just returned from Switzerland. On the ride up Cheget's base double, he adds that my visit gives him an excuse to come home. A native Balkar, Vladimir is 5 feet 7 inches and 150 pounds. He has a reputation as a superb alpinist and has climbed extensively in the surrounding Caucasus, in the Pymirs, and in Nepal. He also has a degree in English literature and, catching the second chair from the Cafe Ai, he tells me, "If you wish to meet other Russian skiers, I have friends from Moscow."

Hospitality is legendary among the Balkars. His friends are Anna Sviatskaya, Anna Sevostianova, and Valeri Akopyan, who have been coming to Cheget for eleven seasons. Transportation from Moscow, three meals a day, room, and lifts for ten days comes to roughly five hundred rubles. I ask Anna Sevostianova, who makes roughly two hundred rubles per month working at a museum, how she can afford to spend 20 percent of her yearly gross on a single ski trip.

"Well, of course, it is impossible to save," she admits.

The group continues to grow. We are joined by Sasha Cama and three other hot-bumps skiers. We ski Cheget's heavily moguled north face until closing; then Comanche leads us down a 3,000-vertical-foot, east-facing bowl beneath Nakaratu.

"Of course, most of the snow has gone," he says, gesturing at large bare spots, "but with new snow it is something I cannot describe."

When we reach the base, Galina tells me we have been invited to dinner by Elbrus's minister of sport. His name is Machmood, and I ask if it would be possible to include a few friends. "Naturally," Galina interprets, and that evening we are driven to a warm streamside dacha, where a traditional Balkar dinner is waiting.

Machmood has a doctorate in education, and as we enter

the dacha he offers a lyric welcoming toast to U.S.-Soviet friendship and his guests, then cuts a small bone from the night's barbecued lamb.

"Whoever breaks this bone becomes Tamadah, chief of the feast," Galina translates as the bone passes between the men. On the third circuit Machmood fractures it with a loud snap. For the rest of the night he is Tamadah, source of wisdom, humor, and favors. We eat, drink, and listen to traditional Balkar stories until late that evening when Tamadah takes the cooked lamb's head and presents the ear to Comanche. It is an honor to be selected, and Tamadah says, "Eat this so you may listen closely and thus know what is truly intended."

The eye goes to Valeri, the nose to Galina, and I receive the brain, "To give you inspiration and to help you describe the warmth of the Balkar people." Toast follows toast, and in closing Tamadah says, "The U.S. and Soviet Union are like two climbers roped together. If one falls both fall, but working together as a team we can conquer any summit."

The following days are spent skiing Cheget and Elbrus. In late March spring is making its presence felt in bare patches and late-afternoon slush, while the nights are filled with private parties and dancing in the Hotel Cheget's lounge. On my last morning Anna, Valeri, and Anna take me to a small local market where local women are selling knitted goods. A beautiful mohair scarf catches my eye, and the trio insists on buying it for "your wife." "That way when you look at her you will not forget us," Anna says as good-bye.

As the crow flies, Dombai Ski Area is only 40 kilometers from Elbrus but it takes nine hours to drive back down the Baksan Valley to Patigorsk, where the road turns west across rolling wheat fields to the Tiberdah River Valley. It is Saturday afternoon in the Soviet Union, and in the small villages along the two-lane road families till private gardens, whitewash tree trunks, and drive huge horse-drawn hay wagons that crowd Tole's van into the oncoming lane. We pass open-air markets where vendors offer produce, books, and knitted goods for sale. Enormous agricultural communes shine like temples upon distant hills, and we pass Russian Orthodox churches and mile upon mile of cypress windrows where rooks circle above crude stick nests.

It is past ten when we climb the twisting road to Dombai. Galina returns to tell me that the resort hotels are "totally" booked. "Our reservations have been made at the Tiberdah Sport Hotel, twenty kilometers back down the valley."

"Twenty kilometers!" I repeat, shaking my head.

"There is not one room. Not one bed. I can, how do you say, make a scene, but it will do no good. It is impossible." Under most circumstances Galina is extremely resourceful, but the word impossible means you have little choice. Because unrestricted travel within the U.S.S.R. has only evolved during the past two years, the system is now forced to work at capacity.

In Tiberdah the apologetic manager of the Sport Hotel admits the Dombai tram starts at 8 A.M. "The local buses are always full," Galina explains. "Tole must return to Elbrus, so somehow we must arrange transportation."

The following morning we catch a ride with a tour group of East Germans. Atsa Sell, an East Berliner in his mid-thirties, tells me the tour is outraged over the Tiberdah Sport Hotel.

MIR Corporation in partnership with the Soviet Central Council for Tourism and Excursions (CCTE) offers ski trips to the **Caucasus Mountains**. During the winter of '90 the first trip ran from February 15 to 28 and toured Moscow, Dombai, and Copenhagen for $2430, which included round-trip airfare on SAS, all meals, guides, and accommodations. The second went from February 27 to March 13 and toured Moscow, Dombai, Leningrad, and Copenhagen with the same inclusions for $2450. For information: MIR Corporation, 85 South Washington Street #210, Seattle, Washington 98104, tel. (206) 624-7289.

★

"Since I have come for the skiing, the rest is not so important," he says in accented English, lowering his voice. "But many of the others do not ski, and, well, the rooms are tiny and cold and the food—well, you have eaten it. . . ." He shrugs. "The cost is two thousand DDR marks—as much we make in a year. So for many they have been saving four years for this holiday."

"Is it true you are an American?" Karin, another Berliner, whispers to me across the aisle. "Perhaps we meet later; I can tell you some things!"

In many ways Dombai resembles a western resort. Located at the head of the Tiberdah Valley, Dombai is composed of five hotels, a few small shops, and three restaurants clustered around the base chair lift and a fifty-person tram. A heavy sleet is falling when the bus struggles up the last grade into town. Stepping into ankle-deep slush, there is some debate about whether it is possible to ski.

"The wind is blowing very hard above," Galina tells me. "Perhaps you do not wish to ski today."

"No, I will ski," I reply. It could always get worse. Half an hour later the base tram rises into a heavy cloud layer toward the upper station 2800 feet above. From there you must pay the attendant sixty kopeks, then load a double chair that rises 1500 vertical feet to another eighty-kopek double that rises a final 1500 to the summit. In 6,000 feet the temperature drops twenty degrees. The top is a total whiteout.

Western lifts unload down slight hills. Soviet chairs unload either onto flats or up gentle hills. To unload you must skate strongly to one side and let it pass. In Dombai the chair frames are covered with oak slats, and over time large splinters have worked free. As you try to skate free, the chair bumps your legs, snagging at your pants.

It is snowing hard on top, and visibility is down to a few feet. Tracks lead downhill, but they could easily belong to someone who have never skied Dombai, and in this whiteout you could easily follow their tracks off a cliff.

Victor, a Dombai ski instructor who has been assigned to guide the East Germans, now appears out of the fog. He has somehow lost the Germans. Lost or ditched—you get the impression Victor is not especially fond of this group.

"Andre," he says now, signaling me to follow him. It is bitterly cold. Dressed in a nylon shell, with no gloves or goggles, he disappears into the whirling snow.

To the right of his tracks the snow is shin deep, and I try not to grin as my knees rise and fall and my skis arc beneath the soft snow. Twenty turns later Victor's track ends in a huge divot, and I find him struggling with his bindings. He waves off any offer of help, and I continue downhill and drop beneath the clouds. From here, 1300 feet to the lifts, the skiing is spectacular. In pockets the snow rises to knee deep, exploding into my face as I dive into a vertical bowl that returns to the chair.

Because of the bitter cold and sporadic visibility, less than a dozen people are skiing the upper lift. Aided by Hollofill, Polypro, and Smith goggles, I have less of a problem than most and catch four untracked runs. On the fifth I toss a ruble at the attendant and load with Atsa Sell.

Atsa's ski suit has been ripped open and is now hanging down the back of his legs. "Za chair grabbed me," he admits, "but, well, the skiing is wonderful, is it not?"

Watching a girl carve round turns in the untracked powder beneath us, I agree it is. We manage to catch her at the bottom. Atsa speaks a little Russian and Elucia Toposkoboya speaks a little English. She says she is a high school science teacher on holiday with two friends from Tyea and asks us to call her Lucy. When I ask her how long she has been skiing, she replies, "Three . . . yes? Three years but no . . . um . . ."

"Snow?" I suggest.

"No . . . snow . . . like . . . this." She smiles in agreement. If that in fact is true, she is a rare natural, and for the rest of the day we ski the upper lift. The clouds hang around until the lifts close. I'm only able to see the lower part of Dombai's front face. Elucia tells us that tomorrow the weather will improve, and on the final run we agree to meet the following day.

Though the snow stops, the clouds linger, and during dinner that night it starts to rain again. Winds close the tram the following morning, and on the chair ride up I meet Igor Maslov, a Moscow engineer who spends his vacation working as a ski patrolman at Dombai. Igor turns out to be an ex-racer and beautiful free skier; we meet Lucy and spend another day skiing run after run in the untracked snow.

Like Alma-Ata and Elbrus, Dombai has plans to expand. One afternoon Evgeniy Koudelia, chairman of the Karachayevo-Cherkessk Tourism, points to the base of the Gorge—a huge east-facing bowl that Evgeniy says offers far more skiable terrain than Dombai. "To develop lifts, hotels, and services would require foreign investment," he says, "but we are now in a position to offer very favorable terms. If a company was interested in trading a block of rooms for a hard-capital investment, well, we are open to any suggestions."

That night a cold wind whistles through the cracks in the Sport Hotel, and the following morning we discover it has scoured the mountain down to its hard blue base. Overnight the powder was blown off the icy bumps, rocks, and crust, and we make one run before it starts to snow.

The storm continues through the day and night. In order to make the flight to Moscow I must catch the afternoon bus to Mineral 'nyie Vody. Early the following morning I am packing when the storm lifts. For the first time in four days, I see the Caucasus shining above Dombai.

Knocking on Galina's door, I tell her I must go skiing.

"If we miss our flight, there might not be an opening for a week," she replies.

Since virtually all flights are booked to capacity and there are only two phone lines out of Dombai, even to inquire about changing flights requires a three-hour wait in line just to reserve a time to make the call. Then you must be at the phone at that time, and then you must reach an Aeroflot agent who is willing to waste time searching for an open seat. And if you are disconnected, well, step to the end of the line.

Galina explains all this to me, but I can't leave without seeing Dombai, and jumping a bus, I meet Lucy in the summit lift line.

It is the kind of day skiers dream of. A foot of fresh powder covers Dombai's huge bowls, and Lucy and I ski beneath the chair line, matching turn for turn down until Igor yells from the chair for us to wait. He catches us in the line below and leads us into huge sunlit bowls that fall to the chair below. One run follows another; we chase untracked lines away from the summit chair where we discover virgin faces and brilliant ridges until only one run remains.

"You must catch the bus," Igor reminds me. "If you miss it, then you would have to stay."

It is 11 A.M. I can think of worse punishments than being stranded in Dombai during a sun storm cycle. I could delay, then try to catch the train back to Moscow. So far, however, our luck has held because we've obeyed Galina's itinerary. Two days before, the hotel manager pulled strings just to get us on

---

SAS Viking Vacations, tel. (800) 344-9099, and Bennett Tours (800) 221-2420 offer package tours to **Gudauri**. Located in the Caucasus approximately 75 miles from Tbilisi, Gudauri is a new resort built by Austrian contractors. Gudauri offers over 3000 vertical feet with modern lifts, enormous terrain, Austrian instructors, and local guides. Optional helicopter skiing goes for $175 per day. Included in the $1410–$1610 double occupancy price is SAS round-trip flight from New York to Helsinki, an Aeroflot charter to Tbilisi, all ground transportation, seven nights at Gudauri, one night in Helsinki, and meals

the bus to Mineral 'nyie Vody. It would tempt fate to let the seat leave empty.

"You will send us photos of today?" Elucia says, writing her address in my notebook. "You will not forget?"

I promise, turn, and feel the skis accelerate toward the distant Tiberdah Valley floor.

REST AND RECUPERATION

Stories of shortages within the Soviet Union are not exaggerated. There is much to do in Moscow where one can enjoy **Red Square**, **Gum Department Store**, the **Bolshoi** or the **Moscow symphony**, the **Pushkin Museum**, and the festival atmosphere on **Arbot Street**. But once you leave the capital, life becomes very basic. Travel from the airport is by bus and once at Alma-Ata, Dombai, or Elbrus, entertainment is heavily weighted toward a basic nightclub or sightseeing. While in Alma-Ata do not miss the **Kazakh Baths** or the local **circus** which can be arranged for at the Hotel Otrar. Shopping is almost nonexistent and goods of less-than-average quality. Lines are long and daunting, but the people are wonderful. Before you arrive stock up on American ski pins, a map of the U.S., chocolate, gum, cassette tapes, film, photo books of your town, ski magazines, and, if you have room, bottles of vodka; it is nearly impossible to obtain any of these in the Soviet Union.

In Elbrus there are small coffee shops and outdoor markets where you can buy homespun, home-woven woolen goods, and in Dombai there are small cafes where you can buy tea and sandwiches. Bring books and recorded music for the flights.

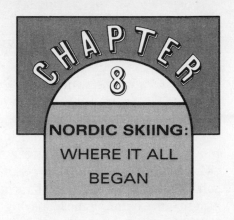

NORDIC SKIING: WHERE IT ALL BEGAN

THE PEER GYNT TRAIL RESEMBLES A NORDIC fairy tale come to life. Named after an eccentric eighteenth-century Oppland farmer who supposedly cavorted with trolls, this 70-mile Nordic track runs from Dalseter in the Espedalen Valley across Norway's Oppland region to Gausdal above Tretten. Though Peer Gynt's wild tales astounded his superstitious neighbors, he might have been forgotten if it hadn't been for the Norwegian playwright Henrik Ibsen and the composer Edvard Grieg, who put Ibsen's *Peer Gynt* to music.

Today Grieg's "Peer Gynt Suite" still evokes the Oppland's rolling hills, deep lakes and meandering rivers. Located 190 kilometers north of Oslo, the Oppland includes the Jotunheimen and Rondane national parks and encompasses two of Norway's highest mountain ranges. Rising to 7600 feet, by European standards these peaks are not high, but this far north the treeline clings to the low gullies, leaving a vast ice-and-snow shield stretching for hundreds of square miles. Generations of Norwegians have broken themselves on this flinty soil, and today only scattered cattle farms and the tourist hotels remain. As soon as winter's snow buries these rolling hills, however, tracks are set and red anoraks flower on the empty plains that run to the horizon.

I cannot take credit for discovering the Peer Gynt. That honor must go to Michael Daley, photographer, musician, and dedicated Nordic skier, who dreamed of skating from resort to resort carrying only a day pack. What he wished to avoid was weight—the extra clothes, shaving kit, and survival gear that would turn a Nordic voyage of discovery into a 70-mile slog. His idea was to travel light, skate along prepared tracks during the day, and sleep on clean sheets at night.

But where?

A Norwegian joke goes, "Why do you think they call it Nordic skiing?" If it loses something in translation, Norwegians do love skinny skis. Oslo alone boasts more than 1000 miles of tracks within the city limits, and that doesn't include any of the outlying resorts, or the Norwegian food, people, or scenery. Thus after a connecting SAS flight to Fornebu Airport outside of Oslo, we took a shuttle to the downtown train station where we caught the evening train to Lillehammer.

SAS offers direct daily flights from Newark, New Jersey, to Oslo; reservations: (800) 221-2350. Daily flights from Seattle, Chicago, and Los Angeles connect to Oslo through Copenhagen. Trains run daily from Oslo to Lillehammer and Vinstra, jumping-off points for the Peer Gynt Road. Shuttles are available at the airport.

Our plan was to spend two days acclimating in Lillehammer (site of the '94 Winter Olympics and nominal capital of the Oppland) before transferring to Dalseter. Including time spent exploring the intermediate resorts of Fefor, Golå and Fager-høy, we figured to ski from Dalseter to Gausdal in four days. These "hotels" are in fact small, self-contained ski centers that offer enormous surrounding webs of maintained ski trails. A major advantage of skiing the Peer Gynt is that our baggage would be shipped from Dalseter to Fefor to Golå to Gausdal, leaving only a lunch and a windbreaker to carry in our day packs. With light loads and tracks linking the hotels, realistically we could cover the distance in two very long days, but that pace would eliminate any chance to commune with the Norwegians and enjoy the local ambiance or ski the surrounding track systems.

Stepping off the train and backing our skis and bags out to the curb, we caught a taxi to Lillehammer's Victoria Rica Hotel where, while registering, the night clerk informed us that there was dessert in the dining room and dancing downstairs. Though we were inclined toward both, it had been a long day. Half an hour later I was dreaming of skating skis and scowling trolls.

Rica Victoria Hotel, 2600 Lillehammer, Norway, tel. 50-049. Amenities: 174 beds, dining room, restaurant, bar, dancing. Terms: write or call for price.

Bellevue Sportell, 2600 Lillehammer, Norway, tel. 50-400. Amenities: 140 rooms, dining room, centrally located. Terms: write for price.

Oppland Turisthotell, 2600 Lillehammer, Norway, tel. 51-528. Amenities: 140 rooms, dining room, restaurant, dancing, lounge. Terms: write for price.

We were up early the following morning, carrying our skis through Lillehammer's silent streets. A light snow had fallen during the night, and the overhanging birches were etched in white. Lillehammer sits on a hill above Mjøsa, Norway's largest lake, which is spiderwebbed with cross-country tracks and im-promptu hockey rinks. Lillehammer is a settled town, with quiet residential streets, a pedestrian-only retail center, mu-seums, and fine old hotels. With the temperature hanging at fifteen above, we climbed past weathered houses and an old man sweeping his front walk, heading for the start of the Nor-dic tracks that climb into the forests above the city.

After 1994 the Olympics will alternate summer and winter games every two years. Known as the "Compact Olympics," with a projected budget of $370 million, the Lillehammer Games will occupy the single transition year.

Organizers insist that the Compact Games are on schedule. '89–'90 was set aside for planning, '90–'92 will see the con-struction phase, with '92–'93 devoted to testing. Recently the International Olympic Committee complimented the IOC for its excellent planning phase. When the facilities are com-pleted, it will be possible to walk to the skating, jumping, luge, and bobsled venues.

But for now Lillehammer's streets are silent, and two kilo-meters above the city center a single groomed track leads to a Nordic interstate with six lanes and merging on-ramps. The sun is not yet up, but skiers are already skating in both direc-tions. These tracks are financed and maintained by Lilleham-mer and circle out to Nordseter and Nevra—towns that sit in the hills above. You can either train or travel through the in-credibly diverse surrounding countryside.

To prepare for the Peer Gynt, I tried to ski 20 kilometers four days per week. By late February I was in fair shape, but com-pared to the Norwegians, I'm dog-slow. The Norwegians start to ski before they learn to walk, and now all the V-shaped guys in stretch Lycra draw a bead on us.

"They're tough," Daley admits, as he leans into his poles, kicks powerfully, and glides along. Daley has been Nordic rac-ing for years, and we jump on the tail end of six skiers who pass on the left. Skating hard, we maintain a fast pace until a gap opens and they slowly pull away.

Most are training for the Birkebeiner, the famous 56-kilometer race from Lillehammer to Rena. In 1206 two Viking Birkebeiner, or "birch leg warriors," carried two-year-old Haakon Haakonsson through a blizzard to safety. This daring act secured the Norwegian succession of kings. The Birkebeiner has been run since 1932 and today attracts five thousand competitors. The history of skiing in Norway, however, is far older. A four-thousand-year-old stone petroglyph shows a stick figure poling along on 10-foot wood slats.

After a fast 15 kilometers, we return to breakfast at the Victoria Rica. If Norwegians invented skiing, they also coined the word smorgasbord. After a brisk workout on the tracks, the Rica's breakfast includes cereal, toast, eggs, bacon, cold cuts, cheeses, fruit, fish, tea, and coffee. Back home this bounty would be more than I'd eat all day, but breakfast pales beside lunch, which is itself simply an appetizer for dinner.

The problem is if you miss one workout, this caloric overload immediately jumps on your waist. The cycle can be vicious. The brisk 15 K's build a huge appetite, which in turn is oversatisfied at the groaning buffet tables, which in turn spawns guilt, which leads to more kilometers, which makes you hungry. The bottom line is, by skiing your brains out, you might only gain ten pounds on the Peer Gynt.

That night we learn it is possible to ski from Nordseter back to Lillehammer, and the following morning we catch a ride up the mountain. It is late morning but still very cold when we step into our skis and skate downhill. During the first kilometers our hands are numb, and we push hard to warm up. From time to time we pass other skiers on the two-lane track that winds through the deep forest, but for most of the two hours it takes to ski the gentle downhill back to Lillehammer, we are alone. The tracks are fast, our glide wax is perfect, and we rejoice in the long shadows, cold air, and sinuous terrain. It is an exhilarating workout, and that afternoon we reluctantly catch the train to Vinstra.

Stepping off the train, we are met by Eric Gillebo who along with his wife Elsa owns the Dalseter Mountain Hotel. Eric helps us load our bags into the hotel van for the hour drive to the Espedal Valley and the start of the Peer Gynt Trail. Melting snow stains the pavement, and Eric tells us that the Gulf Stream, which follows Norway's west coast, helps to maintain

temperatures in the teens and twenties. We pass mountain farms clinging to steep hillsides and moose browsing through the thick birch forests, and by the time we reach Dalseter it is midafternoon and the sun is already hanging above the southern horizon.

You can book the Dalseter or any of the other Peer Gynt hotels by writing Peer Gynt Hotels, P.O. Box 115, N-2647 Hundorp, Norway, tel. 96-000.

Peer Gynt Hotel Dalseter, 2628 Espedal, Norway, tel. 99-910. Amenities: 90 rooms with bath, shower and toilette, sauna, large swimming pool, solarium, weight room, ski school, small alpine hill, bar. Terms: call for price.

★

"You can have your choice," Eric says after we drop our bags in a warm west-facing room. "You can ski on our small alpine hill, you can have a swim and sauna, or you can try our tracks."

We vote for the tracks, and in a few minutes are gliding through a large meadow above the frozen Breidsjoen Lake. In the distance we can see the ice-capped peaks of the Jotunheimen National Park, while above us is the birch-covered ridgeline we must cross tomorrow. Due to improvements in Nordic gear, we have brought skating skis for the Peer Gynt. Except for a short mountainous section from Dalseter to Fefor, the terrain is primarily rolling hills, and with the groomed track we intend to make good time.

The following morning, when we bring our bags to the front desk, Eric is dressed in wool knickers, a traditional Norwegian sweater, and three-pin boots. "Unfortunately a shipping company has booked Fefor for the week," he tells us. "You have reservations at Golå, a few kilometers further along," and then gesturing to his attire adds, "With the hotel demanding so much of my time, I do not get as much exercise as I should. I hope you won't mind if I ski with you for a short distance."

Peer Gynt Hotel Fefor, 2640 Vinstra, Norway, tel. 90-099. Amenities: 115 rooms, fitness room, squash, small alpine hill, bar, beautiful restaurant, main hotel dates from 1891. Terms: call for price.

★

It is a blue sky morning, the snow is hard and fast, and for an hour we climb through a birch forest that gradually opens up onto a south-facing hillside. The untracked snow is covered with breakable crust, and we work our way down to a single-room refuge where Eric produces a thermos of tea, crackers, and cheese. Pointing to a distant southern range we will have to cross, he voices reservations about our skis. "If you have sunshine and hard snow, there is nothing better," he tells us, retrieving one of Michael's skis from the snowbank and turning it to study the base. "But we are here so close to the ocean, storms come quickly, and if you lose the track in light clothes . . . These skis are not made for deep snow. I would prefer to see you with three-pin touring skis and a firm touring boot. That way if a storm comes . . . Well, you understand."

He points to Fefor, which is visible in the distance. "You will have no problem from here. . . . Take care and good luck," he says as he offers his hand and turns to ski the 15 kilometers back to Dalseter.

Including Fefor, the distances between the Peer Gynt resorts average an easy 20 K's per day. Along with an extensive track system, an alpine ski hill, a pool, sauna, wax room, and dancing, Fefor is worth at least two days. Without it, however, the Dalseter-Golå leg is 38 kilometers, which makes a long but not a killer day. After three hours on a track that runs through fir forests, we arrive with enough time left for a sauna before a candlelit dinner.

Built on a wooded rise overlooking Lake Galan, Golå is actually three hotels offering a vast track system, restaurants, weight room, pool, dancing, and a small alpine hill. At dinner it's obvious the Peer Gynt hotels appeal primarily to families. If Norway's sun-worshipping youth prefer the beaches of Greece, North Africa, and Spain to a quiet week of Nordic skiing, once they marry and have children they always return. Seated near the buffet table, I note that a number of tables have three generations seated at dinner. Thus I am not surprised when the nightlife runs toward chess, quiet conversation, books, and

---

Peer Gynt Hotel Golå, 2646 Golå, Norway, tel. 98-109. Amenities: 40 rooms, swimming pool, fitness room, game room, small lounge. Terms: call for price.

★

cheek-to-cheek dancing. No flashing disco lights or straight shots of aquavit here; just early to bed, early to rise and 20 kilometers before breakfast.

A storm moves in during the night, and by dawn visibility is down to 30 feet. Under these conditions, the 35-kilometer stretch to Gausdal is far too dangerous, if not pointless, and we pass the day cycling from Golå's laden smorgasbord tables to the surrounding track system to the swimming pool and weight room. By now I have no willpower. Breakfast, lunch, and dinner seem to follow in two-hour increments. Even worse, however, I've begun to look forward to each meal, and the seconds on pastries, puddings, and evening entrees are starting to have an effect. I am therefore relieved when dawn reveals blue skies and temperatures in the teens.

The fast-moving low pressure system has coated the trees with a glistening rime, the setter has been at work since long before dawn, and now a fresh track runs through lacy arbors, stunted trees, and frozen lakes. It is 9 A.M., and the freezing temperatures cut through our Lycra leggings. Daley skates rapidly away, and I have to work to keep him in sight. A short time later we drop into a wide gully and lose sight of Golå. As we settle into a rhythm the kilometers pass, the grade slowly increases, and we break free of the woods and start across a vast, empty plain. Driving the poles, I see the sun is hanging in the south, casting our long shadows across the undisturbed snow, and we pass deserted summer cottages and small farms until only the track remains pointing across the undisturbed plains.

Studying this vast expanse, I realize how ill-prepared we are for trouble. Without a compass, heavy clothes, extra food, or more than a bottle of water, if a sudden wind would obliterate the track, we would quickly lose the way. This is the stretch Eric Gillebo warned us about, and we maintain a steady pace. Nine A.M. turns to twelve-thirty, and cresting a rise, the track skirts a herder's hut. We tuck down a long downhill descent and in the distance see Fagerhøy Fjellskole.

Built in a remote valley halfway between Golå and Gausdal, this isolated hamlet serves as a private ski school where students from eight to sixteen are taught winter survival techniques. Knocking on the front door, we are greeted by one of the instructors, a striking green-eyed blonde who offers her hand and invites us inside.

"You are skiing the Peer Gynt," she says, leading us into a sunny dining room. "I don't think many Americans do this. In fact, we don't get many visitors at all. So you must join me for lunch and tell me about your adventures."

Michael briefly describes how we heard about the Peer Gynt and his impressions of Lillehammer, the food and skiing, before admitting she probably needn't worry about crowds of Americans suddenly appearing on the horizons.

"Yes, you are probably right," she agrees in flawless English, placing a tray of sliced meats and cheeses, bread, and orange soda on the table. "I cannot remember another American skiing the Peer Gynt. Most ride the tour buses to Bergen or to Trondheim. Or they stay in Oslo. Fagerhøy is not a major stop. . . ." She smiles at her small joke. The next hour passes too quickly, and seated in her sunny breakfast room we linger longer than we should. Too soon she's waving from the front door as Michael and I climb a long grade on the last leg to Gausdal.

For the next hour we ski in silence. From our ski tips to the horizon it is all ice and snow with only the single track lending definition to distant unnamed rises. If we came to Norway to ski, this is as good as it gets. Timing a skating kick to a pole stroke, we are making good time when we are overtaken by one of the instructors from the Fjellskole, who is skiing to Gausdal and back. We keep pace and ask how far the resort is.

"Not far, 12 kilometers maybe," he says, leans into his pole stroke, and gradually pulls away.

The sun starts to settle toward the southwest horizon, the light flares golden across the rolling snowfields, and we encounter four skiers from Gausdal who are telemarking into a shallow gully. From here the grade increases, and half an hour later we are standing at the top of a bluff, looking across to a cluster of hotels, cabins, and a series of chair lifts rising 1050 vertical feet to the Skeikampen summit.

Stepping into a track, we tuck down to the Gausdal Hoifjellshotell where we are shown to large, elegant rooms facing the Skeikampen alpine area. Including the Skeikampen Hoifjellshotell, Gausdal may serve as one end of the Peer Gynt trail, but during the past days I have learned that the beginning and end are less important than what lies between. An afternoon swim and sauna are part of crossing the Peer Gynt, and it is 7:30 when we are shown to a candlelit table. Surrounded by extended families, Daley and I make something of an odd couple, and we nod to the closest diners and regret that tonight marks the end of the track.

The next morning we ski south west toward Austlid. Roughly

Peer Gynt Hotel Skeikampen, 2622 Skeikampen, Norway, tel. 28-505. Amenities: all rooms with bath, shower and toilet, minibars in room, new bar, sauna, solarium, wine cellar, ski school. Terms: call for price.

Peer Gynt Hotel Gausdal, 2622 Skei/Gausdal, Norway, tel. 28-500. Amenities: rooms with bath, toilette and shower, radio, telephone, bar, restaurant, ski to tracks and alpine lifts, disco, swimming pool, solarium, ski school. Terms: call for price.

Austlid Holiday Center, N-2622 Svingvoll, Norway, tel. 28-513. Amenities: 31 rooms with shower and toilet; 25 semi-detached cabins, including kitchens, sitting rooms, video/TV. In main building, disco, an excellent restaurant, lounge; staff speaks excellent English. Terms: call for price.

★

4 kilometers from Gausdal, Austlid is a mountain resort that maintains 150 kilometers of prepared tracks—more than the distance back to Dalseter. Owned by Per and Gro Stephensen, the hotel itself offers a warm, hospitable refuge from the frigid morning air, and we linger over a cup of coffee before returning to the track. World Cup biathalon teams train here, and Michael and I climb steep, forested hillsides to a flat plain where the tracks point to the horizon.

Returning to Skeikampen, we spend the afternoon skiing the Alpine mountain. With eight lifts, 1000 vertical feet, a dozen marked runs that access off-piste skiing, and a base rental shop, Skeikampen offers intermediate alpine skiing, and by the time we take a last run, it is late afternoon, the sun is dropping in the southwest, and dinner is being set.

If all good things must end, by rights the Peer Gynt should be 40 kilometers longer. Or even better there should be a north-south Nordic interconnect that eventually links up with Oslo's city tracks. Instead, the following morning we ride down to Tretten in the Gudbrandsdalen Valley and there catch the Oslo express back to a final night in the city.

REST AND RECUPERATION

Oslo is one of the world's most beautiful cities; you can't come to Norway and ignore its museums, parks, restaurants, and shopping. Oslo has forty islands in its archipelago, one hundred nightclubs and restaurants, four cabarets, cafe theaters, dance groups, and festivals.

Prices in Oslo vary with the dollar/kroner exchange rate, but whether it's favorable or not you don't have to spend a great deal to enjoy this city. While here try to see the **Vigeland Park** filled with the sculptures of Gustav Vigeland. Another diversion is the **Viking ship** museum and near that the **Norwegian Folk and Maritime Museum**. The thirteenth-century **Akershus Castle** sits above Oslo's beautiful harbor. Thor Heyerdahl's **Kon-Tiki Museum** displays his Kon-Tiki raft and the **Edvard Munch Museum** contains 1100 paintings by the artist.

Try the **Grand Cafe** or **Cafe Metropole** on Karl Johans Gate, tel. 42-93-90, which used to be a favorite of Henrik Ibsen. Or the **Restaurant Blum**, which was once a stable and later a gathering place for Oslo artists. Today it caters to Oslo's politicians, artists, and businessmen. Excellent cuisine and extensive wine list at Karl Johans Gate, 41B, tel. 42-73-00.

For more information regarding Oslo, accommodations in Lillehammer, or the Peer Gynt Trail, contact the Norwegian Tourist Board, 655 Third Avenue, New York, New York 10017, tel. (212) 949-2333.

Besides a small alpine ski area above town, Lillehammer also has a large **skating rink**, an excellent **fine arts museum** that displays a range of Norwegian artists, an **automobile museum**, and the **Maihaugen Collection**. Started in 1887 by Anders Sandvig, a Lillehammer dentist who realized that the Gudbrandsdalen Valley contained a wealth of folk art and a distinctive architecture, Maihaugen is a kind of Norwegian Knotts Berry Farm minus the chicken dinners, fruit pies, or train rides.

Influenced by Charles Darwin and the Norwegian sociologist Eilert Sundt, Sandvig originally set out to trace the development of the dwelling house from the most primitive example to the most advanced. What resulted was an outdoor museum that contains over a hundred buildings representing the evolution of local farms, workshops, and a medieval stave church. Today Maihaugen displays the workshops of hatters, coopers, bookbinders, and cobblers working with the old tools as well as guided tours that give insights into the economic, social and religious customs of pre-industrial Norway.

If Oslo and Lillehammer are filled with hundreds of shops, nightclubs, restaurants, museums, and parks, once on the Peer Gynt a day away from the tracks slows to chess games, swimming in the hotel pool, reading, conversation in the solarium, or long naps. At night there is coffee, dancing in the lounge, or a sauna. The emphasis is on exercise, and early to bed and early to rise.

CHAPTER 9

LAKE EFFECTS AND LITTLE COTTONWOOD CANYON, UTAH

EARLY MORNING IN SNOWBIRD. CONCUSSION bombs rattle the Cliff Lodge's windows. Snow falling like purple fog. Sirens of Sno-Cats. The tram climbing into the clouds hiding Hidden Peak. A weather forecast predicts 6 inches in Salt Lake, twice that in the Wasatch Mountains. Forget breakfast or messing with your edges or showering or shaving. Drink black coffee, stretch out, take two aspirin and climb into your Gore-Tex suit of lights.

Rising 2900 vertical feet in eight minutes, the Snowbird tram opens exactly at 9 A.M. It is now 8:45. Outside the ski-scratched windows, dime-sized flakes fall from cloud to the burdened faces above.

Forget the Monashees or Bugaboos. Here between Little Cottonwood Canyon's towering walls, an inch an hour is just another ho-hum day in paradise. To stand out here, a storm has to redline at 3 inches an hour, and you listen to the drumming of plastic boots and titanium pole tips on the tram's concrete floor and wonder what it's doing now.

An inch an hour? At least that. Divide Snowbird's average 500 inches by a five-month season and you come up with 3.3 inches a day. Not so impressive alone, but figure 21 inches a week, 7 feet a month—and that doesn't count the months that get 3 feet and the months that get 11. If other areas brag about their snowfall, Snowbird benefits from a special dispensation.

Standing in line, I know that today, as every day, Snowbird will provide a vertical stage for the exotically dressed actors waiting with me. Snowbird bears a certain similarity to Broadway. A great actor is nothing without a powerful play. You can ski Colorado, California, or New Mexico, but until you open in New York, or catch the Bird on a day when it's pumping 2 inches, it's all just summer stock.

When forecasters speak about lake effects, they're usually referring to Buffalo, New York, or Snowbird, Utah—areas where advancing low pressure sucks moisture from vast inland seas to release it in prolific dumps on downwind towns. In Buffalo's case these enormous snowfalls create 11-foot drifts, bury cars, isolate homes, and bankrupt the city's maintenance budget. Out in Utah the opposite happens. Here snow means big dough. If Utah is known as the "Beehive State," judging from revenues generated by Wasatch ski resorts it should have been named the "Flake State."

It is now 9 A.M. The brightly colored line starts to wind through a pipe labyrinth that switches back on itself. At the end of the labyrinth a yawning Snowbird employee guards a turnstile that regulates an adult version of musical chairs. Those that slip by the green light rejoice and reflexively look back at the anxious faces left behind. Those close to the break point crowd forward, anticipating the red light. Once it flashes, there's no appeal to a higher authority. No offered bribe (unless it's a very big bribe and offered very subtly) will change his mind. I know the break is just in front or just in back of me, but my luck holds and I make the first tram as the turnstile freezes and a disappointed groan ripples down the line.

There is a trick to riding trams. Load first and you get jammed into distant corners away from the doors. Load last and you get jammed against the operator. If you're lucky, you won't be wearing a white jumpsuit and he won't have grease on his jacket. Either way last on means first off, which may not seem like much of an advantage, until you get off last, take a second to knock the snow off your boots, and are forced to follow a flight of over-revved powder hounds down the first 100 vertical feet of Chips Run.

By Utah's standards Salt Lake is a large city, with a population of 250,000. If you settle in for a week or a season, rentals are reasonable, restaurants are basic but plentiful, and even if the state liquor laws do require jumping through flaming hoops for a mixed drink, Alta's inexpensive day pass and Snowbird's tram elevate Little Cottonwood Canyon to one of the top five destinations in the United States.

Another asset is Salt Lake City's international airport. Located 31 miles from Snowbird and serviced by Utah Transit Authority buses, L.A. skiers can quit work at five o'clock Friday and check into Snowbird's Cliff Lodge by 9 P.M. Add Salt Lake's Chicago, Denver, San Francisco, New York, and Seattle step-on, step-off connections, and the Wasatch Mountains could have average snow and still receive rave reviews. Because Little Cot-

---

Alta/Snowbird is one hour from the airport. Buses: Utah Transit Authority connects to both resorts; $6 from airport. For schedule: (801) 262-5626.

Rental Cars: Avis (800-331-1212), Dollar (801-596-2580), Hertz (800-654-3131), National (800-227-7468).

Salt Lake City Airport is serviced by American (800-433-7300), Delta (800-221-1212), and TWA (800-221-2000).

★

tonwood Canyon gets the most print, many out-of-staters assume Snowbird and Alta are the only game in town. It's only after you mention Park City, Sundance, Deer Valley, Snowbasin, and Solitude that the Great Salt Lake starts to resemble a huge snow gun aimed at the Wasatch range.

Oddly enough, many of the skiers who climb these canyons have little or no winter driving experience. Though the state plows usually keep up with storms, at anything over 2 inches an hour the roads turn to vertical ice rinks. Braving Little Cottonwood Canyon without four-wheel drive, chains, or studded snow tires is an object lesson in how the weak, the dumb, and the unfit eliminate themselves from the communal herd. Blue ice, sharp turns, and a mind-blowing grade send inexperienced drivers yawing toward the ditch. Often it's so slick that anything short of a Sno-Cat can't get started once someone stops, and the traffic simply shivers in place. For that reason taking the four-wheel drive airport shuttle and booking Snowbird's Cliff Lodge or one of the other accommodations can eliminate the stress of renting a car, staying in Salt Lake, and risking the road.

The tram rises into gray cotton, and to my left a man in mallard brown and blue studies my Dynamics.

"Do you like those skis in deep snow?" he inquires. I admit I do, to which he replies, "We don't get that much powder in Minnesota. So, do you know anything about these?" He turns his soft flexing Dynastars so I can see the model. I tell him they're probably pretty good.

"Dear, it's not the skis," his wife quietly points out.

"Yesterday we tried Alta and didn't have much luck. So, how do you ski it?" He ignores her. "You sit back?" I tell him it's hard to steer from the tails. It's best to stay centered over the middle of the ski.

"I heard you're supposed to sit back," he replies with the least disappointment. "Well, we'll probably stick to the groomed stuff this first run," he admits.

He'd be well advised to take a powder lesson. Junior Bounous has headed the Snowbird Ski School since 1972 and is a legendary powder skier. Bounous started teaching at Alta in 1948 and is known as a fearless tree skier as well as a zen master of the steep and deep. "Trees tend to steer people away and thus the powder lasts longer there," he admits. "In the trees your mind has to be alert, constantly searching downhill for patterns and escape routes. Conditions can change quickly, especially in pines where the distance between the trees determines whether they can be skied at all."

With one hundred full-time and fifty part-time instructors, Snowbird has one of the largest ski schools in the United States, and among its different programs offers the Mountain Clinic, which is basically an insider's tour of Snowbird's secret runs, its empty runs, hidden faces, and forest glades. Because of the terrain, classes are limited to experienced and confident skiers. To get that experience and confidence many skiers take the Super Clinic, for which the school uses video to visualize specific problems and strengths.

Snowbird also offers one of the most innovative children's programs in the country. Ages run from four-year-olds in Kinderbird's classes to Mountain Adventure for advanced ten-year-olds and up who are introduced to more challenging terrain, race tips, and powder lessons. Like the adult version, the Junior Super Clinics rely on the use of video and are designed for older children and teenagers. During the day instructors videotape students as they ski around the mountain. Then, during breaks, they replay the tape and pinpoint problems. The aim is to avoid burnout on too much clinicking and too little skiing.

Private lesson is $50 per hour. All-day private, $230. Ski clinics: three-hour group lesson, $35; three days, $135; five days, $200. Mountain experience or Super Clinic: one day, $50; five days, $200. Kinderbirds/Children's classes or Mountain Adventure: one day (two hours A.M. and two hours P.M.), $45; three days, $120; five days, $200.

For all my careful positioning in the tram, on top I see there isn't a need to rush. Visibility is down to 20 feet, and I can't see the trail markers. Hesitating only long enough to figure out which way is down, I get passed by two dozen locals who disappear down Chips Run. Kicking the snow off my boots, I step into my bindings. If you normally ski a seven DIN setting, remember ski brakes were never designed to handle Wasatch powder. Powder stresses DIN settings, and when you release the ski typically vectors off beneath the snow.

Everyone has watched overconfident pilgrims searching beneath the chair. At first they're in a hurry, digging frantically along a track that leads to a lone sitzmark. On your next ride the search has expanded to a hundred square feet and in places is down to the grass base. On the third ride the search has expanded to five hundred feet and is now totally random. They're sweating, have stripped to a turtleneck, and are carrying on brief, frustrated conversations with helpful people on the chair above. By the fourth ride they're sitting silently in the snow, staring philosophically down the canyon.

Strong advice offered here: To avoid this scenario stuff powder cords up your pant legs.

From the tram's upper station I take Chips Run. Poor visibility precludes knowing exactly where I am, and as three skiers break down Regulator Johnson into the Gad Valley the thundering pack makes a sweeping left turn, then a sweeping right onto the Cirque Traverse, which leads to the Gad Chutes, Wilbere Chute, and the awesome Mach Schnell. Snowbird's trail map leaves little doubt as to what these yellow triangles with the red exclamation marks designate. "Caution," it says. "Check with ski patrol for current conditions." Unless you are on the U.S. Development Team or a Snowbird local, you had best avoid these cliff faces until the visibility lifts.

I start banging into unseen bumps and stop. Below all I can see is swirling clouds and falling snow, but the slope is untracked and I drop off the cat track, rise over a buried mogul, link a turn, and start through the fog. The skiing is steep, deep, and light as the snow blows past my knees, and my skis float through 16 inches of new powder. I reach for the next turn and the next, sensing this is some kind of fantasy. In a minute I'll awaken, untangle the sheets around my neck, and wonder what possessed me to order the double bean burrito for dinner.

A major advantage Snowbird shares with European resorts is size. Though it claims 2100 acres and 3100 vertical feet serviced by seven double chairs and the single 125-passenger tram, it skis far bigger. In general, near the Hidden Peak summit the terrain runs to open bowls filled with islands of trees. As you descend toward the valley base, the forest intermingles with chutes and cliffs before giving way to open intermediate faces and beginner trails.

Common sense insists open bowls are not the smartest place to be blundering around in a whiteout, and when the shadowy shapes of evergreens appear below, I trace them down to the Little Cloud lift. If the snow is excellent, the visibility is a killer. Increasingly leery about skiing into or off something, I pull out the trail map and take a rough fix on the Gad II chair.

On low visibility days, it can be argued, the protected Gad II offers the best skiing in Snowbird. Rising to the top of Gadzooks, Bananas, and S.T.H., the Gad II services both glade skiing and more traditional trails with an interesting mix of advanced and intermediate terrain. Most of the advanced pitches can be found along a sheer face that runs perpendicular beneath the lift.

Riding the chair, I watch four thirteen-year-old boys sidestep a rock face down into a vertical chute. The first in line sucks up his knees and drops into the deep snow that has blown in next to the trees. Then the rest follow, jumping from turn to turn until the chair crosses the transition and I lose sight of them. What would I have given to attend junior high at the mouth of Little Cottonwood Canyon?

I once skied Snowbird with Mark Harbaugh, who was Nordica's #1 Sales Rep that year. For a big man Harbaugh skis powder with little-boy enthusiasm, jumping off rocks and chancing tight trees, taking risks and grinning through the face shots. For Harbaugh skiing Snowbird was a way to balance the 40,000 miles and six months he spends on the road. It's his reward for living in motels and eating at roadside diners. He was obviously refreshed by the Bird's deep snow and empty lines.

In a meteorological anomaly peculiar to the Wasatch, the sun can be shining in Salt Lake City while it is snowing an inch an hour on Hidden Peak. By following Lower Bassackwards (a reference to Dick Bass, Snowbird's developer and present owner) you can reach the Mid Gad and Gad 1 lifts. The Gad 1 lift rises 1827 feet to a flat above the Little Cloud lift, where it accesses Lunch Run to the Mid Gad Restaurant. The temptation, of course, is to rave on until the final bell. Stopping for lunch means a lost three runs, but your legs are the first to go when you're running on empty, and the Gad lunch line offers a quick in-and-out. Slamming down an all-American "cheeburgerorderfrieskoke'n'candybar," you can still jump into your bindings and loop down Big Emma to the Gad base.

The clouds lift just after noon, and a spot of sunlight explodes onto the burdened faces. The improving visibility sends me racing to the tram. Taking Bass Highway (another nod to Snowbird's fearless leader), I catch the tram during the lunch lull. In spite of Hidden Peak's usual amenities—its toilets, coffee, hot chocolate, and finger foods—I don't dally. Squaring my shoulders to the hill, I follow Chips Run away from the Cirque Traverse down a series of switchbacks to the Peruvian Gulch that looks more like a bowl. Rated intermediate, Chips Run skirts the black diamond Primrose Path and the yellow runs Silver Fox, Great Scott, and Upper Cirque.

No wonder Chips Run attracts more than its share of pressure, for it alternates short faces with flat gullies and open tree glades. Below the Peruvian Gulch it swings back beneath Chips Face, where it picks up Primrose Path. In turn Primrose alternates open trees and broad paths until it intersects the black diamond Adager, lower Silver Fox, and lower Chips Face, which in turn lead back to the tram.

Half the thrill of skiing Snowbird is first tracks. Granted it isn't heli-skiing, where you're guaranteed a minimum untracked vertical, but if it snows hard enough, it can be close. Four tram runs equal a day of heli-skiing at 10 percent of the cost. Here you can traverse to the far right of Peruvian Gulch, where an untracked face drops to a distant tree line. One turn follows another; a crystal contrail lifts behind you as you try to avoid the groomed pistes and hunt for the entrance to the black diamond Chips Face. Here you drop from bump to bump straight at the Cliff Lodge pool.

With a twenty-minute line blocking the tram, I herringbone

up to the Peruvian chair. Admittedly it only gains 1000 vertical feet in six minutes, but with no lift line it's roughly twice as fast as waiting for the tram. On the chair I meet Mike, a twenty-year-old bump skier/model dressed in a multicolored but tattered jumpsuit, who tells me his goal is to make the U.S. Olympic Mogul Team for the '92 Albertville games. To that end he is working in the Cliff Lodge, taking advantage of the pass and night shifts to ski. I ask him how he's been doing in competition.

"Okay," he admits. "Top five . . . which isn't good enough. Snowbird's full of hot skiers, but the trials aren't for a while. . . . We'll see."

I start to follow him, but he dives into Adager's big bumps and when I hesitate, he is gone. I could easily ski the Peruvian double until closing, but the tram line has shrunk to eight minutes; so once on top I follow the Cirque Traverse down a series of stair steps past narrow chutes. This is steep stuff, and I'm about to go left down Wilbere Bowl when a skier in front of me goes right. Here, with the tram passing overhead and the clouds starting to lower, I ski a broad empty bowl back down to Chips. Though I'm not the first, the prior tracks show an expert's symmetry, and I bend my knees, reach downhill, and wish the valley floor were twice as far away.

By the time I reach my room in the Cliff Lodge, I am fried. The storm has resumed outside, the wind is rising, and everything hurts: back, shoulders, and knees. Fortunately Lodge amenities include the Cliff Spa—27,000 square feet on the ninth and tenth floors devoted to the alleviation of pain and age. Figuring to start with the first and work backward, I slip into the Lodge's rooftop pool, crank out twenty laps, then cross over into the Jacuzzi.

Because of Utah's neolithic liquor laws, you're not likely to catch Snowbird guests dancing on the tables. Here ordering a mixed drink involves dragging your own brown-bagged bottle through the restaurant then ordering mixers, garnishes, and the rest. If the brown-bag image is better suited to a skid-row

Full service spa including spa cuisine in the Aerie Restaurant, tel. (801) 742-2222 ext. 5900. Beauty salon and skin-care department, massage, exercise rooms, sauna, swimming pool, weights, and fantastic views. Fitness programs centered around winter skiing and summer hiking and tennis.

habitué, that is partly the intent of the law—to use inconvenience and social stigma to eliminate consumption. As of '88 a new law allows 180 establishments statewide to serve drinks to the table but it is well to heed the bumper sticker: "Eat, drink, and be merry for tomorrow you might be in Utah."

Ski area snow reports often sound like horoscopes. During drought years "skiing is very good on packed powder . . . be alert for unmarked obstacles" bears a striking similarity to "economic future is bright if you can avoid hidden pitfalls." "Our forecast calls for a major storm to move onto the coast" mimics "a strong romantic interest will enter your life soon." In short, when it comes to snow conditions, ski resorts tend to amplify the truth. An exception to this rule is Alta, with an annual snowfall of over 500 inches. "Alta is enjoying a foot of fresh powder on top of yesterday's two feet of new powder" doesn't leave a lot of room for criticism.

If you come to Snowbird you can't miss Alta. Located a short distance up Little Cottonwood Canyon from Snowbird, Alta is ten years behind the times. Here a day ticket for Alta's eight double chairs and three tows accessing the full spectrum of groomed, tree, and mogul runs is only $19. A half day is $14, as is a strict Albion Basin pass, and if you're still skiing at eighty, Alta will comp you a free season's pass—a backhanded tribute to Alf Engen, who was still Alta's ski school director at

---

The **Cliff Lodge at Snowbird**, tel. (800) 453-3000, is a full-service hotel that sits conveniently uphill of the tram. You can ski down in the morning and ride the chair up at day's end. Amenities: deluxe rooms and suites, four restaurants, 27,000-foot spa, pool, sauna, in-house ski rentals, day care, and ski-to-slope access. Terms: double $88–$159.

Lodge at Snowbird, The Inn, Iron Blosam Lodge, tel. (800) 453-3000. Amenities: complete spa, sauna and pool facilities available, walk to bank, post office, medical clinic, pharmacy, and shops. Terms: double $69–$149.

Salt Lake City Marriott, 75 S. West Temple, Salt Lake City, Utah 84144, tel. (801) 531-0800. Amenities: 510 rooms, swimming pool, whirlpool, airport shuttle, hotel courtesy car, two restaurants, access to downtown shopping and restaurants. Terms: double $69–$99.

Information about local motels and prices from the Salt Lake Convention and Visitors Bureau, tel. (801) 831-4332.

Alta Reservation Service, tel. (801) 453-8488, handles reservations for Alta's lodges.

★

---

eighty. A member of the National Skier's Hall of Fame, Engen first skied Alta in 1935 while working for the Civilian Conservation Corps and subsequently played a pivotal role in its development. Engen also worked to organize the Professional Ski Instructors of America and, it can be argued, was the father of modern deep-powder skiing. Like Engen there's a timelessness to Alta, a sense of taking a step back and recalling when wooden skis were still duking it out with the Head Standard and double chairs were engineering miracles.

As I step off the shuttle in front of the ticket office, the day promises marginal visibility and deep powder—a fine trade when you factor Alta's 2000-foot vertical drop, eight double chairs, and vast acreage. The lifts open at 9:30 A.M., but unlike most areas on a powder morning, no one seems to be in a terrible rush. Skiers wander around the base of the Collins Double Lift messing with bindings and cleaning their goggles. I keep waiting for a ground swell to push me into the passing chairs, but at 9:26 the operator sweeps the snow off and loads the first in line. A minute later I'm riding the chair with a Wy-

---

Snowpine Lodge, tel. (801) 742-2000, is the oldest lodge in Alta, recently remodeled, with sunny dining room for breakfast and casual, easy dinner. Rooms are not luxury but are clean and reflect Alta's ambiance.

Rustler Lodge, tel. (801) 742-2200, one of Alta's luxury lodges; dining room, bar, large rooms, and pool.

Alta Lodge, tel. (801) 742-3500, luxury lodge, old and new sections, rustic bar, great food, family operated.

Alta Peruvian Lodge, tel. (801) 742-3000, pool, sunny lobby and dining area, rustic rooms, flavor of Alta.

For more information (801) 942-0404, Alta Lodging Reservations.

---

oming forest ranger who says he's been coming to Alta for twenty-five years.

"Since I was a kid," he admits, adding that the resort's family style and absence of glitz hasn't changed. Now he brings his own family. Son, brothers, and father—three generations convening on this snowy day. "If you're alone, take a run with us," he says. "My brothers and I know some great chutes off Greeley."

I politely decline. It is a reunion and I only have that day to see Alta, but his offer is typical of people who ski this resort.

Bucking the present trend, Alta isn't interested in throwing up trams and quads. Management's reasoning is, better a short line and fantastic skiing than no lines and average conditions. From the Collins double you can ski down to the Germania double, which rises 1,125 feet to the top of the intermediate Mambo and Ballroom. Though these runs aren't showing tracks, turning left I follow the High Traverse then drop into Race Course, which alternates open forest, deep snow, and buried moguls. Knees pumping in the smoky powder, the speed comes up and I float downhill. Powder serves as a buffer against hard moguls and sudden falls. It forces you to loosen up, face downhill, and stand in the center of the ski, and if at times the rhythms of skis and snow seem to beat out of synch, there are also moments when they harmonize, and the resulting melody haunts you for decades.

A line is starting to form, and after a short wait I catch a chair with a New York doctor who is attending a seminar on infectious diseases in Salt Lake City. I query him about AIDS and he asks me about skis.

Leaving him at the top, I drop into Mambo, which has been groomed. The upper section is tracked, and so I ski the trees back to the Germania base. The line is getting longer, and rather than wait I ski Meadow to the lower part of High Rustler and down to the base area's Wild Cat double. Servicing the expert Wild Cat area, the chair rises 1250 vertical to the Peruvian Ridge that separates Alta from Snowbird. Dropping into Punch Bowl, I make a dozen turns and start hitting Rock Gully's enormous moguls, rock outcroppings, and sheer, man-eating faces. I make two more turns and blow it. Savoring how a wing-shot chukar must feel, I tumble down the face. The powder cushions my fall, but I still get the breath knocked out of me. When I finally clear my goggles and shake the snow out of my jacket, my courage is gone. If pride suggests I challenge

Rock Gully again, common sense warns me that small victo-
ries belong to those who live to ski another day. Or in this case
another run, which means catching the Germania chair to the
head of the Albion Valley, where I follow a long traverse to the
Supreme chair.

A guy in full powder assault gear nods in reply to my yell of
"Single!" On the chair Bucky Burrows tells me he recently
moved to Alta from Bethel, Alaska. Burrows worked as a bush
pilot and is now taking a winter off from flying. He exchanges
maintenance at one of the lodges for room and board. The
hours are flexible and allow him to ski days. So of all the
mountains in the Rockies, why did he pick Alta?

"It's got the snow," he says. "It's also got the terrain. It's a
skier's mountain. . . . You don't find many pretenders here."
Succinct, direct; it also turns out that Bucky can ski. During the
ride he suggests the cliff faces to the left of the Supreme chair.
After some discussion we agree on a glade shot off Big Dipper,
which drops back to the chair. On our next run Bucky suggests
we traverse out into the Sunset area, where the trees open into
broad untracked meadow. The snow spills past our knees and
tempts us to hang on long after our screaming thighs and ragged breathing warn of anaerobic overload.

In succession we hit Sunset's powder again and could hit it
all day, but the overcast is growing grayer, and Bucky suggests
we try one of his favorite runs. Traversing to the Sugarloaf
chair, we follow the Devils Elbow into a deep gully that finally
spits us out on an untracked face above the Alpenglow Hut.
Here, beneath the towering Greeley Face, we ski crud down to
an untracked meadow that finally leads to trees and the Albion
base.

If race coaches insist hard snow is better for your skiing,
shots of U.S. team members typically depict guys and gals with
massive legs, huge buttocks, and a pit bull's inbred aggres-
siveness. None of them, however, look as if they're having fun.
It's all big bucks and national pride and a *Gott im Himmel*

grimace. Even so, there aren't many U.S. team members who would trade a Wasatch powder day for an icy racecourse. When storms redline at 3 inches an hour and 56 inches of snow falls in a long weekend, runs replenish themselves, bumps soften into pillows, and skiers submarine beneath the downy surface. If this reads like fiction, the Little Cottonwood Canyon is admittedly a meteorological anomaly. Here, if compasses still point north, snowstorms lose their way, swirl, stagnate, and dump their burden on the Wasatch range below.

REST AND RECUPERATION

If you take a day off from the slopes, you should visit the **Cliff Spa**'s (801-742-2222 ext. 5900) exercise rooms, sauna, and swimming pool. After a workout you might try breakfast at the **Aerie Restaurant**. You can shop beneath the tram base or catch the UTA ski bus down to Salt Lake City, 25 miles away. Once in Salt Lake you should visit **Temple Square**, which includes the Latter Day Saints' Temple, Tabernacle, and gardens. Tours (801-240-2534) are offered from 9 A.M. to 9 P.M. seven days a week. Unless it is on tour, the **Mormon Tabernacle Choir** can be heard twice a week, Sunday at 9:15 A.M. and Thursday at 8 P.M. Organ recitals (801-240-3318) can be heard Monday through Friday at 12 noon. Admission is free.

Visit the **Beehive House** (801-240-2671) at 67 East South Temple, which was built in 1855. It served as a supplementary residence for Brigham Young's large family. Today it is a national historic landmark open Monday through Saturday, 9:30 A.M. to 4:30 P.M. Also try the **Hansen Planetarium** on 15 South State Street (801-538-2098). The **Capitol Theater** (performance schedule, 801-534-4777) on 50 West 200 South is home to a number of modern dance, ballet, and opera companies. The **Utah Museum of Fine Arts** (801-581-7332), on the University of Utah campus, offers touring exhibits. Salt Lake also offers extensive shopping, the **Utah Symphony** (801-533-5626 for performances) at 120 West South Temple, and the **Utah Jazz** basketball games. For more information, contact the Salt Lake Convention and Visitors Bureau, 180 South West Temple, Salt Lake City, Utah 84101, tel. (800) 541-4995.

In Snowbird you must make do with wine coolers and draft beer. Admittedly, bottled Budweiser suits the **Tram Room**'s thunderous rock and roll (521-6040). It also goes well with the **Keyhole Restaurant**'s Mexican food and chirpy waitresses (969-5911). At the **Steak Pit**, 521-6040, you can get a bottle of cabernet at the state package store and a good cut of beef, and though I didn't eat there I heard the **Wildflower Restaurant**'s (521-6040) continental cuisine at the **Iron Blosam Lodge** is worth investigating. With its 4-story glass façade framing the Peruvian Lift, the Cliff Lodge's **Atrium** (742-3434) provides a dramatic setting for breakfast.

CHAPTER

10

BIG SKY,
LONE
MOUNTAIN

D ESPITE THE FACT THAT BIG SKY SITS BETWEEN
the Spanish Peaks Wilderness and Yellowstone, it is also
less than an hour from Bozeman, which is serviced by
Continental, Delta, and Northwest Airlines. If you're driving
north from Idaho Falls, Highway 20 leads to West Yellowstone,
and Highway 191 follows the Gallatin River north past the park.

C ontinental (reservations: 800-524-0280), Delta (reservations: 800-221-1212), Northwest (reservations: 800-225-2525), and Horizon (reservations: 800-547-9308) all
fly into Bozeman. Greyhound also reaches Bozeman, and
regular TW bus service connects to Big Sky (reservations:
307-344-7311).

★

Here the Yellowstone fires of '88 were started by dry lightning. Fueled by the driest summer in a century, pushed by 50-

mile-an-hour winds, and aided by the Park Service's initial "let it burn" policy, the fires raged until late September, when an early snowstorm swept in from the north. One million five hundred thousand acres were affected by eight major fire complexes, and today miles of charred snags from the Wolf Lake and Fan Fires follow the Gallatin River. When the road crests, broad black alleys of burned timber stretch to the horizon. The Park Service regards this holocaust as a blessing in disguise, for new growth will create needed range for bison, elk, and deer.

In winter, however, the snags cast stark shadows across the undisturbed snow, and we're 15 miles out of Big Sky when we pass a moose munching contentedly in a stand of willows. Running down to a corner 7-Eleven for a gallon of milk is a problem when you're located roughly an hour south of Bozeman and about the same from West Yellowstone, but that same inconvenience translates into unbroken horizons, clean air, and empty lifts. Little wonder that NBC newsman Chet Huntley fell in love with the Gallatin Valley.

A Montanan by birth, Huntley hunted and fished out of the 3 Corner Ranch. When he retired from NBC he devoted himself to building a ski resort. With his connections he was able to interest (among others) Burlington Northern, Chrysler, and General Electric, all of whom helped finance the purchase of two ranches totaling 10,000 acres. Construction began in 1970, Big Sky opened in December of 1973, and Chet Huntley died of cancer the following March. Without Huntley's guiding influence, the investors sold the resort in 1976 to Boyne USA Resorts.

Today Big Sky boasts 2800 vertical feet serviced by four double chairs, one double, and two gondolas. It has 55 miles of trails—a mix of fall-line cruisers, broad bowls, and death-defying steeps that are rated 25 percent beginner, 40 percent intermediate, and 35 percent advanced. Here you can snowmobile through Yellowstone or ski Lone Mountain Ranch's groomed Nordic trails. You can photograph moose, deer, bison, and elk, or you can critique Big Sky's restaurants and pervasive cowboy ambiance. Or you can simply hide out from it all.

It is late afternoon when we check into the Huntley Lodge. It's hard to miss the Huntley, since it is fronted by the seven-story Shoshone Condominium Hotel. From a distance the Shoshone resembles the Château Lake Louise in Banff National Park, and when we arrive the lobby is filled with Bozeman's first families attending a dinner/auction to benefit the Special Olympics. Here beneath a huge elk-horn chandelier, cowboy boots, yoke shirts, and spotless Stetsons mix with dark suits

---

The **Shoshone Condominium Hotel**, P.O. Box 1, Big Sky, Montana 59716, tel. (800) 548-4486. Amenities: 94 condominiums managed by hotel staff. Retail space and 20,000 square feet of convention center increasing Big Sky's total to 43,000 feet. Included in this major addition is a 116-seat amphitheater for medical conferences, a 9000-square-foot (1000-seat) central meeting hall, and an indoor/outdoor pool. Other amenities: ski-in ski-out, sauna, Jacuzzi, and cable TV.

Huntley Lodge, P.O. Box 1, Big Sky, Montana 59716, tel. (800) 548-4486. Amenities: 200 rooms, ski-in ski-out, pool/sauna/Jacuzzi, cable TV, two restaurants and Chet's Bar, game room, and fitness center. No dogs. Terms: $89–$149 single, $99–$149 double.

Buck's T-4, Highway 191 south of Big Sky, P.O. Box 279, Big Sky, Montana 59716, tel. (800) 822-4484. Amenities: Jacuzzi, cable TV, restaurant and bar on premises, children free, skier shuttle. Terms: $39–$52 single, $45–$64 double.

Golden Eagle Lodge, P.O. Box 8, Big Sky, Montana 59716, tel. (800) 648-4488. Amenities: Jacuzzi, cable TV, restaurant on premises, skier shuttle, children free. Terms: single $40, double $45–$52.

★

and sequined evening gowns as couples study art depicting Yellowstone Park, western sculpture, fly rods, and float tubes— all necessities for the Montana lifestyle.

Our room faces the aptly named 11,166-foot Lone Mountain. This far north the 11,000-foot spire compares favorably to Switzerland's Matterhorn, which it vaguely resembles. Lone Mountain's height in large part explains why Big Sky averages a seasonal 400 inches of snow. As such, the mountain opens in mid-November and stays open through mid-April, when a simple lack of skiers forces it to close.

Big Sky's lifts start in back of the Shoshone, and before my family unpacks I suggest we take a run to stretch out after the long ride. The boys and Barbara vote for the pool, however, and ten minutes later we're sharing a steaming Jacuzzi with six other guests. One is an Illinois minister chaperoning a troop of Boy Scouts. There is a Wyoming lineman who has just bought a time-share condominium. And there is a Southern California couple who learned of Big Sky's proximity to Yellowstone and hoped to combine a ski vacation with a winter tour of the park.

Not surprisingly, **Yellowstone** is one of Big Sky's major draws. During winter the buffalo and elk descend to the valley floor, where the frigid air and boiling steam create spectacular thermal displays. A morning shuttle to West Yellowstone, snowmobile tours, cross-country skiing, and snow coaches can be booked opposite the Shoshone's front desk. Guests can leave in the morning, hop on a John Deere, and be back before dinner.

The following morning clearing skies reveal a skiff of snow left by a storm that blew through during the night. Though the Huntley Lodge serves an excellent breakfast buffet, we opt instead for a fresh-baked cinnamon roll at Ernie's General Store in the Skiers Mall.

"So how many of these will you serve a day?" I ask the clerk.

"Heck if I know," he admits. "I'd guess Ernie bakes a couple of hundred a day. On some days he could bake a thousand and we'd still run out."

From Ernie's we head to the Explorer chair, which rises up Lone Wolf, to the beginner's slope of White Wing and the lower section of Mr. K. On the chair I tell Robert that Yellowstone Park is thinking about reintroducing wolves. This revelation surprises him, and he stares between his skis at the passing run. "Think we'll see one, Dad?" he inquires.

"Probably not," I admit.

Robert, however, isn't buying it. "Who says?" he wonders.

"Biologists," I reply, using a word he won't understand. Even so, wedging down Lone Wolf, Robert clings to my tails and keeps a close watch on the tree line.

Lone Wolf is a perfect warm-up, but at the base Andrew insists, "Robert skis too slow," and so we split up.

Taking Gondola 1 to the base of the Bowl Area, you have a choice of skiing the intermediate Mr. K. down to the base or riding the Lone Peak triple to 9800 feet. Below the valley is marked by rolling forests, open meadows, a snow-covered Arnold Palmer golf course, private homes, and a single black ribbon of a road—not isolated, but definitely self-sufficient.

From the top of the Lone Peak triple, skiers often climb what would be Lone Mountain's Hornli Ridge. Future plans include a tram to the summit, which would access a huge southeast snowfield and effectively double the terrain. At this time, however, no date for construction has been set.

Accessed by the triple, the bowls are never groomed, and since they catch the morning light, they peak before one o'clock. After that the face lies in shadow, the visibility erodes, and the snow hardens. What we haven't anticipated is that the bowls' combination of fresh snow, hard base, and tight moguls would challenge Andrew's stem turns. He falls often and hard, and by the time we work our way down to the intermediate Upper Morning Star, I am expecting the worst.

In light of his linked crashes, I try to be as diplomatic as possible. "So what'd you think of the bowl?" I ask.

"Good," he shrugs, then suggests we do it again. Do it again?

Not surprisingly Big Sky's most challenging terrain can be found off the Challenger chair. Few runs off Challenger are groomed, for this lift accesses Montana's biggest vertical and its steepest run. Here the north-facing A-Z Chutes plummet into the Nashville Basin. This is expert terrain that returns via a long traverse through Midnight Basin, Moonlight Basin, and Big Rock Tongue to the Challenger. Turning left off the chair, the south faces are somewhat less steep but filled with large bumps, weathered fir, and rock outcroppings that, intermediates will discover, are intolerant of those who attempt to ski above their station. On deep powder days this area offers some of Big Sky's best skiing—steep, sheltered, and north-facing.

While the boys and Barbara stop at Whiskey Jacks for nachos and 7-Ups, I drop by the ski school office. Director Robert Kirchschlager is headed out for a run and invites me along. Born in Austria, Kirchschlager arrived in Big Sky via an instructing job in Boyne Mountain. Now, riding the Rams Head chair, which runs above Ambush's symmetrical moguls, he points out that, though Montana only has 750,000 people, it also has the second lowest income per capita in the United States. The result is that relatively few local skiers come banging on Big Sky's door. Because Bozeman has Bridger Bowl (effectively a municipal resort), a majority of Big Sky's 180,000 skier days come from as far away as Florida, Georgia, Illinois, and Oklahoma. Big Sky's comparatively small number of skiers means there are never lines. Or at most there are five-minute lines at Gondola 1 from nine to ten on Easter weekend.

With Yellowstone out Big Sky's back door, you would think this resort would benefit from the overflow. Taylor Middleton, Big Sky's director of marketing, says that the resort must work for every skier day (bad for the bottom line but great for skiers). With four fifths of its business accounted for by winter, he points out that Big Sky has had four consecutive years of increases as of this writing.

Andesite Mountain serves as an 8800-foot little brother to Lone Mountain. With three chairs, including the new Southern Comfort triple that accesses 160 acres of southeast-facing trails, Andesite offers a variety of intermediate and advanced runs. Kirchschlager suggests Big Horn, and we swing down its groomed length, past thick forests and the occasional rolling moguls to the Mad Wolf double chair.

Riding the chair, Kirchschlager tells me 40 percent of the terrain is groomed, which accounts for Silver Knife's satin surface, one that absorbs our edge sets as we drop toward the Mountain Mall. Back at Whiskey Jacks, the boys are satiated on soft drinks and chips and are scrutinizing a Cape Buffalo when I suggest we try Calamity Jane. As long as it doesn't contain a reference to wolves, Robert is game, and we load the Gondola 2. During the ride I note that my younger son seems a bit tense. It turns out he's worried about what's holding the gondola to the cable.

What?!

Barbara and I pride ourselves on being enlightened parents. We don't tell stories about chainsaw massacres at bedtime. We've unplugged the television. We set aside quality time each day. So why is Robert worried about the gondola crashing into the gully below? It's either a genetic glitch or he's been listening to his older brother.

Calamity Jane's bumps, crud, and varying pitch challenge both boys, and after a final run down Mr. K they stagger off toward the pool.

This being the West (and Montana at that), you would expect the local fare to run toward beef, beef, and more beef with a side order of baked potato. Well, you can get a pretty good beef at Big Sky's Whiskey Jacks, and you can find great Italian in

Naples, New York, and San Francisco, but 50 miles outside of Bozeman? Forget what you expect and try Andiamo.

Owned by the resort, Andiamo 995-2220 owes much of its success to Monique Corne, a twenty-eight-year-old native of Bozeman who studied cooking at the California Culinary Academy in San Francisco. "I refuse to do pizza," she now admits. "Anyway pizza is American and tends to reflect on the rest of the menu. When I lived in San Francisco I ate at a lot of Italian restaurants and now have a pretty good feel if something works. In Big Sky much depends on what's available, and we're fortunate to get fresh seafood flown in daily from Portland."

"Pizza pie," Robert whispers when the menu arrives.

"No pizza," I reply.

"Why not?" he frowns.

"They don't make pizza here" I say.

"No pizza? Dad, what kind of Italian restaurant is this?" Andrew asks.

Since Robert can't read, he thinks we're lying to him about the pizza. Under protest he says he'll try the *Fusilli alla Vesuviana*, which is a spiral pasta with parmesan and mozzarella cheese, topped with fresh basil and tomato sauce. Andrew insists on a salad and side order of mussels; I have the *Rigatoni col Sugo Piccante de Salsiccia*, which turns out to be a tubular pasta served with spicy Italian sausage and tomato sauce, and after much agonizing Barbara decides on the *Bucatini con Aglio*, a tubular pasta with a sauce of olive oil, garlic, and hot pepper tossed with parmesan cheese. All of it is fantastic and far more than we can eat. But with help Andrew finishes the mussels and three-bites-and-I'm-done Robert nearly finishes his fusilli.

Other good restaurants in Big Sky include **First Place,** 995-4244, for continental cuisine and **Edelweiss Restaurant,** 995-4665, for Austrian and German Specialties. There's **Buck's T-4,** 995-4111, on Highway 191 for a good steak, game and seafood. **Levensky's Pizza,** 995-4646, is in the skiers' mall. You should try the **Huntley Lodge** dining room, 995-4211, for dinner, especially Austrian night on Wednesday and the morning buffet. There's **Scissor Bills,** 995-4933, in the Arrowhead Mall for après atmosphere charburgers and **Whiskey Jack,** 995-4211, for African game heads on the wall, finger foods, burgers and steaks. After a day on Lone Mountain you may not feel up to dancing the night away, but if you do, Whiskey Jack's books groups like Nicolette Larson, the Temptations, and the Ozark Mountain Daredevils. At the **Corral,** 995-4249, on Highway 191 couples push the pool table out of the way and country swing to local bands. Wednesday is Austrian Night at the Huntley Lodge Dining Room and Rum Boogie Night is Thursdays at Scissor Bills.

Because the boys have school on Monday and home is a six-hour ride away, we are up early. Five-year-old Robert has had enough of the wolves. No way are we going to get him on the Mad Wolf chair or down Lobo. Seven-year-old Andrew, however, is desperate to ski Ambush's big bumps. No horror story of how big, hard, or impenetrable they are will dissuade him. On the Rams Head chair to the top of Andesite, he is unmoved by the large egg crates passing below us.

A parenting problem here. You know Andrew risks breaking his leg, arm, or worse. You have the experience, the authority, to say no, but you don't want to rob him of his self-confidence. Do you flatly refuse, offer a bribe, or try to distract him? Do you turn down the groomed Elk Park Ridge that drops to the Mad Wolf chair and hope he forgets this mogul madness? I try the latter. Andrew is unimpressed. On the ride up, he insists we ski Mad Wolf, which pretty well describes how it looks. Crazy Raven is even worse, and forget Snake Pit. Andrew refuses to be fooled a second time, and so we traverse into the lower section of Mad Wolf, where he takes a beating.

"Let's do it again," he says.

"Son . . ." I protest.

"Dad, I'm getting better," he insists.

On the next run I note a small improvement. He takes another beating. We do it again. My thighs start to burn. Andrew keeps plugging away. We ski Big Horn and then Mad Wolf again. Andrew gets better. With time running out we ski North Ambush to the base. By now he's unweighting and almost disappearing between the bumps. I try to imagine where this will end. In another decade will he blow through the bumps, leaving me to stagger along behind? Will he become the instructor and I the student?

And so at two that afternoon we're back on 191 headed south toward West Yellowstone past the Corral Restaurant. Inside, a bunch of hunting-and-fishing outfitters are watching a Mets game, and we order the Corral Burger and study the bear skulls, branching antlers, and period firearms. With video games along one wall and horseshoes for door handles, a pool table in front of the bar, and signs that say "Does" and "Bucks" on the bathroom doors, the boys think this is the best restaurant in the state.

"So what did you think of the skiing?" I inquire.

Andrew takes a bite of the cherry pie and nods. "I told you Ambush wasn't that hard," he says.

REST AND RECUPERATION

Big Sky's relative isolation results in simple, off-day pleasures. Besides the Shoshone's swim-in swim-out pool and Jacuzzi, you can shop in the slope-side Mountain Mall or Arrowhead Mall. The **Lone Mountain Ranch**, (406) 995-4644, offers 45 miles of groomed cross-country trails, rentals, sales, and sleigh ride dinners. If you only take one day off, however, I would strongly suggest taking the bus to Yellowstone and there, depending on your sense of adventure, renting a snowmobile or taking **TW Services Snowcoach** tours. If you hurry it takes roughly three hours to travel out and back to **Old Faithful**, which, unlike many park services, does not close for winter. Tours to Yellowstone can be booked at the Shoshone's main desk. Or **Two Top Snowmobile Rental**, (800) 522-7802, offers a 10 percent saving for a Big Sky skiers' special.

Mountain sheep winter just above the turnoff to Big Sky and can be photographed as they come down to feed. Moose can be observed feeding along Highway 191 to West Yellowstone.

With the help of guides supplied by the Bozeman Chamber of Commerce, 1205 East Main, you can explore the city's historic sections. Also do not miss the Gallatin country **Pioneer Museum** on 317 West Main or the **Museum of the Rockies** paleontology, Native American artifacts, and antique vehicles on the Montana State University campus (994-2251); hours 9–5 Tuesday through Sunday.

CHAPTER 11

HELI-SKIING PARADISAICAL NEW ZEALAND

T IS RAINING DURING AIR NEW ZEALAND'S SIN-gle stop in Papeete, Tahiti, and, sprinting for cover, I miss the sign for the transit lounge. I end up with a tour group, and a stunning Tahitian girl steps into my path.

"Aloha," she says, placing a lei around my neck and kissing me on both cheeks.

As the exotic smell of plumeria wells into my face, I manage a passable "Merci," then notice the "Nothing to Declare" sign. I've stumbled into arrivals!

"Excuse me, I'm sorry," I say, trying to return the lei; but the girl has seen it before and tiredly refuses. Finding my way into Duty Free's relative anonymity, I order a three-dollar orange soda and wonder what to do with my flowered necklace.

"Fragrant piece of work, that," a silver-haired New Zealander sitting at the bar ventures.

"Yes, it is," I agree.

"Generous people these Tahitians, absolutely wonderful," he observes. "You knew our Marys sailed from here?"

"No, I didn't," I reply, wondering what a Mary is.

"Oh yes, they named our South Island, Aorataranga. It means Land of the Long Cloud." He pauses to empty his beer into a glass. "Tahiti's prices'll kill you. Our dollar's not worth a damn."

"Nor ours," I agree. "You were saying the Land of the Long Cloud?"

"Right, the Marys didn't know the cloud was the Southern Alps. None of 'em had ever seen snow before!"

Now, with Air New Zealand's domestic Flight 523 on final approach into Christchurch, I can't shake an image of Mary (read Maori) explorers sailing toward a glistening cloud. Legend claims a storm blew these voyaging Tahitians off course and, looking out the window at the Southern Alps, I see a deep ocean swell lift the canoe out of a trough. The canoe hangs on the crest, and the Tahitians try to make sense of the shining peaks, blue glaciers, and dark canyons. Perhaps it is a spirit cloud, the navigator speculates as the canoe slides into the next trough.

Feeling the nose drop toward Christchurch, I suspect that the Southern Alps have always defied description. Erupting out of the Canterbury Plains, dozens of snow-covered summits give way to beech forets, which in turn drop to rolling green

---

Air New Zealand offers daily flights from Los Angeles to Auckland with hourly connections to Christchurch. Air New Zealand also has a four-stop ticket that includes Honolulu, Fiji, Rarotonga, Tahiti, and Auckland. Reservations: (800) 262-1234. Flights are also available on United (800-241-6522), Continental (800-525-0280), and Quantas (800-622-0850). Most rental car companies are represented in Christchurch, and if you plan on skiing both Wanaka and Mt. Cook, hiring one is recommended.

★

foothills. It's possible that the Southern Alps are an optical illusion. Or perhaps they aren't all that steep. Or perhaps they are every bit that steep and New Zealand skiers learn to wedge turn on triple black diamond runs with names like Lamb's Lane, Kiwi Kruiser, or Totally Beechin'.

Either way means trouble. Too heart-stopping steep and all you remember is one survival turn after another. Too forgiving and the real excitement begins in the pub—after the lifts close. Buckling the seat belt and raising the tray table, I don't know what to expect from Wanaka or Mt. Cook, but if the South Island's skiing approximates these mountains, you can fix this summer for the duration. At some point well into the twenty-first century, my heirs will say "Grandpa? Are you awake?" and I will straighten and point out, "Ah yes, that was the summer I skied New Zealand."

By the time I clear customs, collect my bags, and take care of the rental car, it is midafternoon. The rental clerk takes a Christchurch city map, draws a bright red line toward Timaru, then says something about not missing the turn to Lake Pukaki and Wanaka.

"And do remember," she adds, offering the key, "to drive on the left."

After two practice laps around Christchurch International, I start the six-hour drive to Wanaka by taking Highway 1, which heads south down the east coast.

Lesson one. Do not make left-hand turns into right-hand lanes. It upsets the locals. If you survive those first critical miles, try to relax and enjoy New Zealand's cypress windrows, emerald pastures and sheared sheep, uniformed school kids, tractors, and brick farmhouses. Three hours later you'll come around a corner and nearly have a head-on with the alpenglow on Mt. Cook's 12,349-foot summit. At times like this, you wonder if the South Island's light is weird or if you've just been up too long. Turquoise lakes, snow covered peaks, green pastures, stone churches, and muddy sheep: it's more than your

light meter can handle, and you'll find yourself firing frame
after frame.

Clear and cold is fine August weather in New Zealand, but
it's raining hard when I check into the THC Hotel in Wanaka.
Even so, rain offers a fine portent for tomorrow morning. A
thousand feet above—still well below Wanaka's Treble Cone
Ski Area—it's snowing: good news for Paul Scaife's Harris
Mountain Heli-skiing's Figure Eight contest. With 250 runs on
120 peaks in six separate mountain ranges, if there's a drainage Harris Mountain doesn't ski, it's not worth skiing. Dunedin's forecasters are predicting "fine" weather by morning, and
it is well past midnight when I fall asleep, counting turns instead of sheep, hundreds upon hundreds scattered across as-
yet-unseen slopes.

THC Wanaka, Helwick St., Wanaka, New Zealand, tel.
(02943) 7826. Amenities: 46 rooms, restaurant, bar, private toilet and bath, tea and coffeepot, telephone. Terms:
NZ$71.50 double.

The **Edgewater Resort**, Sargood Drive, Ripponlea,
Wanaka, tel. (02943) 8311. Amenities: 132 rooms, restaurant, bar, toilet and bath, coffeepots, telephones, spa,
sauna, public transport. Terms: NZ$125 double.

And just as predicted, the dawn is fine. Across Lake Wanaka
the Harris Mountains brighten by degrees, and I skip breakfast, throw my skis in the car, and accelerate toward Treble
Cone. No one warns me about the road to the ski area—a serpentine, ice-covered, red dirt miracle of modern engineering
that starts in soggy sheep pasture and levels out in a foot of
fresh powder.

From Treble Cone north Lake Wanaka serves as an enormous mirror for the glistening Southern Alps. Believe everything you've heard about New Zealand's views; "spectacular"

does this country an injustice. If you judge Treble Cone by its double chair, two T-bars, one platter, and beginner tow, the area seems small. What it lacks in numbers of lifts, however, it compensates for in vertical feet, accessible acres, and non-existent lines. Except for the obvious size difference, Treble Cone resembles Lake Tahoe's Heavenly Valley.

New Zealand's winter is August, the sun rises in the north-east, south slopes are shadowed, and storms spin clockwise. So how does this affect the snow? Is it heavier? Softer? Deeper? White or blue? Ten turns will convince you: powder is one of nature's few constants. Without a video as witness, no one is going to believe Treble Cone. I float from one turn to the next down Sinclair's Run, which drops back to the two-story day lodge. With Lake Wanaka at your feet, the Southern Alps at your back, and the rising sun tinting the unbroken snowfields a salmon pink, there ought to be a way to jam the solar clock-works—hit the freeze-frame button and drag this moment out until the player overheats and the cassette ejects.

A pair of Queenstown instructors are down a short face. Per-fect round turn follows perfect round turn, but they are unim-pressed.

"You're rushing your rights. . . ." one comments as they study their tracks.

"I'm also dragging my pole," he admits.

Big trouble for two guys who will go *mano a mano* against ex–U.S. Ski team member Steve Bounous and his wife Sue of Snowbird, Utah. Team Bounous are hosting their "Kiwi to Fiji Ski Adventure" and entered the figure eights as a lark. After their first set of turns on Black Peak, however, they're ranked among the top five. For most of the day a dozen teams will cut serpentine eights down a shadowed south bowl. When the Jet Ranger deposits the finalists on an untracked face, the differ-ence between the Team Bounous and Werner Hanni (President of the New Zealand Ski Federation) and Wolfgang Kiehne (a Queenstown instructor/heliguide) is one flawed turn.

That night the weather holds, and early the following morn-

ing Scaife meets a mixed group of Americans, New Zealanders, and Australians for a stream-fording, rock-bashing safari
up the Matukituki River Valley. At one time Scaife's family
owned a 50,000-acre ranch near Wanaka, but by the age of
eighteen young Paul had seen enough sheep to last a lifetime.
Forsaking the family business, he started to climb, first in the
Harrises, then in Mt. Cook National Park, where he completed
the first traverse of the Main Divide from Elie de Beaumont to
Copland Pass. Fame eluded him, however, until he scaled the
Sydney Opera House.

"There was this intriguing pattern to the overlying tiles,"
Scaife recalls, "and after a couple of failures, I discovered a
route." With the local constables using a bullhorn to read him
his rights, Scaife sat on the roof, enjoying the view. The police
wanted to make an example out of him (You can't just have
these looney Kiwis bouldering about on Sydney's buildings),
but it wasn't clear if Scaife had broken a law, and so they eventually let him go.

This morning Scaife's objective is the remote Tyndall Glacier.
Located within the boundaries of Mt. Aspiring National Park,
the Tyndall serves as HMH's crème de la crème—in keeping
with the southern hemisphere, a kind of dessert before dinner.
Scaife points out that because storms move quickly in the
Southern Alps, to ski the Tyndall you need a forecast of absolutely fine weather. Meeting at eight at Harris Mountain Heli-
skiing's Wanaka office a short time later. Scaife's rusted Land
Cruiser is rattling down a dirt road beside the braided Matukituki River. For the next hour we open and close pasture gates,
wind through the beech forests, and study the brilliant blue
skies between the canyon's glaciated walls. When the track
peters out, Scaife pulls into a meadow and starts throwing gear
off the roof rack. Seconds later the sound of the helicopter's
rotor echoes off the canyon walls as it banks around a bend
and flares against the bright morning sun.

Skis and skiers are quickly loaded, the pilot pulls pitch, and the ground quickly falls away. During the twelve minutes it takes to fly to the Tyndall, the lush beech forests change to black rock faces, then to a convoluted blue glacier. Below the skids the early loads are standing on a wide saddle. The sunny north face drops to a rocky scree slope. To the south the Tyndall appears equally uninviting. We glimpse a vertical face flaring above the saddle that leads to a series of black crevasses.

Bending to clear the rotor, we get a grip on our hats and packs; the air fills with a blinding blizzard, and the pilot pulls pitch. The silence is sudden and startling. With the Southern Alps stretching to the north and the sun glinting off the surrounding snowfields, Scaife steps into his skis and studies the shadowed face below.

"Let's do this one at a time," he says, "Please, keep to the left of my tracks! And please, no one below me." He pokes at the surface with his pole, then carefully pushes over the edge, sinks to his knees, unweights, and sinks again. Establishing a rhythm, he links thirty turns, the fresh snow blowing up his thighs before he pulls to one side and signals us to follow.

If New Zealand is seventeen hours and eleven hundred dollars away, the Tyndall pays the bill in full. Skirting a yawning blue crevasse to link powder turns on an untouched snowfield, it's hard to admit that in six hours this adventure will come to an abrupt end. Whether you work to attain a state of perfect grace or whoop, holler, and race the other skiers in your group for the best lines will make no difference. No matter how much you would like to double each hour or quadruple the vertical, each turn signals an electric click in your watch's silicon chip, and you wish there were a more dependable way than pure memory to store the glacial ice, black cliff faces, and untouched snow for future reference.

From the Tyndall the Ranger crosses the valley to Shotover Ridge, where the terrain changes from shadowed glacier to sunlit faces, banked hollows, and broad snowfields. The variety is enormous. Here you can challenge one of a thousand lines down to the pickup point, until the shadows start to creep up the Tyndall's north face and Scaife says, "Anyone care for an extra run on Headlong?"

At an added cost of NZ$90, the last run on Headlong Peak's 4000-vertical-foot southwest face rivals the first on Tyndall. With the afternoon sun filling the bowls with long shadows and the steeps set at two DIN numbers below raw intimidation, I wish there were a way to slow the pace. By now however I've learned that heli-skiers are a greedy bunch, and aside from a wistful glance at the distant Tasman Sea and a pause to photograph Mt. Aspiring's distant spire, the group behaves as if the untracked snow and golden light will last forever. Sunset, however, inevitably follows, and we buckle into the Jet Ranger. The turbine starts to scream, the pitch increases, and I console myself that there is always tomorrow.

To account for every run during the next three days would require as many words as there were turns—and there were

---

When weather shuts the heli-skiing down, New Zealand has excellent ski resorts. Close to the Harris Mountain Heli-skiing, **Treble Cone** has one double chair, two T-bars, and one platter, two-story base lodge, snack shop at top of chair, live music, barbecues.

Cardrona Ski Area, 33 kilometers from Wanaka, 57 kilometers from Queenstown (transportation available), has two quad chairs, one double chair, two cafeterias, ski school, and rentals.

Cornet Peak, 18 kilometers from Queenstown, one triple, one double, two T-bars, 1500 vertical feet, night skiing, fully licensed restaurant, rentals.

The Remarkables, 10 kilometers from Queenstown, two quad chairs, one double chair, main lodge, ski rental, ski school, cross-country skiing.

★

many. The weather miraculously holds above the steep south faces of Fog and Niger peaks in the Harris Mountains and the convoluted west faces of Visual Overload, Mt. Alta, and Matukituki in the Buchanans. When the weather finally does close out I thank Scaife, reluctantly bid Treble Cone, Wanaka, and the Harris Mountains good-bye, and use the day to make the three-hour drive to Mt. Cook.

The following morning a storm is raging over Mt. Cook's Hermitage Hotel. Rain hammers on the dining room windows, and on the opposite scree face avalanches suddenly appear as brilliant white streaks cascading through the cloud cover. South of the fortieth parallel, weather is serious business: between the Southern Alps and South Africa there is no major land mass to slow the rush of wind and waves. It's either Cape Horn or Mt. Cook, and if you can believe New Zealand's National Weather Service, in the next forty-eight hours Cook can count on a blow.

Known as Aorangi or "Cloud Piercer," to the native Maori, during winter Mt. Cook experiences some of the harshest conditions on earth—fifty feet of snow per year and hundred-mile-an-hour winds. Little wonder that the neighboring Ben Ohau Range offers some of the world's best heli-skiing—if you're lucky enough to hit clear skies.

Gathering in the Hermitage's lobby, Bryan Carter, head of Mt. Cook's Alpine Guides, tells the Australian, Japanese, American, and New Zealand clients that the storm center is still over the Tasman Sea.

"There is a chance it will clear tomorrow," he says.

But one day turns to two. When weather closes in over Mt. Cook, you can read, run in the rain, hike to Kea Point overlooking the Mueller Glacier, take gray photographs of the Hermitage, do chin-ups on the door trim, stare out the window, watch videos, study the historical photos, write postcards, drink coffee and drink sodas, eat kiwis, and the following morning haunt the Alpine Guides' main office.

"Well, what's the forecast?" I ask Mark Whetu, a Scotch-Maori heliguide.

"No good," he admits. "We're expecting at least another twelve hours of the same thing," he tells me.

This is a major disappointment. "So how long can these storms last?" I persist.

"Hard to say, mate," he shrugs. "A day, two days, a week . . . It depends on the storm." Easy enough for Whetu to say when he's got the entire winter to wait. Four days makes a big difference, and committing to a week at any one of the heli-skiing operations is an iffy decision. If you book the skiing on a day-by-day basis, it'll cost a little more; but if the weather craps out at least you can drive to Oamaru, Dunedin, or Invercargill — sightsee, shop, and dine until the storm abates — then hustle back to catch the first load out.

Harris Mountain Heliskiing, P.O. Box 177, Wanaka, New Zealand, tel. (02943) 7930/7277, offers runs throughout the Remarkables, Harrises, Tyndall Glacier, and Buchanans. Depending on the area, a day of heli-skiing will run NZ$350—NZ$500, which basically includes four to five runs, approximately 10,000 vertical feet, alpine lunch, guides, and instruction. Harris also offers **Odyssey Weeks** which include 50,000 or 100,000 vertical feet, seven days/eight nights accommodations, ground transport, breakfasts, lunches, and two dinners. Terms: NZ$3695 (50,000) or NZ$6150, (100,000) double occupancy; includes bed and breakfast.

And so a second sleety day passes. That evening the heli-skiers have given up hope when the weather system suddenly accelerates. Though no one places any faith in this latest development, there is a chance that by morning we'll see the Main Divide. Wakened before dawn by a ravenous Kea parrot eyeing the safety straps on my skis, I stumble to the window.

No dice. Cook is still shrouded in clouds. Breakfast is dragging through a fourth cup of coffee when sunlight suddenly explodes onto the valley floor. Twenty minutes later Alpine Guides is full of skiers, all staring up at Cook, Sefton, and six other 10,000-foot peaks.

Now is the time for speed! After the three-day wait, it's important to be on the first load out, to get the show on the road, to ski powder up to my eyeballs, to fix New Zealand into the coming century with this single incandescent day. I'm ready, willing, and able! And yet, arriving at the heliport in Glentanner, I see fifty other skiers have the same idea. While I watch for the first hint of approaching low pressure, Pieps transceiver rescue beacon drills are run, equipment checked, and helicopter loads sorted out. As necessary as all this might seem, at any minute I expect to see the first horse tails waving above the Main Divide.

In due time Whetu introduces two Japanese who don't speak English; retired American businessman Jim; James Kay, an American photographer; and his wife, Suzy. Together our group makes two helicopter loads, and on the second flight out I buckle in and feel my stomach sink as the Airespecial surges off the pad.

South Wales Run is one vertical and five linear miles from Glentanner. In that distance the terrain changes from a grassy meadow to a rubble-filled stream to enormous bowls and finally to a knife-edge ridge where the Airespecial flares in 14 inches of fresh powder. At 7000 feet the views will make you pause in wonder. To the north are Cook, Haast, Douglas, and a dozen other peaks that form part of the South Island's Main Divide. Filling the valley below, the glacial Lake Pukaki offers a startling, milky blue contrast to the untracked basin at your feet. And in the distance huge glacial rubble piles, braided river valleys, and jagged snow-covered summits stretch to the horizon.

The helicopter is soon lost against these enormous vistas,

and pushing his pole into the new snow, Whetu observes, "It should be stable, but for this first run let's go one at a time please." Whetu is an exceptional skier. Even with a sixty-pound pack, each pole plant, unweight, and edge change is a study in control.

It's unclear whether this "one at a time" business is for safety or to separate the weak from the strong. Either way I make three turns and am rocked onto the tails as the snow turns to crust. The culprit is wind and, as the surface fractures into square-foot slabs, the sensation is similar to skiing on rails. To turn you must throw all the switches, jump clear, reverse direction, and maintain speed.

Except for Whetu no one really shreds it up, and he quickly leads us into a hollow where it's shin deep and air light and I relax and float from turn to turn. With 4000 feet South Wales is a classic powder run, neither too steep nor too shallow, with minor pitch changes among the shadowed swales, and open bowls. Along sheltered rises my knees disappear beneath the untracked surface; the snow slides up my thighs and splashes against my jacket.

It takes us an hour to reach the pickup point, where Ron Small is waiting with the helicopter. On the flight up Whetu says Small was named "Member of the British Empire" for his rescue of two climbers stranded on Mt. Cook.

"They reached the summit just as a storm was moving in and couldn't down-climb," Small would later admit. "And then a lack of visibility grounded us for almost a week. When it cleared enough to fly, it was blowing too hard to land. By some miracle they stuck it out in a crevasse, and with a 100-mile-an-hour wind blowing us across the summit, we were just able to push supplies out." Eventually Small was able to land and, though severely frostbitten, the two climbers survived.

Now he sets down on an untouched face down the ridge from the South Wales banks and drops back to the streambed. With fifty skiers and three helicopters working this drainage, there should be an ongoing dogfight for untracked lines. But other than a few rotored mosquitoes buzzing down the immense ridge, we are alone.

If the first run down Wales offered a consistent pitch, the second drops precipitously to a wide plateau that in turn plunges down a long, changeable face to the pickup. Following Whetu, I try to copy his form. Impossible! He is far too good. Whether it is a function of youth, strength, timing, or simply 10 million vertical feet in every condition, the guide is flawless. During those two runs (and for that matter the next three days) he never falls—but, even more disgusting, he never makes a bad turn.

Lunch is a fine affair. Sandwiches, fruit, cookies, drinks, and condiments appear out of a large cooler. Whetu passes the Vegemite, which the New Zealanders substitute for ketchup. Taking a sniff, it's hard to believe they actually like this stuff. They obviously eat it like Sonoran chilies, Rocky Mountain oysters, or other delicacies of brutal texture and questionable nutrition—simply to flaunt a repressed machismo.

Located in Mt. Cook Village, **Alpine Guides**, P.O. Box 20, Mount Cook, New Zealand, fax (05621) 898, tel. (05621) 834 or 833, offers guided heli-skiing in the Ben Oahus, Richardson Glacier, and Jollie Ranges. Dates run roughly from mid-July to late September. A week of skiing includes 60,000 vertical feet, seven nights accommodations, all breakfasts and lunch, and transport to and from heli-skiing. Terms: NZ$3690.

★

Improved weather has a remarkable effect in the Hermitage disco. By nature the Australians have happy feet but no rhythm. It would be out of character for them not to sing, buy drinks for the house, and dance up a storm. It's the Japanese who seem out of character. If they tend to covey up, at least its an elegant covey. No Korean imitations for this group. Its Gucci, Laurent, and Laura Ashley, all of whom represent pocket change for these yen-rich children of the rising sun. Polite to a fault, though, they stop well short of doing the Funky Chicken or Bunny Hop through the Hermitage's fireside bar. In

a refined Oriental way, they do let their black hair down. Especially on the slopes above, where their untranslatable "yippy!" and frequent half bows leave little doubt about what they think of the skiing.

T he **Hermitage**, Mt. Cook, New Zealand, tel. (05621) 809. Amenities: 104 rooms, en suite bathrooms, Jacuzzi, restaurant, coffee shop, bar, shops, large reception room, spectacular views. Terms: NZ$203.50 double occupancy.

Glencoe Lodge, Mt. Cook, New Zealand, tel. (05621) 809. Amenities: 55 rooms, en suite bathrooms, restaurant, bar. Terms: NZ$165 double occupancy.

Morning's first light turns Mt. Cook into a 12,000-foot torch.

I use a crust from breakfast to ransom my skis from the marauding Kea parrots and run toward Alpine Guides. A majority of the previous day's skiers had been hanging on, waiting for the storm to dissipate so they could claim a single day. Now most have departed for Christchurch, and when I arrive at Glentanner, the numbers are down by half. Loading into the Airespecial, the Kays, Whetu, and I climb vertically away from Glentanner and minutes later land on Mt. Mary.

"Mary" seems like a funny name for a ski run. Since we don't see it in print, Whetu might be saying Mary and meaning Maori. Either way it doesn't sound that challenging. In fact, even before we make a first turn, I figure it's a gift to one or two in the group who go bug-eyed on the steeps. This Mary run can't be nearly as good as yesterday's Mt. Dark, 4000 vertical feet past towering black cliffs and silent blue glaciers. Dark's a macho run, a man's rawhide run that skis just like Darth Vader looks. Another bold name is Cardiopulmonary Resuscitation, and though no one was foolish enough to nonstop its 4000 feet, the mere attempt is a tune-up for a heart attack.

And yet, for all its allusions to lambs, Mary's doesn't start well. Perhaps the instructions don't translate, for one of the Japanese sits back and promptly rockets out in front of the guides. Dangerous mistake. Our group edges cautiously away from the resulting uproar and starts down a wide, untracked bowl that falls directly toward Lake Pukaki. At the very least Mt. Mary deserves style points for the visuals. Then again, the snow on its upper faces and hollows isn't bad. A thousand feet lower we're still dropping down off camber faces to half-pipe curls, to bowls and ridges, and though I try, it's almost impossible to choke down a convulsive "yippy!"

Mary or Maori turns out to be a classic run, one of many we wish we could ski again. But in the following two days before the next storm closes Glentanner down, we travel across the Ben Oahus. Skiing a dozen runs with names like Zodiac, Darkies, Jacks, Flamingo, and Stoneys, we live in a world of hanging glaciers, black cliffs, and the best snow of our lives.

Riding from edge to edge toward the waiting Airespecial, I wonder what it takes to become a New Zealand heliguide. I suspect, like Whetu, you have to be a flawless deep-snow skier. So I guess the only question is, how do I talk Barbara and the boys into moving to New Zealand?

REST AND RECUPERATION

Weather is changeable on the South Island and if you have to sit, Wanaka offers numerous diversions. Just outside of Wanaka proper is the **Wanaka Maze and Puzzle Shop**, which offers an excellent maze that takes from twenty to forty-five minutes to find your way out of. There are also hundreds of puzzles that you are invited to solve. New Zealand is also known for its woolen goods, and the **Perendale Wool Shop** (tel. 7294) in Wanaka's downtown section offers excellent homespun, hand-knitted sweaters at fair prices. You can fish on **Lake Wanaka** or, if the weather really falls apart, travel to Queenstown for a day's shopping or a dinner cruise on the **TSS Earnslaw**, also known as the "Lady of the Lake." Sheep are always being sheared, and inquiries at the hotel can earn you an invitation to watch the process.

Because of Mt. Cook's relative isolation, when the weather fails most skiers settle in with books in front of the lodge fires or the evening movie in the lounge. You can run to stay in shape, take hikes in the snow, Jacuzzi in the Hermitage, or compose fervent prayers for the return of high pressure.

CHAPTER 12

FAMILY SKIING ON MT. BACHELOR

N WINTER THE SIMPLEST WAY TO GET TO BEND, Oregon, is to catch the Horizon Airlines commuter to Roberts Field in Redmond. Or if you're comfortable at 75 miles per hour, can afford the speeding ticket, and aren't spooked by icy roads in the Cascades, from Portland you can take Highway 26 to 97 at Madras. Alternatively Highway 22 cuts southeast from Salem over Santiam Pass, Highway 20 out of Corvallis crosses Tombstone Summit, and Highway 97 runs due north from Klamath Falls. Not too many skiers, however, come out of the Oregon desert.

"What part of Idaho you folks from?" the pump jockey in Burns asked.

"Sun Valley," Robert, my five-year-old, volunteered from the backseat.

"Dad, why is he pumping our gas?" seven-year-old Andrew asked, looking up from a book.

"It's a state law," the attendant replied, glancing at the skis. "Where you going skiing?"

"Bachelor," I replied, handing him a credit card.

"Bachelor? Why would you come from Sun Valley to go skiing in Bachelor?"

Good question, especially on the empty 43-mile stretch from Brothers to Bend. Robert and Andrew have exhausted all the diversions psychologists recommend for stressless family travel. They've read all the books, worked all the puzzles, done battle with their Ninja Turtles, beaten the electronic video games, and transformed their transformers. They've stuck plastic locusts to the windows, eaten Ritz crackers, and spread crumbs over the backseat. They've counted horses, pointed out hawks, and read road signs, and now they're playing their favorite game. In honor of the town we've just left, it's called "Bug your Brother."

The rules are simple. Start by repeating everything your brother says until Dad says stop. Then take something that belongs to him and dispute its ownership. Wait a minute then reach across and touch him. You know he hates this. Then when Dad says don't touch him, accidentally touch him. Dad will say "Don't even accidentally touch him," so let your foot cross the imaginary dividing line in the backseat and almost touch him. Dad says don't even almost touch him. When Dad says he's going to stop the car, make up a tuneless song about your brother's breath, then take offense when he suggests Dad sell you to the lowest bidder.

"That's enough, boys," Barbara says, waking from a nap in the passenger seat. "Where are we?" she yawns. On the horizon Mt. Bachelor's snow-covered cone is barely visible above the unbroken cedar forests. You would think that some sign of human endeavor would mark this 9060-foot extinct volcano. Even at this distance you should be able to see a clear-cut alley that reveals a ski run. Or maybe a column of wood smoke rising above a mountain restaurant. But other than the vast cone's glistening symmetry, nothing catches your eye. And extinct? That's what locals at Spirit Lake were claiming just before Mt. St. Helens blew its top. Now most Bend locals knock on wood or whisper when they use the word.

East of Bend the country bears evidence of Bachelor's once-violent nature. Large pumice boulders lie scattered across the red, iron-rich soil, and distant rises look suspiciously like ancient flows. Even without its volcanic nature, Bachelor's statistics are impressive. With three double chairs, five triples, and four quads to service 3200 skiable acres, a 3100-foot vertical drop, and an average annual snowfall of 190 inches, Bachelor hits all the right notes.

In contrast a number of midwest ski resorts have labored for fifty years to build their own slopes. Some have waited until a major city produced a pile of old newspapers, refrigerators, and tires then covered it with topsoil and planted grass, trees, and a dozen lifts. If the tires had a tendency to eddy to the surface, it didn't affect the skiing. Other areas used huge earth movers to transport glacial gravel to the top of an existing bump surrounded by Minnesota farmland. The point is that both of these projects—the garbage and gravel—took decades to produce 300 vertical. On the other hand there is still some debate about how long Bachelor's been working on its 3000, or whether the project is complete.

Arriving from the east, Bend, Oregon, is indistinguishable from a hundred other West Coast towns that have sold their historical character to the franchise frenzy. That is, the urban-strip sprawl shouldn't come as a surprise but does. Here, surrounding the intersection of Highways 20 and 97, a variety of fast-food drive-ins, car parts, shopping centers, car lots, gas stations, and doughnut shops compete for attention. Granted this complaint has the disingenuous ring of an expatriate flower child, but Oregon is a leader in the ecological movement. We have this sparsely populated northwest state to thank for glass and aluminum recycling. In the name of cheap electricity and a dimly held vision of irrigated fields stretching from The Dalles to Klamath Falls, Oregon, did allow the Co-

lumbia to be repeatedly dammed between Umatilla and Portland. Idaho and Washington, however, made the same mistake
in the name of progress, and at least Oregon once advertised
its deep woods, clear lakes, and unspoiled mountains with the
slogan "Come visit but don't move here."

Bachelor is served by Alaska/Horizon Air; reservations:
(800) 426-0333. United Express offers nonstop daily
flights from Los Angeles, San Francisco, Seattle, and Portland; reservations: (800) 241-6522. Rental cars, bus, and
limo services are available from Redmond/Bend Airport.

What has happened since those distant days when people
were tuning in and dropping out? Blame it on the Californians,
those hordes of South Bay burnouts who find Bend's clean
river and cheap land a heady alternative to life below the border—the Oregon-California border, that is.

Fortunately Bend's character rapidly changes as you follow
Greenwood Avenue west onto Bond and Wall streets. Here in
Bend's renovated downtown a thriving business community
quickly erases any earlier impression of a town built on a foundation of double burgers, maple bars, and discount plumbing
supplies. With the Deschutes River sweeping around Drake
Park before it flows beneath the Newport Avenue bridge, bookstores, banks, and beauty shops mix with pharmacies and
honest-to-God furniture and shoe stores. In contrast to Highway 97, Wall Street gives the impression of a stable town with
a stable working population that raises kids, pays mortgages,
and occasionally, just occasionally, skis the "extinct" volcano
20 miles to the west.

After a stroll down Wall Street and a great roast beef sandwich and bowl of clam chowder at Pastries by Hans on Northwest Wall Street, we headed for our rented condominium.

There are numerous motels, hotels, condos, and B-and-B's in the Bend area. For a complete list contact the Central Oregon Reservation Center, tel. (800) 547-6858.

Situated near downtown Bend on the river next to Pioneer Park is the **Bend Riverside**, 1565 N.W. Hill Street, Bend, Oregon 97701, tel. (800) 546-0892. Amenities: 100 units, kitchens, covered heated swimming pool, sauna, Jacuzzi, hot tub, telephones, televisions, laundry facilities, close to restaurants and shopping. Terms: $38–$58 double.

The River House, 3075 N. Highway 97, Bend, Oregon 97701, tel. (800) 547-3928. Amenities: 208 units overlooking the Deschutes River, sauna, indoor/outdoor pools, hot tub, Jacuzzi, kitchens, spa, fireplace units, three restaurants, exercise room, small pets okay. Terms: $44–$54 double.

On the road to Bachelor is the **Inn of the Seventh Mountain**, P.O. Box 1207, Bend, Oregon 97709, tel. (800) 452-6810. Amenities: 332 units, popular family resort, swimming pool, sauna, hot tub, Jacuzzi, three restaurants, stables, skating, TV, telephones. Terms: $52–$122 double.

Mt. Bachelor Ski Area is famous for both its long season and family terrain. With an average of 200 inches of snow per year, the season extends from November to July. For most resorts, advertising a July closing date is economic suicide. No one skis in July, and it's hard to find snow if they want to. Bachelor, however, seems to be the exception to the rule. Blame central Oregon's outdoor mentality for the race camps, spring skiing, shred boarders et al. who are still cutting it up when the rest of the country is into burned wieners, watermelon, and the rockets' red glare.

Never having skied Bachelor on July Fourth, I can't comment on the late season, but as for the family terrain, testers Andrew and Robert had promised to share their opinion. So picture on this snowy morning of February 12 the typical American family: Mom, Dad, two boys and a Ford station wagon parked in

the West Village parking lot. What had started as a light snow is getting serious as deep gray cumuli roll across Bachelor's Summit Express quad. By the time the boys are into their boots and ski suits, the clouds have lowered to the top of the Pine Marten Super Express, which reaches the tree line.

Having been born and raised in Sun Valley, Robert and Andrew have something of an advantage over most skiers their age. Andrew is game for anything short of black diamond steeps, likes to drag me into the moguls, and at this point is learning to ski untracked snow. With a great wedge-to-parallel move, Robert is not far behind. He's unafraid of most conditions but favors groomed intermediate runs.

With intermittent fog rolling across the base area, we load the Yellow Chair in front of the West Village Day Lodge. Climbing leisurely to a knoll above the base area, this short lift is perfect for beginners. The cats have rolled the slope, which has set up during the night. Andrew has no problem with it, but the icy corduroy rattles young Robert into submission. Because he relishes having Mom to himself, and because Andrew is dragging me toward the Pine Marten Express, we split up.

Built in 1986 to replace the aging Black Chair, the P.M. Express is one of Bachelor's key lifts. From it you can take the Summit Crossover to the Skyliner Express quad, the Sunrise chair, Summit Express, and the Sunrise Lodge. Riding a left edge, you can dive into the empty intermediate cruisers of Avalanche, Cliffs Run, and Dentist's. A little sharper left off Pine Marten onto Skyliner will take you down the fall line Canyon to Tippytoe, or alternatively Coffee Run. If that's not enough, a right off the P.M. Express connects to the Outback Express quad and the broad north-facing runs of Kangaroo, Bushwhacker, and Down Under. Only the Outback Express quad returns directly to the P.M. Express, and though Andrew and I both want to explore, with the fog limiting visibility to the tree line we take Canyon, a rated blue run, back to the West Village base.

It is now snowing hard. A wind is kicking up, and the temperature is falling. Barely visible in the swirling clouds, Andrew looks like a red neon stick figure with goggles over his eyes and a rime-crusted scarf across his mouth. The snow is growing deeper by the minute, and skiing as much by intuition as by the soggy, wind-whipped trail map, we accidentally turn down the black Canyon.

The pitch gradually increases, and when we drop out of clouds, we're hanging above steep powdery bumps. I slow to check it out, and Andrew goes by me, riding the bumps as he traverses from side to side. My first impulse is to catch him, warn him to slow down, to stifle his self-confidence in a futile effort to protect him. Unfortunately falling is part of learning, and instead I watch him change edges, note where he holds his hands, and envy his youthful determination. Starting children in this sport is similar to rolling a rock downhill. Most have a wonderful stance, natural balance, and an almost total lack of fear.

Watching Andrew ski Canyon's face, I recall a distant Sunday when I, too, traversed from crash to crash. On that, my first day on skis, if someone had suggested I would one day be skiing with my son, I would have dismissed it as a poor attempt at humor. During those first frustrating runs, who would believe that skiing would mark the success or failure of the next two decades? Meager savings account aside, if I measure assets and liabilities solely in terms of days spent skiing the world's dark forests, deep powder, and sun-baked bowls, I am rich beyond measure.

Now, watching my seven-year-old son set an edge on a face that would intimidate most adults, I realize if adults use skiing as a synonym for freedom, a seven-year-old quickly discovers it's a perfect opportunity to assert his independence.

When Dad yells "Slow down!" you speed up, then claim you didn't hear him.

Dropping down the face after him, my Dynamic slaloms switch from powder to underlying base with equal ease. Soon I am matching him turn for turn, running interference against foreign objects that might come rocketing out of the fog onto that steep face.

If I had been alone I could have skied Canyon faster, but not much faster, and when we reach the base we join a short line on Pine Marten Express, where we catch the intermediate Coffee Run. The fog is still hanging at mid-mountain, it is starting to snow heavily, and after skiing Coffee's faces and flats, in succession we ski Skyliner over to Old Skyliner.

Shortly before noon we find Robert and Barbara sharing a hot chocolate in the West Village Lodge. A glass wall faces the mountain across a snow-covered deck and the Lodge is mobbed with people seeking shelter from the elements. The storm is intensifying, and we vacillate between taking another run or retreating to a hot tub and exploring downtown Bend.

Mt. Bachelor's exposure to the Pacific is the reason for its long season. Any storm that comes across the beach invariably hits this cone. If this were Utah, where temperatures hang in the twenties and the desert humidity can age you ten years in a single night, Bachelor's 200 inches would rise like puff pastry. But the marine air is moist, storms are frequent, and the top of the mountain is well above tree line. Which means luck has much to do with catching Bachelor under clear skies. On average the Summit quad is open 48 percent of the season, but the loss of this upper lift cuts the skiable terrain by two thirds. Storms are known to orbit around this summit for weeks—bad news if you're checking in at the same time the cloud layer begins to descend.

The hot chocolate builds a fire under the boys, and in spite of the weather we ride the Pine Marten Express back up to the Summit Traverse. Here, in a cottony world of falling snow and fog, we ski the Summit Crossover to the green-rated Marshmallow that drops to the Sunrise Lodge. If Andrew looks like a neon stick figure on skis, Robert is even smaller. For his age he is strong, fearless, and can link wedge turns on anything short of black faces. His problem is traverses, the occasional narrow trail that leads to whoop-de-do's. As we approach the Summit Express's base station, he refuses to hang onto my pole and pays the penalty. As soon as he takes off I know I've made a mistake. Robert speeds down the trail, slams into the first bump, explodes out of his skis, and starts to slide. When I catch him, he is crying.

"Daddy," he sobs, blaming me for his fall, "why did you let me do that?" Relieved he's not hurt, I willingly accept responsibility. I help piece him back together then lead him down Crossover to Marshmallow. A marshmallow is both a fine image for kids and an apt description of this run's gentle pitch. By now it's obvious that skiing on a volcano means that the majority of runs follow the fall line. At Bachelor there's no hanging on one edge in a V-shaped gulch. The volcano falls away at a consistent pitch that gradually flattens out at the base. Very roughly speaking the expert terrain surrounds the

summit, the intermediate covers the mid-mountain, and beginners will love the base.

The weather continues to close in, the snow keeps improving, and by one-thirty the kids have had enough. Besides
Marshmallow we have skied Roostertail and Carnival top to
bottom. Barbara offers to take the boys back to the condo
while I make a few runs alone. Leaving them at the West Village, I load the Pine Marten quad then turn right at the rime-
crusted upper station onto Bushwhacker, one of Bachelor's famous Outback runs. Dropping between towering spruce and
fir trees, the intermediate Bushwhacker offers a variety of terrain, steeps and flats and sweeping turns. For the first time
that day I relax, let my skis run, and burn vertical.

If I enjoyed the Canyon I love the deserted Outback runs.
The only problem is, they're too deserted. Riding the Outback
Express quad 1780 vertical feet back to the Pine Marten Lodge,
I'm the only one on the lift for as far as I can see. Granted the
weather is getting downright ugly, the rime has claimed my
jacket, scarf, and ski hat, and my fingers are numb in my
gloves; but the skiing is fantastic, and as long as the visibility
holds I'll stick it out until the lift closes. In succession I ski
Boomerang and Down Under, wondering why Bachelor picked
Aussie names for Oregon ski runs.

Riding the quad for the fourth time, my hands and feet blink
off line, and I hobble into the Pine Marten Lodge to warm up.
Though this modernistic stone, steel, concrete, and glass edi-
fice shelters both a bakery and gourmet dining, it's too late to
think about breakfast rolls or a three-course lunch. I order a
mocha and watch the storm rage outside.

Catching the Bachelor shuttle to Bend, I'm back at the condo
by four. Barbara and the boys have already hot-tubbed,
dressed, and are waiting for me to go to town. Walking down
Wall Street, Andrew sees a mad bomber replica World War I
pilot's helmet and must have it. Count it an early birthday gift,
he says. What if we take money out of his college fund to help
with the cost? His entreaties are creative and heartfelt. Step-

ping inside, I feel as if I'm asking, "How much for the doggy in the window?"

"Forty dollars!" Barbara mouths to me as Andrew lovingly strokes the rabbit-fur liner. She rolls her eyes, then whispers, "We'll think about it," to Andrew.

"Think about it?" he says, truly disappointed.

Outside he's broken-hearted—he really loves that hat more than anything, his head is always cold, it matches his red jacket. . . . Protests continue until we cross the street to the Stuft Pizza Restaurant. Inside a pizza chef is throwing dough into the air, where it barely clears a rotating ceiling fan. Forgetting the hat, the boys pounce upon this scene as fine participatory theater. Sooner or later the chef's going to sling it into the whirling blades. In spite of our stern insistence they stay at the table, they slip away to press their noses against the glass partition, gape, and giggle at each near miss. Wednesday comedy acts are scheduled from 9 P.M. to closing, but after a full day the boys can't keep their eyes open, and by the time we reach the condo we have to carry them upstairs.

For dancing try **McKensey's**, 388-3891, at 1033 N.W. Bond; **E. L. Benders**, 382-2867, on 3rd Street; or **The River House**, 389-8810, on Highway 97. For live theater, **Magic Circle Theatre**, 385-5511, or **Community Theatre of the Cascades**, 389-0803. Balloon flights are at the **Morning Glory Balloon Company**, 389-8739.

The following morning we're riding Bachelor's Rainbow chair under blue skies. To pass the time I asked Robert which run he likes best.

"Marshmallow," he replies earnestly. And so it is Marshmallow, with me following him down the Sunrise area green runs then cutting in turn across to the Flying Dutchman, which was rolled the night before and is now littered with death cookies. Robert falls and votes loudly for something green. Andrew is getting bored and so again we split up. Andrew and I take the West Village Getback traverse to D.S.Q. down to the Skyliner quad. Bachelor's size works in its favor. Tucking the traverses between the base areas is a grand adventure, and dropping into the quad, Andrew squirms with delight.

On the next run we ski the side of Cliffhanger next to the dark evergreens. I suspect Andrew likes the name as much as he likes the broad run itself, for he asks to do it again. These intermediate runs are fun, but Bachelor is far more than its lower runs, and as we ski past the Summit Express I notice the chairs are running and a fleet of cats is packing out Healy Heights and Beverly Hills. So the question is, will the summit open today?

We are having lunch in the Sunrise Lodge when word circulates that the top has opened. Grabbing my goggles, gloves, and hat I promise to relieve Barbara in an hour. The Summit quad is an exposed chair, and at the upper station it's obvious I'm late. Tracks web down the named runs and into the broad snowfields' lines. I have heard the West Ridge Run that drops toward the Outback area offers 3200 feet of untracked vertical. But this afternoon the West Ridge is closed and crusty.

What to ski, what to ski?

I'm starting to panic. With a choice of 360 degrees, which way do you turn? Locals slalom around me on their way to secret lines, the quad is loaded, and I still can't make up my mind. At this point making the wrong choice is preferable to making no choice at all. I follow the line of least resistance and allow gravity to pull me down East Healy Heights. During the storm, this sheltered swale served as a snow sink, which now blows around me as I find a tentative rhythm and float toward the distant tree line.

One of Bachelor's brochures shows a skier getting air off a quadruple-scoop ice cream cone. The top scoop is a picture of Mt. Bachelor and the subliminal message is "Come to Bend for cones, quads, and skiing." The message that Bachelor's powder is dessert is lost on most of the people who flip quickly to the inside trail map. Though I had promised Barbara I'd spell her, I'm twenty minutes late.

Family vacations are fun, but at some point Mom and Dad have to get away. We are lucky to have an old friend living in Bend who helps us find a baby-sitter. Tonight we treat ourselves to McKensey's Ore House. Along with a huge salad bar it hosts live entertainment on Thursday through Saturday nights. We listen to a hot country band's first set then cross Bond street to the Deschutes Brewery, which serves a variety of locally distilled beers and ales. The Deschutes appeals to a local mix of college kids, loggers, and skiers in various states of distress.

McKensey's, 1033 Northwest Bond downtown, 388-3891. Owned by Jim and Judy Weaver and serving a variety of seafood, game, steaks, and prime rib, McKensey's is Bend's most popular restaurant/nightclub.

Cyrano's, 119 Northwest Minnesota, 389-6276. Steaks, daily seafood specialties, coffees.

Pastries by Hans, 915 Northwest Wall Street, 389-9700. Sandwiches made on their own fresh-baked bread, French pastries, espresso.

Pine Tavern Restaurant, 967 Northwest Brooks, 382-5581. Prime rib, steaks, fresh seafood, lamb, trout, reservations suggested.

Giuseppe's, 932 Bond Street, 389-8899. Fresh pasta, Italian specialties, espresso, and cappuccino.

Stuft Pizza Restaurant, 125 Northwest Oregon Avenue, 382-4022. Hand-tossed Sicilian crust pizza. Live comedy Saturday and Sunday nights.

Tito's Mexican Restaurante, 3081 North Highway 97, 388-3198. Freshly prepared Mexican menu.

★

Most of the loggers appear to favor the Deschutes lager, and as we sit in the corner and watch couples swing around the dance floor, I calculate that if it takes nine hours to drive to Bend, barring bad weather we would be home by early afternoon. In all honesty I probably wouldn't make that drive in the middle of winter. Idaho's midwinter skiing is a powerful inducement to stay home, but Sun Valley historically closes about the time Bend is breaking into its best season, and Central Oregon has other inducements like state parks, the lava cast forest, lava caves, and clear lakes. Keeping that in mind, I know what the boys would say about taking a ski trip for summer vacation.

REST AND RECUPERATION

If you take a day off, you can tour the **Deschutes Historical Center** (389-1813) on the corner of Wall and Idaho streets, which displays Indian artifacts, a pioneer schoolroom, relics from the timber industry, and historic photos. Or try the **Lava Butte and Lava Lands Visitor Center** (eleven miles south on Highway 97) which includes a tour of Lava Butte and interpretive slide shows describing the history of the lava areas. Ten miles north of Bend on Highway 97 are the **Petersen Rock Gardens**, a four-acre park of miniature bridges, towers, and buildings all made from different types of rocks. Then 18 miles northwest of Bend on Highway 126 is the **Reindeer Ranch**, which is home to over one hundred domesticated reindeer. Admission is free.

On the first and third Saturdays of the month you can squaredance at the **Bachelor Beauts Square Dance Club** at Fox Hall, 2525 Northeast Studio Road (382-7461). Snowmobile tours and ice skating are available at the **Inn of the Seventh Mountain** (382-8711). A few of the area lakes and streams are open for fishing; check with the Oregon Department of Fish and Wildlife (388-6363). You can swim at the **Juniper Aquatic Center**; it has indoor and outdoor pools at 800 Northeast Sixth Street (389-POOL).

CHAPTER 13

SHAKESPEARE ON THE SLOPES: ASHLAND, OREGON

I AM SKIING DREAM, A FLAT, STEEPLY PITCHED run covered with a lush carpet of rolled snow. My skis are articulate, edge to edge, the tips biting, the slalom waist carrying the carve through the tails. Left to right, right to left, around an island, off a bump, knees ten feet in the air, left to right right to left. Dream rates a 6 on a scale of 10, and it isn't even the big draw. So far I've hit Ado, Tempest, Balcony, Romeo, and Juliet and if this sounds like the Literature category on "Wheel of Fortune," add a W, C, and A for Winter, Circe, and Avon and slam the buzzer.

"Is it Ashland and the Shakespeare Festival?"

"YOU'RE UNBELIEVABLE," Pat exults.

Camera to Vanna who smiles dazzlingly in agreement.

"Well," Pat continues, "you've won a three-day, all-expenses-paid vacation to Ashland, Oregon, where you'll ski Ashland during the day and listen to Shakespeare at night   "

"Shakespeare?" you wonder.

If 3000-foot groomed runs and discoing beneath mirrored balls has started to feel like "sweets grown common" (Sonnet 102), then Ski Ashland and Oregon's Shakespeare Festival can make for "brisk and giddy-paced times."

Located 18 miles above town, exactly halfway between Portland and San Francisco, and serviced by Horizon Air's daily flights to Medford, Ski Ashland offers an alternative to the traditional ski vacation of max vertical and après overindulgence. I think I've worked out the perfect itinerary. Fly into Medford on Friday afternoon and rent a car. Drive the 17 miles to Ashland and check into a room in the Winchester Inn. Claim reserved tickets for Saturday and Sunday nights' performances (hopefully for one Shakespearean and one contemporary play), and ski Ashland's four chairs, twenty-two runs, and 1150 vertical feet during the day. I suspect those two days will pass as "swift as a shadow, short as any dream" (*A Midsummer's Night's Dream*).

By car Ashland is five and a half hours from Portland, Oregon, and six and a half hours from San Francisco. United (reservations: 800-241-6522), Horizon Airline (reservations: 800-547-9308), and Continental Airlines (reservations: 800-525-0280) fly into Jackson County Airport in Medford. Car rentals are available at the airport.

Located in the Rogue Valley near the California/Oregon border, Ashland is surrounded by fruit orchards and the Rogue River National Forest. This city of sixteen thousand started as a lumber mill, added a flour mill, planted orchards, built a college, and though all five still play major roles, it was Angus L. Bowmer who put Ashland on the map.

In 1935 Bowmer produced the Festival's first play, an event that has grown into a $50-million-per-year industry. Today, with the Angus Bowmer Theater, the Elizabethan Stage, and the Black Swan, the Festival is able to stage diverse offerings. In early February it doesn't take an overactive imagination to confuse Ashland with England. Not with Stratford-upon-Avon, perhaps, but with Ashland's Shakespearean names, country inns, and theater crowds in capes, tweeds, and overcoats, it could be "this blessed plot, this earth, this realm, this England" (*Richard II*). All right, that's enough, no more Shakespeare! Get focused here!

Ashland hotels also offer ski/lodging packages. Rates are per person, per day, based on double occupancy, and include one all-day lift ticket. Lodging can also be booked through Southern Oregon Reservations, tel. (800) 547-8052, or in Oregon, tel. (800) 533-1311. For brochures and more information: Ashland Chamber of Commerce, 110 E. Main Street, P.O. Box 606, Ashland, Oregon 97520, tel. (503) 482-3486.

The **Winchester Inn**, 35 South Second Street, Ashland, Oregon 97520, tel. (503) 488-1113. Amenities: restored Victorian home built in 1886, bed-and-breakfast inn, seven rooms with private bath, restaurant with full breakfast, two blocks to theater. Terms: $45—$65.

Ashland Hills Inn, 2525 Ashland Street, Ashland, Oregon 97520, tel. (800) 547-4747. Amenities: 159 rooms, full-service motor inn, restaurant, cable TV. Terms: $26 weekday, $32 weekend.

Stratford Inn, 555 Siskiyou Boulevard, Ashland, Oregon 97520, tel. (800) 547-4741. Amenities: 53 units, five blocks to the theaters, indoor pool, whirlpool, free coffee, ski lockers, cable TV. Terms $28.55—$34.55.

Mt. Ashland Inn, 5550 Mt. Ashland Road, Ashland, Oregon 97520, tel. (503) 482-8707. Amenities: log bed-and-breakfast inn, fireplace, views, private baths, hearty breakfasts. Terms: $40—$90.

★

I'm on my way to see Brendan Behan's *The Hostage*. Born in 1923, Behan was an Irish playwright who was imprisoned for Irish Republican Army activities. *The Hostage* is an expression of Behan's profound nationalism—a subject that, I suspect, should have little appeal for an American audience. But on Friday night, it is a measure of the Festival's reputation that the Angus Bowmer Theater is full.

Information and tickets may be obtained from the **Oregon Shakespeare Festival**, Box 158, Ashland, Oregon 97520, tel. (503) 482-4311.

★

If I questioned the wisdom of American actors doing Behan in front of an American audience, I was wrong. It is a wonderful performance, and after the final curtain call, I follow the crowd out. Though past 11 P.M. it seems early, and I walk past the dance halls on Main Street that are filled with Southern Oregon State College students. Behind the steamed windows, shadows move to the thumping of an amplified base, and I continue to walk along the sidewalk, under a canopy of heraldic banners.

Try the **Ashland Bakery and Cafe**, 482-2117, for fresh baked bread, pastry, and espresso. **Beasy's Back Room**, 482-2141, for Texas hill-style cookin'. There's **Change of Heart**, 288-0235, for a romantic setting and French and American dishes; the **Chateaulin Restaurant and Cafe**, 482-2264, for fine French cuisine and after-theater hot drinks. **Gepetto's** on Main, 482-1138, for Italian. The **Underground Deli**, 488-2595, breakfast, lunch, and dinner. Make sure to try the **Winchester Inn**, 488-1115, for fine dining in a restored Victorian home.

★

The Chateaulin is one of Ashland's best French restaurants. Here among art nouveau appointments I order an Irish coffee and study the crowd. Tonight it has the cool, sophisticated feel of a popular New York theater club. Ursula Meyer, who plays the servant girl in *The Hostage*, arrives with a bouquet of roses, smiling in response to scattered applause. A few minutes later, Douglas Markkanen, who plays the lead, enters and sits among a table of admirers. Swirling his cape about, he is still too keyed up and glances restlessly around the room, then finally stands and drifts toward the door.

To reach Ski Ashland you take Interstate 5 up the Siskiyou Summit grade to a marked off-ramp that heads west out a twisting, two-lane road. Because it is the highest peak west of the Cascades, Mt. Ashland receives an average annual snowfall of 300 inches, and the banks increase until you're driving between two white walls.

It is Saturday morning but the area is almost deserted. I meet Gene Landsman, Ski Ashland's director of skiing, at the base lodge, and a short time later we load the Windsor chair, where he gives me a thumbnail sketch of the area. "Ski Ashland started in '63, when Rogue Valley locals underwrote the cost of lifts and run clearing," he says. "At that time skiers used to drive up the Mt. Ashland loop road by Lithia Park. It was so

narrow we had to make it one way up in the morning and one way down in the afternoon."

At the upper station, Gene bends to buckle a boot, taps his poles together, and drops into Bottom. With southern Oregon filling the distant horizons and the morning sun casting long shadows across the run, we ski the left side next to the trees. For a big man Gene gets on and off his edges with quick, almost audible pops.

Though Mt. Ashland attracts families, it is not a beginner's mountain. 47 percent of the terrain is rated advanced/expert with 27 percent more given over to advanced/intermediates, and on the next run we hit Winter, a moderately steep fall line run with perfect snow that returns to the Windsor chair.

With no lift lines on the Windsor and night skiing on Thursday through Saturday, vertical is not a problem. On the ride up, Landsman admits that a big weekday is two thousand skiers, an average weekend fifteen hundred.

We traverse over to the Ariel chair, which accesses the summit runs Upper Balcony, Upper Dream, Upper Tempest, Circe, and Bowl. The nod goes to Bowl, and we join a group of teenagers staring down the precipitous drop. Someone is going to blow it here, but before I figure out exactly who, a sixteen-year-old in yellow rolls over the edge and tucks the incline.

Big mistake! By a combination of youthful reactions and luck he survives the upper section, carries enormous speed into the compression, almost pulls it off, then hits a rut. Skis, poles, hat, and gloves explode away, and we watch him go head-feet, head-feet, back-stomach-shoulder-hip-head-feet, until it hurts just to watch. When we reach him, he's staggering around telling his buddies he's fine, no problem. "Anyone see where my skis went?" he inquires, staring dazedly out of his broken goggles.

If Ashland claims 1150 vertical feet, its grade and fall-line runs make it ski much bigger. A lack of lift lines help, as do a variety of bump and swale runs off the Ariel chair. I forget to watch the clock, ski until the lifts close, stop for an après beer at the base lodge, and then must speed back to Ashland. By the time I sit down to dinner at the Winchester Inn, I've got half an hour before the start of *Richard II* and must rush to finish.

I am moving toward my seat when the Bowmer Theater goes dark. When the stage lights come up, the actors are in place. How to describe *Richard II*? You must give Shakespeare's dialogue your undivided concentration. Then you must adjust to the rich mix of metaphor and pun. And you should read the play beforehand, for there is power in the story of Richard's loss of England to his cousin Bolingbroke. Richard violates ancient laws of inheritance by exiling Bolingbroke and seizing his lands to finance a foreign war. Having broken the law, Richard forfeits its protection, and Bolingbroke returns to claim not just his land, but Richard's crown as well.

Long before the lights fall on the final act, I have a profound respect for the actors' talents. When the final dance of death circles around the stage, I am tempted to drop this writing game and apply for the job of grip, lighting hand, or perhaps one of the mute soldiers on stage—anything to be part of the process.

On Friday night I watch Terri McMahon play Colette, a whore with standards in *The Hostage*. If I brought one image of her away from Behan's play, I discover a much different one on Sunday morning when she and Assistant Prop Master Jonathan Pierce conduct an intelligent tour of the three theaters. Indeed, I am like the prodigal son who has heeded his father's warnings about the dangers of the stage and now regrets having wasted his life on more mundane pursuits. McMahon and Pierce's knowledge of set, scene, and dialogue convinces me that I have made a mistake. I should have studied drama instead of literature.

And so the day passes too quickly. Bagels for breakfast at the Key of "C" Coffee House, a stroll through Lithia Park, four hours up at Ski Ashland, and a rush to make my flight in Medford.

Two and a half days is perfect. And watching the lights fall beneath the wing, I realize it's futile to compete. If I struggle to phrase a line, work to frame a scene, Shakespeare will always say it better. With the nose up and Ashland dropping behind, I turn again to William:

> *The setting sun, and music at the close,*
> *As the last taste of sweets is sweetest last,*
> *Writ in remembrance more than things long past.*

REST AND RECUPERATION

On an off day take **The Backstage Tour** of the Festival's theaters with the actors involved with the play. Tours last two hours and start at 10 A.M. each performance day. Call 482-4331 for reservations. Also you might be interested in the **Oregon Cabaret Theatre,** 488-2902, which combines plays with hors d'oeuvres, desserts, and beverages. The **Shakespeare Art Museum,** 482-3865, features archives of texts, plays, and royal genealogies as well as paintings. Or the **Ashland Vineyards and Winery,** 488-0088, for tastings, tours, and wine sales. And finally take Lithia Park's mile-long **Woodland Trail,** which passes by numerous marked native, ornamental, and exotic plants, waterfowl, ponds, and fountains.

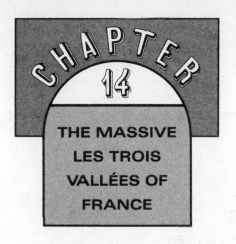

CHAPTER 14

THE MASSIVE LES TROIS VALLÉES OF FRANCE

PRIOR TO THE 1992 OLYMPICS, LES TROIS VAL-lées might just as well have been a rap band. If Chamonix or Courchevel were part of Les Trois Vallées, U.S. skiers would already know that it lies in the Savoie above Moutiers. Over the years both Chamonix and Courchevel have gotten reams of press, and if skiers still can't find either on a map, they probably can't find the capital of Canada either. The truth is, Courchevel is within Les Trois Vallées, and Chamonix is two hours away by car. Both are part of the French Alps, and both offer ready access to international airports, great accommodations, and arguably the best lift-assisted skiing in the world.

One look at Les Trois Vallées trail map will make you pause in wonder. It takes six full folds to cover the three valleys' nine separate villages. Even a six-folder, however, can't do justice to Les Trois Vallées' two hundred lifts and 1000 square miles of terrain! To put that in perspective, 1000 square miles reduces to one run 100 feet wide by 52,000 miles long! True, a portion

The French Government Tourist Office offers brochures on hotels, restaurants, and maps of Les Trois Vallées. In New York: 610 Fifth Avenue, Suite 222, New York, New York 10020, tel. (212) 315-0888; Dallas: 2305 Cedar Springs Road, Suite 205, Dallas, Texas 75201, tel. (214) 720-4010; Los Angeles: 9454 Wilshire Bouelvard, Suite 303, Beverly Hills, California 90212, tel. (213) 272-2661.

of those miles are rocks, cliffs, trees, and glacial ice, but even with it reduced by 10 percent you could still ski around the world. Twice! Add a lift capacity of 180,000 skiers per hour and 1100 lift operators to catch the chairs, trams, and platters and no wonder Les Trois Vallées claims it's "The World's Largest Ski Area." Even if you never turn off-piste, these three valleys are enormous. With a total of 260 named runs that amount to a total of 340 miles, you're still looking at roughly the distance from New York City to Killington, Vermont.

If Les Trois Vallées is still virtually unknown in the United States, it's not because of the number of lifts or size of the area. It can't be blamed on the exchange rates or the food, the scenery or the water, the locals or hotels. Which leaves the language barrier. A certain nativistic reasoning goes, if you can't speak the language, you can't reserve a room, order a meal, or ski the pistes—and since no one in France speaks English you'd best book Colorado or Utah.

Except that the French do quite well with English. The typical restaurant exchange goes: "Pardon, do you speak English?"

"Yes, a leetle."

You point to the menu tentatively. "I was wondering what this means."

"The pasta with mussels and cream sauce? It is a favorite of mine, but you might also like the cheeken, or here, the pepper steak with a green salad and a red wine. This one is good."

Because Lyon-Satolas International Airport will serve as Air France's Olympic hub, the airport has effectively doubled in size. With direct daily flights from New York's JFK, and connections from Boston, San Francisco, Los Angeles, Houston, and Miami through Paris, Air France passengers can catch the TGV Bullet train from Lyon to Moutiers at the head of Les Trois Vallées. For reservations: (800) 237-2747.

Geneva-Cointrin airport is serviced by direct flights on Swissair from New York and connections through Zurich from Los Angeles, Chicago, and Boston. Swissair recently completed a comprehensive alliance with Scandinavian Air System (SAS) that will cover hotels, in-flight catering, aircraft maintenance, and staff training as well transferring passengers into reciprocal routes. Once in Geneva, Frossard buses and Tourist Car buses will handle the roughly two-and-a-half-hour leg to Albertville and Moutiers. For reservations: (800) 221-4750.

I am not exaggerating. During December of '89 I spent ten days in Les Trois Vallées. Because mid-December was low season and because France was in the midst of a major drought, the resorts were empty, and what little snow cover existed was blown from guns. Worse, the day after I arrived even this dense surface was erased by heavy rain. Since skiing was impossible, I spent most of my time negotiating the serpentine Tarentaise roads and exploring the soggy streets of Courchevel, Moutiers, Les Menuires, Val Thorens, Méribel and Mottaret. Admittedly mine was less than a brilliant first impression. Most of the restaurants were closed, the natives were justifiably depressed, and I never saw the sun or the tops of the peaks.

And yet I returned — three months later to be exact, dragging along my wife Barbara and close friends Chip and Susan Stanek for moral support. Delta Airlines had a $520 round-trip fare from Salt Lake to Geneva, Chip had just celebrated his forty-fifth birthday, and since he had never been to Europe, skiing in France made an enlightening gift.

Because we planned to ski Val-d'Isère and La Plagne as well as Les Trois Vallées, we rented a midsize Opel station wagon with a ski rack. With baggage piled to the roof and a dozen bars of Swiss chocolate for emergency rations, we took N201 to the French border. There the French customs agent waved our Swiss plate by without asking for passports, and we continued on N201 through Cerne and Cruseilles to Annecy.

On your first day in France, resist the temptation to sleep. A week in Les Trois Vallées is little enough time to lose a day. Instead, stop in Annecy, have a cup of strong French coffee, change money, eat ice cream, window-shop, or explore le Château d'Annecy, which dominates the promontory above the old city. Annecy is wonderfully photogenic, and there is a temptation to burn rolls of film on children in school uniforms skipping down the narrow streets, or on the numerous cathedral façades, or on the play of light on Le Palais de L'Isle, the prow-shaped fifteenth-century residence of the Chatelain of Annecy that splits the Thiou Canal.

Locally known as the Venice of France, **Annecy** is the capital of the Haute Savoie and sits on Lac Annecy. Annecy's beautiful, narrow streets, fifteenth-century buildings, hilltop château, and sparkling canals combine the best of Old World France with an inland lake resort. For information about hotels and excursions: Syndicat d'Initiative d'Annecy, Bonlieu 1, rue Jean-Jaures, 7400 Annecy, France, tel. 50-45-00-33; telex 309-347.

With two hours to Méribel time was dear, and so we caught N508 along Lac Annecy to Faverges, Ugine, and Albertville.

From February of '92 on, Albertville will be tied inextricably to the winter Olympics. Mention its name in twenty years and people will remember the athlete heroes and the single best, or worst, feature of the city. It's a bit unfair to come directly to Albertville from Annecy. One ranks among the most beautiful cities in France, while the other is a booming center of light industry. If Albertville had a sister city, it would be Anytown, Illinois, where in spite of the outlying furniture centers, plumbing supply outlets, and heavy equipment depots, the old town retains a certain provincial charm. The Arly and Isère rivers skirt the city, Fort du Mont dominates a rocky knob above the N90 highway to Moutiers, and mature trees line the main streets. Most of the downtown buildings are weathered but not dilapidated, and the Olympic rings hanging above the main street offer a marked contrast to memorials for those killed in the first and second world wars.

Albertville is a blue-collar town with white-collar aspirations. Prior to the Olympics, Albertville had a total of 180 hotel beds, of which COJO (the French Olympic Organizing Committee) reserved 150. Since no major hotel building is planned, Albertville will pick up where it left off after the Olympics. It is not a resort, and in all likelihood will not become one. Rather it's a Savoie hub with one spoke leading back to Geneva, another to Chamonix, one to Méribel and Les Trois Vallées, and another to Lyons.

Skiers who come to the Olympics will benefit from the massive road construction undertaken by both the federal and Savoie state governments. To ensure traffic doesn't become gridlocked below the Val-d'Isère, Courchevel, Méribel, or Les Menuires venues, millions have been spent on a four-lane freeway that serves Chambéry and Albertville and Moutiers.

With the sun sinking beneath the western ridge, the two-lane road from Moutiers to Méribel snakes up through Les Allues with its domed church. This small farming hamlot appears to have changed little in the past fifty years, and a few kilometers later, Méribel appears. If we anticipated a ramshackle collection of herder's huts and cow barns standing hip to gable with weathered hotels and century-old restaurants, we instead discovered a busy wood, stone, and plate-glass retail center displaying everything from neon snowboards to aged hams and French pastry.

Located in the Allues Valley, Méribel has strict zoning laws that encourage a style of mountain château that defines the village center as well as the private homes and hotels on the west-facing hillside above. For this modern Méribel owes much to Peter Lindsay, a Scot who arrived in 1936 and fell in love with the Savoie Alps. With the help of engineer Émile Al-

Located in Belvédère above Méribel in the middle of the ski slopes, **Hôtel Allodis,** 73550 Méribel, France, tel. 79-00-56-00, fax 79-00-59-28, is a reproduction of an old French mountain château. Amenities: 41 rooms, sauna, pool, fitness room, restaurant, bar, ski to lifts, and excellent views. No dogs. Terms: $144 per person per day with half pension.

Le Chalet in Méribel Centre, 73550 Méribel, France, tel. 79-00-55-71, fax 79-00-56-22. Amenities: 36 rooms, sauna, pool, Jacuzzi, video, radios, ski to lifts, TV, dogs okay. Terms: $170 per person per day with half pension.

Information: **Méribel Office du Tourisme,** 73550 Méribel, Savoie, France. The Office du Tourisme offers a central reservations service for hotels or apartments: tel. 79-00-50-00.

Transportation is by train or bus from Geneva/Lyon to Moutiers then bus to Méribel. Train reservations: tel. 79-24-01-11; buses: Geneva-Méribel—Société Touristcar, tel. 50-43-60-02; Lyon-Méribel—Cars Philibert, tel. 78-23-10-56; Moutiers-Méribel—Cariane Alpes, tel. 79-24-03-31. Taxis: tel. 79-08-65-10.

★

lias and architect Christian Durupt, Lindsay built the first fixed-grip drag lift in 1938, and following World War Two returned to develop the resort. Using the local mountain architecture as a model, he introduced the use of Méribel's natural materials and gable-roofed theme. Half a century later the English continue to influence this French valley. There are three English pubs in town, English is second only to French, and British travel agencies book busloads of package skiers into the local hotels.

By now all Chip, Sue, Barbara, and I want is a quick dinner and a warm bed, so we check into the Hotel Allodis. Owned and managed by twenty-five-year-old François Front, the Allodis is located a thousand feet above Méribel's commercial center in the Belvedere district. Opened in the winter of '89, the Allodis offers spectacular views of the women's Olympic downhill course, a swimming pool, weight room, fine dining, large rooms, and ski-to-the-lifts access to the slopes. Little wonder CBS booked the entire hotel for their Olympic stay.

There is something special about a French morning that has much to do with the fresh croissants and strong coffee from room service. When you open the shades to the morning sun playing on the surrounding snowfields and watch the ski patrol and lift operators tuck by on their way to work, you realize that France is, well, France—a country populated by staunch individualists who love fine art, wine, and snow-covered steeps. Time is short, and while the Allodis still lies in shadow we step into our skis and follow the dark pine forests toward the Tougnète tram.

Temperatures the previous day in the mid-fifties have turned the spring snow to ice, which causes our edges to scratch and rattle as we skirt Méribel's private châteaux to a cat track above the Olympic hockey rink. From here you can ski to the base of the Tougnète tram and Méribel's main ticket office. I recommend buying a five-day pass. It's only slightly more expensive than the individual area tickets, and you get to ski all three valleys.

The snow is softer on the east-facing slopes, and we catch the Tougnète tram to the 8000-foot ridgeline between Méribel and Les Menuires. Here a sign points toward Le Gros Tougne traverse to Les Menuires and Val Thorens, but the snow is still hard in those west-facing shadows and we drop back toward Méribel. Skiing in France offers a strong contrast to skiing the

American West. Most of the West is marked by wide runs cut through evergreen forests, while the vast majority of Les Trois Vallées is above tree line, and the vast snowfields, brilliant sun, and softening conditions tempt us to push the limits, to arc down unfamiliar faces, dive off-piste into untracked hollows and search for shadowed lines through the valley forests.

With trams that climb out of sight and chairs that streak toward distant ridgelines, Les Trois Vallées tempt you to over-indulge—to burn calories in a vain attempt to see it all and ski it all before the snow softens to slush. This morning we stick to the Tougnète tram and the Roc de Fier poma. In three hours we do not stand in a single line or share a run. We are alone in La Face and the women's downhill. Bernhard Russi helped de-sign this course, and starting down the first steep pitch toward Méribel it's obvious this is not a waxer's or glider's course. With its radical upper section, midcourse bumps, and lower high-speed corners, this downhill favors the strong, the fearless, and those who rejoice in big air.

As long as you keep one of the villages in sight (and as long as you know which one you're looking at), you can pretty much get around Les Trois Vallées by dead reckoning. Start grabbing lifts and diving down seductive swales, however, and what you thought was Les Menuires turns out to be St.-Martin-de-Belleville, and the last 1000 vertical feet requires a half-hour hike in your ski boots.

That same element of adventure, however, can work to your advantage. Once the sun knocks the bottom out of the east faces, we cross the ridge and follow Le Gros Tougne traverse to Les Menuires.

If you're searching for the French definition of quaint, you won't find it in Les Menuires or, for that matter, Val Thorens. These two resorts sit at the head of the Vallée des Belleville and make no apologies for monolithic condos, connecting catwalks, labyrinthine malls, pools, tennis courts, health clubs, or lifts and runs that start and end in the resort core.

Built on the hillside and scheduled to host the men's special slalom in the '92 Olympics, Les Menuires is composed of seven levels. Named after a beach in Cannes, La Croisette is the commercial center of Les Menuires where the office of tourism is located. Surrounding La Croisette are Brelin, Reberty 2000 (and the new Club Med), Reberty 1850, Les Bruyères, Les Fontanettes, and Preyerand. Free buses run between these areas; all have shopping centers, restaurants, hotels, and access to lifts and runs. Though Les Menuires is fairly compact, if you were staying in Reberty 2000, missed the bus, and wanted to get to Preyerand, you're looking at a twenty-minute walk. Because of altitude and winter weather, shopping takes place in strategic indoor malls where you can find ski shops, pharmacies, groceries, and souvenirs as well as the unexpected sidewalk creperie. Les Menuires offers great hotels like the Alten in Les Bruyères, the Les Menuires in Preyerand, and the Club

Med in Reberty 2000; unlimited intermediate skiing on Leo Lacroix off the Mont de la Chambre gondola; and a range of dining at the better hotels (again the Altea) and cafes like Les Pub facing the pool and slopes in Les Bruyères.

Hôtel Altea Les Bruyères, tel. 79-00-75-10. Amenities: Centrally located, ski to lifts, private baths, TV, piano bar, restaurant, and phones. Terms: $75 per person, bed and breakfast.

    Hôtel Les Menuires, tel. 79-00-60-33. Amenities: Centrally located, ski to lifts, color TV, phones. Terms: $65 per person with half pension.

    Central reservations for Val Thorens, St.-Martin-de-Belleville, and Les Menuires: Les Menuires Office du Tourisme, B.P. 22, 73440 Les Menuires, Savoie, France, tel. 79-00-79-79.

    Transportation: railway office, tel. 79-00-63-90; Buses from Lyon, Chambéry, and Geneva airports, tel. 79-00-61-38; taxis from Moutiers, tel. 79-00-69-54.

If you stay in Méribel, the Mont de la Chambre gondola back closes at 5:10 P.M., and thus it is impossible to ski all of Les Menuires' runs. To do that requires at least two days. Instead take La Masse gondolas to the 9200-foot summit on Pointe de la Masse. Here the marked runs of Rocher Noir, Les Enverses, and La Dame Blanche cut through thousands of acres of off-piste skiing. While Barbara and Sue follow the groomed runs, Chip and I explore the untracked faces where unmarked cliffs, ridges, and swales lead back to the Lac Noir chair.

Later, with the sun hanging above the western ridge, the four of us linger over a glass of red wine on the deck at La Croisette and watch the crowds cross the ski stadium's Olympic finish line. The poetry of spoken French, the lingering warmth of the sun—which even now is gilding the west-facing snowfields above—make us deliberately ignore the time. But the bus ride to Méribel takes two and a half hours, and shortly before five we load the La Chambre gondola, which rises to the ridge between Les Menuires and Val Thorens. With the higher lifts starting to close, we cross into Vallée des Allues, where we ski the high, hard bumps beneath the 9700-foot Mont Vallon down to Mottaret.

Located a few kilometers up the valley from Méribel, Mottaret's small business core is surrounded by new hotels, apartments, and condominiums. With its ski-to-lift access and a short walk to restaurants and shops, Mottaret leans toward function over form. If accruing the maximum amount of vertical in the minimum time is important, stay in Mottaret. This station alone offers direct lifts to Les Menuires, Val Thorens, Mont Vallon, and Courchevel.

The sun is casting alpenglow onto the west faces, and the cats are starting to groom the slopes above us. We catch the Table Verte chair, skiing Les Bosses' hardening bumps down to Méribel, where we step into the eight-person Burgin-Saulire 1 gondola to the upper station above the Hôtel Allodis.

Dinner that night is at Le Cro Magnon, an unlikely name for a family restaurant but known for good food at reasonable prices. Located on the road between Méribel and Belvédère, the Cro Magnon is a local favorite. With wine, mineral water, dessert, and tip, the bill comes to $18 per person.

At 10 A.M. the following morning we recross the ridge to Les Menuires, where we catch the La Chambre gondola to the Goitschel traverse to Val Thorens. Skiing into Val Thorens is a rare experience, for you come off a high ridge along an undulating piste that suddenly falls away to reveal an Alpine outpost set in a treeless, glistening bowl. With its surrounding net of trams, gondolas, and chairs Val Thorens could have been lifted intact from a sci-fi thriller about a Venusian ski resort where a couple sleeps late, throws open the shades, and comes face-to-face with an extraterrestrial in a red jumpsuit and fluorescent lime-green snowboard riding the Plein Sud chair through town. The emphasis here is on action sports, fine world dining, and shop till you drop. With a base at 7554 feet Val Thorens is famous for early snow and makes no pretense of being any more or less than a four-season resort. At one time herders ran sheep through the upper Vallée de Belleville, but yesterday's stone huts have been replaced by retail shops, apartments, and hotels like the four-star Fitzroy.

Fitzroy Hotel, 73440 Val Thorens, Savoie, France, tel. 79-00-04-78. Amenities: 33 rooms, 6 suites, private bathrooms with whirlpools. Indoor swimming pool, sauna, exercise room and massage. Beauty salon. Dining room. Book early. Terms: $110–$172 per person per day, half pension included.

Le Val Thorens, tel. 79-00-04-33. Amenities: sauna, whirlpool, fitness club, TV, shopping, no dogs. Terms: $63–$112 per person per day with half pension.

La Sherpa, tel. 79-00-00-70. Amenities: sauna, fitness club, telephone but no TV, no dogs. Terms: $50–$72 per person, with half pension.

Surrounded by this vast bowl of ice, snow, and bare rock, Val Thorens is shiny new and a little brazen and offers some of the best skiing in the world. From the 10,500-foot Cime de Caron to the ridge below the towering 11,500-foot Aiguille de Péclet to the Mont de Pect ridge that leads back to the headwaters of the Vallée des Allues, this area alone would dwarf all but the largest U.S. resorts. With the addition of the Rosael detachable quad in the Maurienne Vallée to the west, Val Thorens has taken the first step into turning Les Trois Vallées into 4.

In '89 Val Thorens also added Le Funitel de Péclet—a state-of-the-art, double-cable gondola that rises 2300 feet to the Péclet Glacier. Each gondola carries thirty people, for a total of three thousand an hour, and the addition of the Tête Ronde run adds 26 acres to Val Thorens' enormous network of runs. Confronted by this vast bowl, Sue, Chip, Barbara, and I let them run. Somewhere below us was another untouched face, another three hundred turns of sunny corn snow, a mountain restaurant, or some futuristic gondola waiting to launch us at a distant peak. In Val Thorens you can take a lesson from former world champion mogul skier Eric Berthon or learn to paraglide with Daniel Millet and his Yuriken school. Or if you're fit and into adventure, you can book a twelve-valley ski tour that starts in Val Thorens, crosses eight passes, stops in eight resorts, and finishes in Val-d'Isère a week later.

Central reservations: 79-00-79-79. Val Thorens Office du Tourisme: tel. 79-00-08-08.

Transportation: Train to Moutiers, then bus (Cars des Belleville) to Val Thorens, tel. 79-00-61-38. Station taxi from Moutiers, tel. 79-00-63-41.

The problem with Les Trois Vallées is that if you try to see it all in a week you risk turning your vacation into a parody of "If it's Wednesday this must be Val Thorens." Or Courchevel, or for that matter any of the other nine resorts. To truly explore Val Thorens you need 210 cm giant slaloms or even 223 downhills, for the area rewards high speeds with enormous vertical. If congestion exists, we did not encounter it, and we skied the gentle Croissant to the Cime de Caron—a 10,500-foot peak to the west of the resort—when we had to turn back.

It's times like this when I regret I don't own an obese wallet. If francs were funny money, or if Visa were free, we could have skied off the back of Caron down the Col de Lauzon and back to Val Thorens. For once we could ignore the clock. When the lifts closed we'd check into the Fitzroy, call room service for razors, toothbrushes, and floss, outfit ourselves at a très chic boutique, and tell François at the Allodis not to wait up.

In reality, if we miss the last lift out of Val Thorens we will face a long bus ride back to Méribel. With luck we might make it back to the Allodis before 9:00 P.M., and so we gaze wistfully at the distant slopes and jump on the Télésiège des Trois Vallées (three-valley chair) to the Mont de Péclet ridge above Mottaret. As the shadows deepen, we race to catch the Burgin-Saulire gondola.

That evening we study Méribel's English expatriates over a Watney's Ale at The Pub before driving to the French Connection near Belvédère. Both bars are filled with young British tourists who revel in the hard rock and absence of spoken Frnech. For dinner, locals recommend the Petite Rosière, which is booked, and the Jardin d'Hiver, which isn't.

Le Cro Magnon, Plateau de Morel—Méribel. Daily specials in comfortable atmosphere, tel. 79-00-57-38. Le Jardin d'Hiver is located above Méribel's commercial center. Open for lunch and dinner, original French cuisine featuring a grill with fondue and fish, reservations required, tel. 79-08-64-62. La Petite Rosière, located between Méribel and Mottaret, winter dinner only, gourmet dining in a charming chalet, reservations required, tel. 79-00-41-46.

During the night temperatures drop into the twenties, and the following morning we catch the Burgin-Saulire tram to the 8850-foot La Saulire station above Courchevel 1850. Here on the sunlit east faces, beneath the 10,000-foot Aiguille du Fruit, yesterday's silky corn has metamorphosed into glaze. At best the off-piste skiing is technical, and the crowds quickly congregate on the groomed pistes where the tiller cats have provided a welcome cushion for beginners who hurtle by on their tails. Near-misses are common, and after a frightening 1000 vertical feet we start looking for the next lift out.

We find it in a double chair to the Col de Chanrossa. The Col is a narrow pass below the 8960-foot Roc Merlet, and here on a long traverse onto a sheltered east face the snow suddenly softens. With Barbara and Sue leading we drop 500 feet down to the Plan Mugnier, where we grab chairs and palmas until we have scribed a large circle around to Les Verdons between the Saulire summit and Courchevel 1850.

Before coming to Les Trois Vallées, Chip had never seen Europe. He is used to one chair accessing two runs; if the size of Val Thorens, Les Menuires, and the Méribel Valley does not leave him speechless, it does affect his fluency. "I never dreamed it was this damned big!" he keeps saying as we transfer from chair to chair.

"Well, I told you," I said.

"Yes, but you never said it was THIS BIG!"

If you're not an expert skier, this same size can lead you into trouble. Cliff areas are marked with signs but not impenetrable barriers. Thus it's wise to look before you leap. Coming off the Aiguille du Fruit chair above the Chalets des Creux, we ski into a steep, icy chute and find a ski pole. Immediately below is another and below that are two skis and another pole and more skis and finally a middle-aged Chinese man falling downhill in his ski boots. At the very bottom a woman is sitting in a mogul, holding both arms in the air. Her elbows have been shredded by a slide out of the chute, and now surrounded by her son and daughter, she is bleeding profusely, waiting for the ski patrol to arrive.

We drop their gear next to them and call the patrol at the bottom of the next lift. When we encounter the man later in Courchevel, he tells us that he and his family have come from Hong Kong for two weeks. "But we are not that good of skiers," he admits. But, except for her lacerated arms, his wife is okay.

U.S. skiers love nonstoppers. Too often breakfast is a cup of coffee, lunch is a brownie on a chair, and any conversation must fit in the few minutes it takes to ride a detachable quad. Courchevel's pace matches its complimentary suntan. Forget that business about ozone depletion and subcutaneous damage. Sun blocks, hats, and full-face scarfs are only partially effective in these solar bowls, and after a week in Les Trois Vallées you'll pass for a chocolate éclair. Deep tans are de rigueur. Aristocratic anemia is out. Flaunt a few carats of jewelery and a camel jacket and leather pants and French tourists will ask for your autograph.

The closer you get to Courchevel 1850 the bigger the lifts get. The biggest of all is the Saulire tram, a veritable Greyhound bus suspended from a wrist-thick cable. Except for the views, which aren't quite what you'd expect, the Saulire's silent running reminds us of an elevator. The French call trams *téléphériques* (tell-a-freaks), which describes how some skiers react to the tram's 36-foot-per-second rise to the distant ridge. The ground falls away, skiers shrink to ants, and any acrophobics crowd to the center.

When you speak of Courchevel, which has a sister-city arrangement with Park City, Utah, you're speaking of four centers: Courchevel 1850 (1850 meters), Courchevel 1650, Courchevel 1550, and Le Praz, the site of the 1992 Olympic jumping competition. With fifty-four hotels, sixty restaurants, and a 450-instructor ski school, each of these areas is linked to Les Trois Vallées, and each offers the usual amenities. To a large extent where you stay depends on your budget. Though we did not get a chance to do more than drive through the lower resorts, Le Praz has the reputation of being a typical Savoyard village, 1550 is weighted toward families, 1650 is a modern resort set on a plateau, and 1850 has a reputation as a destination for the rich and famous.

In the past few years many of Courchevel's hotels have turned away from the heavy industry style of architecture. Hotels at all levels are remodeling in wood and stone in an attempt to recreate the feel of a Savoyard village. In 1850 Michelin-rated restaurants combine with four-star hotels and shopping in L'Espace Diamont. Other advantages of 1850 are that the major gondolas converge beneath the tourist office on the Rue de Forum and an airport above allows direct access from Paris and Lyon.

Generally, the higher you go, the more lodging costs. **The Bellecôte,** tel. 79-08-10-19, fax 79-08-17-16, in Courchevel 1850. Amenities: Weight room, pool, phones, TV, access to slopes, beauty salon, no pets. Terms: $200—$250 per person per day.

The **Byblos des Neiges,** tel. 79-08-12-12, fax 79-08-19-38. Amenities: 69 rooms, weight room, beauty salon, parking, piano bar, indoor and outdoor pools, TV, video, minibar, dogs okay. Terms: $220—$345.

If this sounds steep, you're paying for the name, location, and service. Fewer stars rate fewer francs. **Courcheneige** in 1850, tel. 79-08-02-59, fax 79-08-11-79. Amenities: 83 rooms, Jacuzzi, TV, weight room, currency exchange, bar, dogs okay. Terms: $85—$97, half board included.

Or try central reservations, tel. 79-08-00-29.

Transportation: Train to Moutiers then regular buses departing for Courchevel.

See Méribel for complete transportation.

Standing our skis in a snowbank, we look for lunch. With an exchange rate of 5.5 francs per dollar (in 1991), a plate of spaghetti, a side order of fries, and a small Coke cost $12. You can waste time worrying about the prices, but Courchevel is a long way from Anytown, U.S.A.: it's a fine, sunny deck, the food is warm, and the waiter speaks cheerful English.

Besides the 90- and 120-meter Olympic jumps in Le Praz, in

1992 Courchevel will also host the combined Nordic and ice hockey training. To that end, 1850 is building the Forum, a $32-million, 200,000-square-foot entertainment and sports center across from the gondola base. Besides an Olympic-size ice arena, the Forum will include a shopping mall, a 250-seat restaurant, parking, and a medical center.

Following lunch we buy fresh strawberry tarts in a pastry shop on the Rue des Verdons then window-shop along the Rue du Rocher back to the Verdons gondola. Shadows are lengthening off the 8990-foot Croix de Verdon that towers over the lower runs, and we ride the gondola up to the Saulire tram. Now we have a choice: dive back into Les Creux, ski until the last possible second, and risk missing the final tram out; or play it safe, drop into Méribel, and ski the mid-mountain chairs. It's a split vote, with the nod going to Méribel, and we turn down a run called Chamois. A few hundred vertical feet later, when the piste bends downhill, we continue along the Croix de Verdon's west face. Riding a left edge through the soft corn, in time the tracks end and we find ourselves above a broad, sunlit slope that drops to Le Grand Plan below.

In the American West we would have raged until the lowest chair stopped running. But with high pressure dominating the Alps, we still have a few days left to explore Les Vallées Méribel, Val Thorens, and Courchevel. There are cocktails at the Allodis pool to think about and dinner at La Petite Rosière. Making a first turn in the trackless corn, we realize it is physically impossible to ski all of Les Trois Vallées. In this vast interconnect you could devote a lifetime of vacations to these slopes and still lose ground to the yearly additions. As we reach the piste that leads down to the Allodis, we realize that it is impossible to ride every lift that reaches for the horizon or eat at every restaurant worth its Michelin stars. Instead, we behave like the French, taking Les Trois Vallées' 1000 miles of runs one turn at a time.

REST AND RECUPERATION

Les Trois Vallées is two hours from both Geneva, Switzerland, and Lyon, France, and four and a half hours on the TGV Bullet train from Paris. Add a six-hour flight from New York and the travel time compares favorably to Colorado. Air France (reservations and flight information: 800-237-2747) offers direct flights to Lyon from New York. Geneva is a major hub for Swissair (reservations: 800-221-4750). Both offer connecting ground transportation to the Tarentaise. Trains run from Lyon to Albertville and Moutiers. Taxis or buses connect to Les Menuires, Méribel, and Courchevel.

In winter Geneva's **Old Town** offers a fascinating look back with its Escalade Celebration. There are numerous museums, parks and art galleries, five-star restaurants and hotels, and some of the world's best shopping on the Rue du Rhône and the Rue de la Croix-d'Or. The United Nations, the World Health Center, and the International Red Cross are based here, and beneath the international airport is a train station that connects to the rest of Europe.

On a larger but less expensive scale Lyon also offers a range of hotels, a history reflected in its walled city, weathered façades, and hotels. The **Rhône River** runs through parks, and though the airport, which is undergoing extensive remodeling for the Olympics, sits 20 kilometers outside the city center, buses connect to the city every fifteen minutes. Contact: French Government Tourist Office, 610 Fifth Avenue, Suite 222, New York, New York 10020, tel. (212) 315-0888.

I can't believe anyone would take a day off from Les Trois Vallées' endless pistes, but if the weather really craps out, you can shop in the enclosed malls. Once you bust your budget, there are fitness centers in Méribel, Courchevel, and Les Menuires/Val Thorens. In Les Menuires, **Le Capricorne,** (tel. 79-00-65-10) includes saunas, sun beds, Turkish baths, and a health bar for FF85. If you speak French there are two cinemas, and if you dance, two discos in both Croisette and Les Bruyères. In Les Menuires, you can take a snowboard lesson, Nordic ski or snowmobile. Have your hair styled the French way at **Snow Hair** (tel. 79-00-64-29) in Les Bruyères.

In Méribel do not miss the **Night of Dreams** at the Méribel's new planetarium. The show lasts two hours, is held every Friday night

at nine and costs FF60. Reservations required (tel. 79-00-55-40).
The **Astronomical Center** (tel. 79-00-47-17) is open every day but
Saturday from 11 A.M. to 7 P.M., FF20. Following the Olympics,
Méribel's enclosed **ice rink** will be converted to a public sports
center with swimming, bowling, and an on-site restaurant. There
are many hikes around Méribel, and information can be obtained
at the tourist office. In the evening there are Scrabble and Trivial
Pursuit matches, many against English-speaking Brit locals. Or,
you can take a hang-gliding lesson from the top of the Saulire.
Information at the Méribel tourist office in the town square.

And in Courchevel it would be difficult to experience the shops,
piano bars or discos. If you're staying at **Les Byblos** there is no
reason to leave the hotel in search of a sauna, weight room, or
pool. Courchevel also has a bridge club, chess clubs, numerous
arts and crafts exhibitions, and even language courses. For details
contact the tourist office at the base of the lifts in 1850 (tel. 79-
08-00-29).

CHAPTER 15

GETTING TO KNOW SQUAW VALLEY

HE FIRST TIME I HEARD ABOUT SQUAW VALLEY, I was living in Hempstead, Long Island. The year was 1960, I was twelve years old, and the winter Olympics were on TV. Squaw Valley, California! The name evoked images of a distant West Coast and the Golden State's snow-filled valleys. Seated in front of our black-and-white Zenith, I watched the opening ceremonies, the parade of nations, and a young U.S. hockey team's "miracle on ice" victory over the invincible U.S.S.R. Jean Vuarnet (now of Vuarnet Glasses) won the men's downhill, and Penny Pitou took the silver in the women's downhill and giant slalom.

In June of that year we moved to Palto Alto, California. Starting Wilbur Junior High School, I soon discovered that all my classmates skied. No matter that none of them could drive, much less drive to the mountains: everyone dressed, talked, and pantomimed ski moves. At lunch or in the halls, students assumed a basic bent-legged parallel stance, set imaginary edges, and reached with invisible poles for the next turn. To a newcomer from New York, it seemed that everyone had long since mastered this wondrous sport.

Everyone, that is, but me. My problem was that Mom didn't ski and feared driving in the snow. So for my three years in Wilbur I listened to people talk about Squaw and Heavenly, Headwall and Gunbarrel as if they were tenants in a strange California religion that used leather boots, wooden skis, and deep snow in a ritualistic sacrifice to the gods of winter.

I didn't start skiing until my sophomore year at Palo Alto High School and then only on rented equipment at Dodge Ridge, a small family resort out of Sonora. Riding a Lutheran Church bus through the darkened Central Valley only confirmed my first impression that skiing and religion enjoyed some sort of symbiotic relationship. And if I took horrible beatings on Dodge's intermediate runs, I regarded it as penitence. Someday I would attain Squaw and Heavenly and would ski in a state of grace.

That day occurred during my sophomore year at the University of California, when Bud Hoffacker and I set off for Donner Summit in my '67 VW Bug. The thing I remember most about the drive from Berkeley to Tahoe was Bud's lush white Irish sweater. I also remember the wide-mouthed bottle of Welch's Grape Juice. Bud's a meticulous guy, and during the 200-mile ride he didn't spill a drop. In my rush to be in line when Squaw's lifts opened, however, I flattened a turn on the east side of Donner Summit and at 75 miles an hour dropped the VW's right front tire onto a grated culvert. Bud had been tilting the grape juice bottle toward his lips, and though the tie-dyed looked was still years in the future, that day he made fashion history, staring bleakly at the purple stains and inquiring, "Do you think it'll come out?"

In the years since I have neglected Squaw, Heavenly, Incline, Homewood, and Kirkwood in favor of more exotic, far-flung mountains. In many ways the Tahoe resorts were like old friends, and even if I hadn't received a Christmas card from them in years, I knew if I ever dropped by, we'd quickly settle into the same familiar routines, the good jokes and old memories. Squaw, Heavenly, Incline, and the rest had profited from the years. If I was a better skier, Squaw and the North Shore resorts had grown to 14,000 acres and seventy-seven lifts all serviced by an interchangeable "Ski Tahoe North" ticket. On the South Shore, Heavenly had added more runs, faster lifts, and better grooming.

Real estate agents claim "location, location, and location," are the secrets to business success, and Squaw Valley qualifies on all three counts. Situated between Truckee and Tahoe City, a short drive off Highway 80—the nation's coast-to-coast ar-

---

Reno Airport is serviced by American Airlines (reservations: 800-433-7300), America West (reservations: 800-247-5692, Continental Airlines (reservations: 800-525-0280), Delta (reservations: 800-221-1212), United (reservations: 800-241-6522), Sky West (reservations: 800-453-9417), USAir (reservations: 800-435-9772).

Shuttles from airport: (916) 583-5585.

South Lake Tahoe Airport also is serviced by American Airlines, reservations: (800) 433-7300.

AMTRAK (reservations: 800-USA RAIL), stops at the Truckee rail station, and Greyhound stops in Truckee.

Because North Lake Tahoe is spread out, taxis are expensive and the TART public shuttle stops runnning at 6:30 P.M. The North Lake Tahoe Visitor's Bureau recommends renting a car. Avis, (800) 331-1212; Hertz, (800) 654-3131; National, (800) 824-6348; Thrifty, (916) 583-5585. Average price is $138 a week, unlimited mileage.

North Lake Tahoe has a booking service covering accommodations, flights, and ground transportation: tel. (800) TAHOE-4-U.

★

tery—Squaw is 40 miles from Reno, 120 from Sacramento, and 200 from the San Francisco Bay area. Then, too, Highway 50 runs from Sacramento directly to South Lake Tahoe and on to Carson City and Reno's major airport. All this means that Tahoe is close enough to attract day skiers and yet sufficiently isolated to avoid killer lines—although that doesn't always hold true for Christmas, when the Sierras have 12 feet of snow, or Presidents Day weekend, when every college and high school student between Reno and San Jose is trying to get one last run before hanging up their skis for summer.

With a top at 9050 feet and a base at 6200, Squaw falls nickels and dimes short of the magic 3000. Not that anyone ever complains, for with a 150-passenger tram, a six-passenger gondola, and twenty-six chairs including three quads, seven triples, and sixteen doubles, Squaw offers a money-back guarantee if your average stand in line is longer than ten minutes. The reason Squaw climbs out on this limb is it claims a dazzling lift capacity of 47,370 skiers per hour, which during a single business day will approach the population of Sacramento. That's big capacity matched to Squaw's 8300 acres of skiable terrain, and if you avoid the Siberian Express at midday or the Emigrant Peak chairs (Emigrant, Gold Coast, and Mainline in the afternoon or the base lifts from nine-thirty to ten), you can basically fall into chairs and ski until your thighs spontaneously combust.

Today, twenty years after the grape juice debacle, Bud owns a condominium at Squaw. From his living room window you can see the 8200-foot KT-22 peak with its intimidating West Face and below that the Red Dog faces. To the south is Squaw Peak's 8900-foot summit with its Sun and Siberia bowls—the latter once referred to simply as Siberia, where errant comrades were re-educated in the importance of edge sets on sheer faces and unweights in vertical bumps.

Fortunately passing a day in a tie-dyed sweater didn't prejudice Bud against skiing in general or Squaw Valley in particular. Though he still lives in the San Francisco Bay area, he manages a respectable forty days a season—with all but 10 percent of those devoted to Squaw. Now, on this sunny mid-March morning, he behaves as if we're about to sneak out of bounds. Though the valley is still in shadow and the lifts won't open for half an hour, at eight-thirty we start toward the Olympic Plaza's adjacent Cable Car Building. It hasn't snowed in the past week, during the night temps dipped to the low twenties, and if Squaw Peak doesn't glisten, it's soberingly hard. So why are we waiting in line to catch the first tram up?

"For the view," Bud admits.

As the tram climbs away from the valley floor, there is no denying the Tahoe Basin is beautiful. I had forgotten how the lake's startling deep blue color reflects the surrounding forest and snow-covered peaks. A common misconception is that Tahoe was once an ancient volcano. The basin, however, was formed by faulting—the same process that leveled parts of Santa Cruz, Los Gatos, and San Francisco in '89. Coincident to the birth of the Sierra Nevada, the Tahoe Basin has been sculpted by glaciers, dammed by volcanoes, and cut by rivers, creating the third deepest lake in North American—22 miles long, 12 miles wide, with a maximum depth of 1645 feet.

If this seems like a lot of irrelevant information, Squaw and Heavenly Valley's success is due in large part to Tahoe's rare combination of blue water and deep snow. Whether charging down Heavenly's Gunbarrel or cruising around Squaw's Emigrant Peak, a single glance says Tahoe. Aside from New Zealand's Mt. Cook, Queenstown, and Wanaka; or Argentina's Bariloche, the Tahoe resort's combination of big vertical, superb snow, and runs that fall toward the lake's placid surface is unique in the world.

Another thing unique to Squaw Valley is its lack of named runs. Here there is no trail map dunning the Indian theme. No Pocahontas beginner run, or Sitting Bull expert face. True, locals have names for the extreme chutes, gullies, and tree runs, but none have been committed to a map. Thus skiers are limited to the generic names: Sun Bowl, Siberia Bowl, Backside, etc.

Straddling the ridge between the Gold Cost, Emigrant, and Shirley Lake areas, High Camp, the tram's upper station, is adding an Olympic-size ice rink and six tennis courts. High Camp offers super views of the ski area, the arriving and departing tram, and the surrounding Tahoe Basin. Renamed the Bath and Tennis Club (which sounds like a snooty San Diego social club and at best is going to confuse the hell out of skiers), its future plans call for a series of swimming lagoons, spas, a mid-mountain hotel, and a golf course in what owner Alex Cushing promises will be the U.S.'s only two-level resort.

From High Camp you must traverse to reach the Emigrant triple. Pushing on a left edge past the beginner Belmont, Links and East Broadway chairs, and the Gold Coast mid-mountain complex, I feel an anemic warmth eddy into my legs and wish that the cup of coffee for breakfast had landed on something

In North Shore **Pete and Peters**, 395 North Lake Boulevard, 583-2400, is a local's bar; in back of that is **Za's**, 583-1812, for inexpensive classic Italian cuisine. **Jakes on the Lake**, 780 North Lake Boulevard, 583-0188, is known for its fresh fish, steaks, chef's specials, and lakeside dining. Try the **Hacienda Del Lago**, 760 North Lake Boulevard, 583-0358, for Mexican; the **Mackinaw Inn**, 700 North Lake Boulevard, 583-0233, for a wood-fired rotisserie and fresh fish, game, local produce, and lakeside views. There's the **Bridgetender**, 30 West Lake Boulevard, 583-3342, for burgers; **Le Petit Pier**, 7252 North Lake Boulevard, 546-4464, for gourmet French cuisine; and for something special, Tommy Cortopassi's **La Clemince** in Kings Beach, 546-4322, for classic French.

★

more substantial than an empty stomach. If Bud weren't on a mission, I'd detour through Gold Coast for breakfast. With its 32,000 square feet, the Gold Coast (which also serves as the Gondola's upper station) seats two thousand in its various restaurants and bars. The Oasis, with its Mermaid and Waterfall bars and buffet restaurant, fills the upper level, while on the ground floor there is a choice of an outdoor barbecue, a hofbrau, or various lunchrooms.

Catching the Emigrant triple lift, I note that the chairs in front are empty. The Sierra sun is starting to warm runs that were groomed the night before. Even if ski resorts in the Sierra and Cascades coastal ranges are exposed to the Pacific Ocean, Squaw's 450 inches of snow per season is nothing short of remarkable—especially when compared to Alta, Utah's, upper bench mark of 500 inches. There's an equation for how temperature affects snow volume, and if Tahoe storms averaged even three degrees cooler than Squaw's twenty-five-degree mean it would offer some of the best powder skiing in the hemisphere.

Until that happens, the Sierras will continue to produce enormous bases and some of the West's best spring skiing. For two years after moving to Idaho, I couldn't understand how you could hit rocks in December. In one Sierra storm alone 4 feet of snow fell in thirty-six hours—roughly 1.5 inches an hour without letup. We couldn't get out of the driveway, much less down the street and out to the highway, until the rotary plow rumbled by a day later.

Beneath Emigrant Peak, the Shirley Lake complex offers groomed runs, forgiving fall lines, and open meadows. Shirley used to be something of a secret, with silent glades falling to a single double chair and, depending on the snow, either no lines or enormous lines. With a little searching, you can still find untracked pokes off the Solitude triple chair close to the area boundary.

Today, with the morning cold evaporating from Emigrant's northeast face, we skate away from the chair and down a gentle groomed swale to the Siberia Express chair. Siberia is an old adversary, and I study its convex bowl, where I once followed a cornice traverse onto a line of survivor bumps, made two turns, went over my tips, and landed somewhere beyond the transition. Today with a pair of torsion-box slalom skis and flexible front-buckle boots, Siberia Bowl is technical but not the killer run of my youth, and once clear of its upper bump fields I drop to the Headwall double chair.

So far I've been content to follow Bud, who continues to lead with an insider's tour of the upper basin and ridge above the Sun Bowl. The morning sun has softened this open east face, and the ripening corn snow lets us drop our inhibitions, load our edges, and spring from one turn to the next. The years melt away, we're nineteen again, and before the sun turns the face to slush, we race down to the Cornice II double to hit it again.

KT-22's 8200-foot summit rises like a vertical mine field above the Olympic House and Plaza. In the past I mostly survived KT. Then nineteen and brimming with bravado, there was only one run on KT worth my time: the West Face. There are other famous west, north, and east faces, but then "The West Face" meant Squaw's KT-22, and simply surviving 1700 feet of enormous moguls and unrelenting pitch granted you bragging rights on the long ride home. This is expert terrain, and any desire to put notches on your poles recording how many times you skied KT-22 sets you up for the fractures, jambs, and tears this granite peak exacts as its daily tribute. You do not want to ski KT-22 when it sits in shadow and the mountain is hard and cold. Pick a time when the powder is pouring around your knees or when the corn is deep and consistent.

Squaw rates its chairs. On the map KT-22 is considered black, Emigrant is blue, and East Broadway is green—for advanced, intermediate, or beginner. That, however, doesn't always hold true, for within each are faces that serve as major exceptions to the rule. For that reason Squaw requires a strong dose of common sense. Just as there are no beginner escape routes off the KT-22 chair, a number of double black pitches can be found off the Siberia chair, and to risk one or the other for future bragging rights is the definition of dumb.

Beneath KT-22 is the Red Dog Peak, one of the exceptions to Squaw's colored chairs. Between the expert faces are intermediate lines and a new lift that leads to the new $100-million resort at Squaw Creek.

Scheduled to open in December of '90, **The Resort at Squaw Creek**, tel. (800)-3Creek3, will offer 636 acres of year-round recreational activity. Amenities: 405 guest rooms, some of which will include work/study areas, demi-kitchens, which include microwave, two-burner stove, and refrigerator, two TVs, and spectacular views. There are also twenty-four conference rooms for a total of 33,000 square feet, four restaurants, a Nordic ski center, a Robert Trent Jones golf course, three swimming pools, eight tennis courts, a fitness center, ice skating pavilion, and an equestrian center. Terms: high season double $235 per night. Or for a suite with living room figure $300–$350 per night.

Where to stay? Before winter sports arrived in Tahoe it was famous for its summers and gambling. Summer is still Tahoe's biggest season, and as such there are tons of motels, casinos, and restaurants. Tahoe City and Truckee are about equidistant from Squaw, with the former serving as the resort's major kitchen-and-bedroom community. Admittedly I remember Tahoe City circa 1968 and thus recoil from its strip zoning, with the ubiquitous hamburger stands, gas stations, and cheesy clothing stores. But even Tahoe City is mild compared to South Lake Tahoe, which has long since traded its character for the retail clutter of Highway 50. You can't have it all, and if Tahoe's major towns fall far short of a quaint alpine village, it's got beds galore, a cornucopia of restaurants, and the chance to make five straight passes at craps.

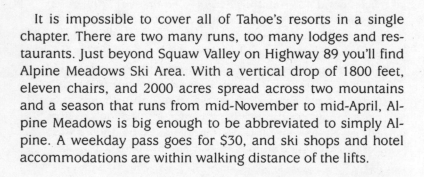

North Shore also has over eighty-five hotels, motels, condos, and bed-and-breakfast inns, as well as a central booking agency that can handle flights, rental cars, and accommodations. The bureau accepts Visa, MasterCard, and American Express. For more information: tel. (800) TA-HOE-4-U.

It is impossible to cover all of Tahoe's resorts in a single chapter. There are two many runs, too many lodges and restaurants. Just beyond Squaw Valley on Highway 89 you'll find Alpine Meadows Ski Area. With a vertical drop of 1800 feet, eleven chairs, and 2000 acres spread across two mountains and a season that runs from mid-November to mid-April, Alpine Meadows is big enough to be abbreviated to simply Alpine. A weekday pass goes for $30, and ski shops and hotel accommodations are within walking distance of the lifts.

Turning right on Highway 89 in Tahoe City will take you past Homewood Ski Area. With a summit at 7880 feet, a 1600-foot vertical drop, five chairs including one quad, and terrain split among 15 percent beginner, 50 percent intermediate and 35 percent advanced, Homewood offers a respectable 1260 acres of north-facing terrain.

Winter usually closes Highway 89's Emerald Bay section. Thus to reach South Shore you must take Highway 28 forty-two miles through Tahoe City, Kings Beach, and Incline. Incline Ski Area is halfway between South and North Shore. Incline's Diamond Peak boasts a vertical drop of 1840 feet, snowmaking over 80 percent of its developed terrain, a lopsided balance of 33 percent advanced and 49 percent intermediate runs serviced by six double chairs and a single quad. Millions have been spent renovating the North Shore casinos, which are open twenty-four hours a day and offer gambling, dancing, and live shows.

Continuing around the lake through the Lake Tahoe Nevada State Park, Cave Rock, and Zephyr Cove, you arrive in South Lake Tahoe where the glittering electric façades of Harrah's, Harvey's, the Sierra Casino, and Caesar's contrast with the blue lake, green forests, and snow-covered peaks. Towering above the casinos, Heavenly Valley's Gunbarrel resembles a spotlight announcing a grand opening. Neither movie nor mall, this heavily moguled run can be seen from around the lake. It is Heavenly's best advertisement and draws skiers from across the country. Getting to Heavenly from Reno is no problem. From Carson City west, Highway 50 is four-lane and well maintained.

Coming from California, however, is another story. The problem is that Highway 50 starts from Sacramento as a four-lane road then shrinks to two lanes 46 miles short of the lake. In summer Highway 50 turns into a parking lot; during winter storms, a skating rink. Still, Heavenly's combination of 12,000 skiable acres, lift capacity, proximity to après ski entertainment, and the fact that it straddles the California/Nevada line more than compensate for the wagon road up.

Figure Heavenly's 3600-foot drop toward Tahoe, 2900 into Nevada, and 12,800 skiable acres, and you have to be hardcore to cover this resort's marked runs in two days. Forget the miles of off-piste pokes that exist between. In contrast to most areas, Heavenly's lower California face is capital *E* expert, while the mountain's upper section is heavily weighted toward intermediate terrain, broad runs, and numerous chairs.

Surveys of the nation's most technical bump runs consistently place Heavenly's face in the top ten. Load the morning tram, Gunbarrel and East Bowl mutely inquire if you're tough enough or technical enough to best their consistently steep pitch and enormous moguls. In fact, only A+ experts do more than survive Heavenly's face, and a cadre of Tahoe skiers known as the "Face Rats" only ski the face.

As soon as you unload it's best to turn your back on the lake and coast down Patsy's to the Waterfall triple. From here follow Maggie's to the Sky triple, which climbs to Heavenly's 10,040-foot summit.

If it seems that you've ridden chairs half the morning, the reward soon becomes self-evident. Liz's is groomed nightly and falls straight at the dark blue lake. Here you don't have to be technically flawless. With the sun sparkling off the lake and the temperature hanging in the twenties, you can slide your tails around or swing your shoulders and no one will be the wiser. Display bad habit in big bumps and you'll be taken for a ride, but here the snow resembles an old Italian ski instructor who wonders aloud, "So what you worried for? A little skid, a little shoulder swing, who cares?"

And most assuredly no one does, as the smell of pine fills the cold wind on your face and your skis accelerate across the fall line. Intermediates will be hard-pressed to better the skiing accessed off Heavenly's Sky, Canyon, and Ridge chairs. Here Canyon, Betty's, Ridge, and the more technical Ellie's fill a northwest face with wide trails, rolling drops, and wonderful glade skiing. It's easy to get hung up here, lunch on the Sky Meadow's deck at the base of the Sky chair, and forget about Heavenly's Nevada face.

Along with a certain emotional satisfaction, skiing two states in a single day offers an enormous latitude. The Sky chair places you at the beginning of the Skyline Trail, a gentle traverse that crosses into Nevada. As the grade increases, hang a right into Milkyway Bowl which, though rated black, is closer to a deep blue and generally holds excellent snow. From here, 2900 vertical feet down to the Boulder Base Lodge, the terrain is generally intermediate—broad, gentle runs snaking through ponderosa pine toward the distant Nevada desert.

Heavenly recently added to its existing network the Comet quad, the Boulder triple, and Olympic and North Bowl double chairs, which access the intermediate Orion, Jacks, Comet, Crossover, and the Olympic Downhill and effectively pull crowds from the California side. Nevada is Heavenly's sunny face, and like the California side, you could spend the entire day here and never cross the intervening ridge. In fact, an alternative to South Shore is staying in Reno, where the winter season resembles off season, the gambling, shows, and casino restaurants are plentiful, and Heavenly's east-slope Stage Coach and Boulder Base Lodge offer excellent access.

Known as "The Biggest Little City in the World," **Reno** is thirty to ninety minutes from seventeen major ski resorts. Its airport is serviced by the major carriers, rental car companies, and shuttles (see transportation above). It has world-class entertainment, casinos that never close, and 25,000 hotel and motel rooms, many of which include ski/lodging packages. For reservations and ski package information, tel (800) FOR RENO

One of Heavenly's major bonuses is tree skiing in glades that drop between the California Trail and Ellie's run, in chutes that squirt down the face off Roundabout, in meadows between California Trail and Maggie's, that shelter a dozen turns between crowded runs. Eastern tree skiers would go crazy here; during a Heavenly powder storm you can ski all day and never have to chance more than a 10-foot slot between ponderosas.

Heavenly is open nine to four from mid-November to May, and at the end of the day you may choose to adjourn to the Top of the Tram and there watch the sun set across Lake Tahoe from the Governor's Room Restaurant and Cocktail Lounge. With the brightly lit casinos rising out of the forests and the lake reflecting the sun's last flare, dinner could be cold canned chili and you'd never notice. Fortunately the food compares favorably to the view. The only problem is that once the ski patrol sweeps Gunbarrel you've got to ride the tram down. Don't tempt the face after the area closes. Even a sprained ankle means big trouble with night coming on and temperatures dropping. And if in the course of dinner you exceed California's legal limit, the designated tram operator satisfies both the spirit and letter of the law.

So much to do, so much to ski. Because it's not technically part of the Lake Tahoe basin, and because it's relatively isolated, Kirkwood's 2000 vertical feet, fifty runs, and ten chairs are rarely crowded. Add an annual snowfall of 450 inches a season that runs from mid-November to mid-April, and South Lake Tahoe locals are willing to risk State 89's 7735-foot Luther Pass and 88's 8573-foot Carson Pass for a chance at Kirkwood's upper expert terrain.

If Lake Tahoe offers a sublime natural beauty, the casinos are high tech. Banks of one-armed bandits ring and buzz and blink, or more often stand silently, as a gamblers deposit quarter after quarter after quarter in the hope that the precise pull, the sudden meshing of odds, or a synchronism in the internal weights, will reward both their patience and purse. The bigger

In South Lake Tahoe I would definitely stay at one of the casinos. Not only do they offer ready access to the gaming, shows, and restaurants, but shuttles are also available. Rising above Lake Tahoe, the casinos straddle South Shore's famous "Stateline" and offer great transportation/lodging/dining/skiing packages.

Caesar's Tahoe Resort, Highway 50, P.O. Box 5800, South Lake Tahoe, Nevada, tel. (800) 648-3353, is reminiscent of a Northern Italian lake resort, complete with waitresses in togas. Amenities: 440 rooms, huge circular tubs, lake and mountain views, comedy, music and revues in Caesar's Cabaret, complete health spa, racquetball, tennis courts, saunas, fitness machines, six theme restaurants. Terms: ski packages start at $359 per person, lift tickets included.

Harrah's Lake Tahoe Resort, P.O. Box 8, Lake Tahoe, Nevada 89449, tel. (800) 648-3773. Amenities: 540 rooms, each with two bathrooms and in-room beverage dispenser. Sixteenth-floor suites also offer personalized butler service. Five restaurants, entertainment in the South Shore room and Stateline Cabaret, bars and lounges, eighteen hundred slot machines, 170 gaming tables, health clubs, glass-enclosed swimming pool, suntan center, children's arcade, pet kennel. Terms: ski packages start at $119, excluding ski tickets.

Harvey's Resort Hotel, P.O. Box 128, Lake Tahoe, Nevada 89449, tel. (800) 648-3361. Amenities: 636 rooms with French provincial decor, cable TV and refreshment centers, lake and mountain views. Also Harvey's has six restaurants, nine cocktail lounges, new swimming pool, health club, wedding chapel, Top of the Wheel Restaurant for continental, steak and seafood in the Sage Room, Szechuan in the Seafood Grotto. Terms: packages start at $128, lift tickets included.

★

the slots get the better . . . until they approximate gaudy bank vaults, enormous blocks of chrome and glass that convert silver dollars into spinning wheels and the promise of matching fruit, bells, or numbers. The rationale insists the more you bet the more you win. Little wonder Circus Circus is one of Reno's most popular casinos, for its tumbling and highwire acts, its bottle and ring toss and its stuffed pandas differ only in wager and reward from the slot machines and rows of blackjack, roulette, and craps tables.

Gambling is Tahoe's major draw, with the casino's floor shows, lounges, and dance floors close behind. Reno/Tahoe is known for its revues—floor shows that rely on skimpily clad showgirls to support the transparent story line. If the costumes are rarely suited to winter wear, the glitter, glamour, and strategic sequins suit this South Shore's unique energy. Titles like "Shocked" and "Passion" compete with established stars like Dolly Parton, the Moscow Circus, various comedians, bands, and impersonators. The casinos also offer a range of restaurants (inexpensive roast beef, lobsters, fruit buffets, and breakfasts are major draws), prices are reasonable, and you can play Keno from your table.

For all the expected reasons, when skiers travel out of state they rarely travel to Tahoe. Colorado is the big draw with Utah close behind. But you have to jump through flaming hoops to buy a drink in Utah, and you can't play craps in Colorado. Then again, neither place has Lake Tahoe, or the shows, or California's climate, and those reasons alone stack the odds in your favor.

REST AND RECUPERATION

A glance at the casino amenities suggest that there is no reason to venture beyond Stateline. Here you can see shows, dine, gamble, and get married at any one of twenty chapels. You can cross-country ski on **Kirkwood Ski Area**'s (209-258-6000) 75 kilometers of groomed tracks or **Spooner Lake**'s (702-749-5349) 55 kilometers. The **Husky Express** (916-577-8557) will take you for a half- or full hour dogsled ride. There is snowmobiling at the **Lake Tahoe Winter Sports Center** (916-577-2940). Besides the casinos there is the **South Tahoe Fitness Center** (916-544-6222) with a range of Nautilis equipment, Universal, and free weights at 2565 Lake Tahoe Boulevard. You can take an evening cruise on the Tahoe Queen or Miss Tahoe paddle wheeler at the **Ski Run Marina** (916-541-3364). There are teen dances sponsored by the City of South Lake Tahoe Recreation Department (916-541-4611), indoor golf at the High Sierra Hotel/Casino at Highway 50 on Stateline (702-588-6211). There are hikes and arcades and more shopping than you can possibly stand. And none of this includes Reno, a short drive down the mountain.

CHAPTER 16

CHARMED BY THE ENCHANTED CIRCLE OF NEW MEXICO

A N ICE STORM IS QUITTING NEW MEXICO WHEN the Air West 737 touches down at Albuquerque's international airport. As I step off the portable ramp and onto the gleaming ice, my dress shoes revolt, forcing me to shuffle carefully toward the passenger lounge. It is nearly midnight when I stop at Avis to claim the rental car. "So what's the road like to Taos?" I ask the clerk behind the desk.

"Taos?" she replies, looking up from the forms. "In this ice storm? You'd be smart to wait until tomorrow." Then, glancing at the make and model, she adds, "Especially with this compact you've reserved."

With four days to ski four resorts, waiting is not an option. I'm tempted to rent the biggest four-wheel drive on the lot, but the weekly rate would give a Saudi prince pause, and so I upgrade to a Dodge Safari, claim my skis, and get on the road. It is now past midnight and accelerating onto Interstate 25 to Santa Fe, for the second time that night I research the definition of slick. Hitting 40 miles per hour down the on-ramp and onto the freeway, the van slides across the right and middle lanes before grabbing traction a few feet short of the median guardrail.

This is not starting well.

I tune into the local rock station. A smoky-voiced DJ says it's bad out here. "Folks, the roads are a nightmare," he admits. "Albuquerque Police report a number of fender benders and an injury accident on San Mateo Boulevard."

Backing off to 30 miles per hour, it's obvious you set yourself up for a certain amount of hardship when you search for the Holy Grail. Or, in this case, the Enchanted Circle. It's not clear how this phrase evolved. Though it suggests a Pueblo Indian rain dance, the Enchanted Circle is in fact four ski areas scattered around northern New Mexico's Wheeler Peak. Starting with Taos at 6 and running clockwise, Ski Rio would be at 12, Red River would be at 1 and Angel Fire would be at 4. With its concentration of lifts, runs, restaurants, and hotels, Enchanted Circle hoped to lure skiers away from Colorado's Summit County.

American reservations: (800-433-7300) and America West airlines (reservations: 800-247-5962) fly into Albuquerque; from which city Mesa (reservations: 800-637-2247) connects to Taos. Shuttles are available from Albuquerque to Taos and Angel Fire. Rental cars at Albuquerque and Taos.

And it still might, but New Mexico has this image problem. If Idaho is often confused with Iowa and Ohio, New Mexico is similarly mistaken for a new state in Old Mexico. Part of New Mexico's problem is it shares thirty-five degrees north latitude with Algeria, Syria, Iraq, and Iran and thus when skiers think of New Mexico they think of Taos, or they think of Montezuma's revenge, red chilies, and velvet nudes.

In more than one way, however, this southern desert is a blessing. With little beside sage, sand, and dry washes between Southern California's beaches and New Mexico's 13,000-foot Sangre de Cristos, winter storms marshal their strength. In an average winter 400 inches of snow will fall on Wheeler Peak—an unbelievable 27 feet—of which a 10-inch skiff would offer sufficient reason to dog the state sand truck. With Interstate 25 in terminal shape, I give up on Taos and at 3 A.M. seek refuge in a Santa Fe motel.

The following morning on State Highway 3 heading toward Ski Rio, the road follows the ice-choked Rio Grande past fruit stands selling 6-foot ropes of red chilies. As the miles unfold past snow-covered mesas, stunted mesquite, bald eagles, and adobe ruins, I start to get a feel for New Mexico. An hour later I'm in Costilla, asking directions.

"Ticket office? Sure thing, right at the top 'a the hill," two high school girls reply in thick Texas drawls. Then, obviously troubled by my own accent, they ask "Say, are y'all n'merican?"

Ski Rio is isolated. Three and a half hours and 178 miles from Albuquerque, a little more from Colorado Springs, the turnoff on State 522 through Costilla isn't even marked on the Rand McNally Atlas. Serious skiers will count this oversight a blessing, for if Ski Rio requires a certain perseverance, it offers equivalent rewards. From the top of its summit double chair you can see north into Colorado, where Culebra Peak rises to 14,047 feet. To the west high plateaus give way to dark forests and finally the snow-covered San Juan Mountains.

With six inches of new snow and 2150 vertical feet, on my first run I explore Marinated, a moderately steep cruiser that intersects Rito Cordova, which in turns drops to the summit double chair. A major forest fire roared through here in 1952, and a crown of charred deads now rings the summit. Blackened trunks stand in stark contrast to the new snow, and I push from edge to edge and wonder at the surrounding silence. It is almost 11 A.M., and though Marinated is tracked, along the left side I discover an undisturbed line. With a base to push off, and the snow spilling around my ankles, I carry air off a bump and nearly blow the landing.

When you have an entire run to yourself, you start to wonder about numbers. Joe Quintana, Ski Rio's director of marketing, says that an average day is six hundred skiers, which when distributed among three chairs and fifty-six runs makes crowds almost nonexistent. Added to this is an average snow-fall of 270 inches (which divides out to 20 feet a year). If you're lucky enough to catch a single foot of this bounty, you can pretty much ski untracked powder until the elk come home.

Turning right off the Summit double chair, I follow Footloose down the ridge to a pony tow that accesses the top part of Sudden Impact and Tightrope. These two expert-rated runs drop through the north-facing Douglas fir to Solitaire, which in turn traverses back to the summit double. The single flaw in Ski Rio is a missing chair lift to this Tightrope ridge, for along with Shredder and Runaway it offers some of the mountain's best skiing.

The **Milagro Inn,** P.O. Box 59, Costilla, New Mexico 87524, tel. (800) 722-LIFT. Amenities: half mile from base area, kitchenettes, dining areas, hot tubs, sauna, and nearby restaurant. Terms: $65–$120 double occupancy.

Or the **Silvertree at Rio,** same address, tel. (800) 722-LIFT. Amenities: two-bedroom, two-bath condominiums, kiva fireplaces, viga ceilings, hot tub. Terms: condos, $150–$200; queen units, $63–$100; king units, $105–$135.

Dining: **Mercado,** sandwiches, soups, salads, and ice cream shop. **Day Lodge Cafeteria,** snacks, drinks, sandwiches, salads. **Rio Grande Grill,** steaks, seafood, and southwestern-style barbecue.

★

For most of the day I ride the summit double and in turn hit Spanish Eyes, which runs through the open trees, down to Hard to Hold. This is starting to sound like a Spanish potboiler, and on successive runs I ski Body Heat and Que Pasa, intermediate rollers that circle back to the double. If keeping all these names straight presents a problem, Ski Rio is in fact a large bowl with a series of intervening ridges and gullys. Run-

ning from left to right, the Spanish Eyes meadows change to the steep Marinated summit runs, which return to open Body Heat meadows and finally the perfect-pitch Tightrope section.

The mountains are casting purple shadows across the Rio Grande when I make a left at Costilla's lone, two-pump gas station back onto Highway 3 toward Red River.

It takes forty-five minutes to drive from Rio to the town of Red River, and it is dark when I stop in front of Texas Reds Steak House. Locals say not to miss Texas Reds because owner Bill Gill serves the world's best steak.

"What's your secret?" I ask as Bill Gill lays a sirloin on the grill.

"Well . . ." he says, taking a moment to think about it,

". . . a lot of people have asked me that. . . ." And then he flips the sirloin, salts it, and smiles.

Texas Reds, (505) 754-2964, is owned by Bill Gill and serves steak, ham steak, pork chops, prime rib, chicken, lamb chops. Old-time western decor, hours 5–9 P.M.

Founded by nineteen-century gold miners and alternately dependent on silver, molybdenum, and more recently tourism, the Sangre de Cristos surrounding Red River were once known as outlaw country. From a boom-town population of over three thousand in the 1890s, Red River has shrunk to a mere three hundred and fifty. The bartender at Texas Reds tells me that during Red River's early years, Billy the Kid, Jesse James, Kit Carson, and Sheriff Pat Garrett once frequented the adjacent Moreno Valley.

Now ghost towns fill the surrounding hills, and if four-wheel-drive pickup trucks and snowmobiles have replaced horses, there is a lingering authenticity about this town, a sense of

---

Alpine Lodge, Box 67, Main Street, Red River, New Mexico 87558, tel. (800) 252-2333. Amenities: across stream from ski lift, restaurant, kitchenettes. Terms: $44–$60 double.

Golden Eagle Lodge, Main Street, Red River, New Mexico 87558, tel. (800) 621-4046. Amenities: fireplaces, free snowshoes and sleds, ski shuttle, pets accepted, some kitchenettes. Terms: $29–$36 double.

Riverside Lodge, Box 249, Red River, New Mexico 87558, tel. (800) 432-9999. Amenities: hot tub, barbecue area, honeymoon suites, cabins, condos, fireplaces, and dishwashers. Terms: $42–$56 double.

history preserved in its weathered storefronts. The best part of Red River is it doesn't feel like a resort. In fact, from Main Street you might miss the ski runs on Mt. Wheeler's northwest flank.

Red River Ski Area has been in operation since 1959, when the first chair lift was strung between a line of oil derricks. Today the derricks are gone, but the area has expanded to 1600 vertical feet and twenty-seven runs serviced by one triple and three double chairs.

During the night the temperature plummets, and the following morning I load the Red chair with General Manager Drew Judycki. The Red chair is by far Red River's longest. Rising from base to summit in twelve minutes, it accesses Red River's intermediate Bobcat and Broadway as well as the expert Lift Line, Catskinner, Mine Shaft, and Powder Keg—primarily north-facing tree runs that offer rolling bumps and steep fall lines.

Judycki used to race on the Southwest Pro Tour and now competes in the Masters Class. Skating away from the chair, he starts down Bob Cat, picks up speed, and accelerates down Broadway. No short swing turns here, for the run has been groomed, the snow is hard, and the wind makes my eyes water as we ricochet from tree line to tree line. It turns into a fine warm-up, and we skate between the empty lift ropes and drop into the Red chair.

"Basically we're a family resort," Judycki says. "You can turn the kids loose in Red River and not worry. We have a great Kinderski program, kids under twelve ski and sleep for free at participating lodges, and the Playhouse offers pinball, miniature golf, roller skating, and teen dances."

On top the Red chair accesses the shadowed Catskinner. Dark spruce crowd the edges, and though it was groomed a few days before, the snow is hard and moguls are starting to dominate the centers. With the cold morning air on our faces and knees riding up and down, edge set follows edge set. While an internal rhythm beats in time to the changing terrain, we follow the shifting fall line back to red Avenue, which traverses back to Red chair.

Catskinner is next with a variation down the shadowed Powder Keg. Alternating the sunny intermediate runs with the shadowed expert runs makes a fine day, and it is dark when we quit Red River's Motherlode Saloon and start down the road to Angel Fire.

Angel Fire is located exactly halfway (or about 35 miles) between Taos and Red River in the broad Moreno Valley. The name Angel Fire has been variously attributed to the Ute Indians, Franciscan Friars, and Kit Carson but the harder anyone tries to pin down the source, the more elusive it becomes—like alpenglow on snow-covered trees, a haunting image. If Red River has echoes of a riotous past, Angel Fire's Legends Hotel is sparkling new. Here you can leave your bags in an enormous room and wander down to the country and western bar, where couples in cowboy shirts, Levi's, and Tony Lama boots sip white wine.

The **Legends Hotel and Conference Center,** P.O. Drawer B, Angel Fire, New Mexico 87710, tel. (800) 633-7463. Amenities: 157 rooms, ski to slopes, queen beds, color cable TV, restaurants, swimming pool, Jacuzzi, shops on premises, bell service. Terms: call.

   The Inn at Angel Fire, Highway 434, Angel Fire, New Mexico 87710, tel. (800) 666-1949. Amenities: 33 rooms (singles, doubles, suites, and dorms), shuttle to ski lifts, 21 miles from Taos, TV, sauna, game room, ski movies, free kennels. Terms: $79 for a double.

It is easy to tune into the Enchanted Circle. Add the discovery of a new resort to new lifts, new runs, changing vistas, different restaurants, and après' crowds—for a skier it's a kid-in-a-candy-store kind of hedonism. With so much ground to cover, it's difficult to say no to any of it, and so you stay up too late, ski runs you shouldn't, and forget the sun block.

A majority of Angel Fire's fifteen hundred skiers per day come from the neighboring Lone Star State, and if you hang around long enough you find words like "howdy," "y'all," and "much obliged" infecting your vocabulary.

It's best to take a warm-up down Exhibition first thing in the morning, then transfer to the number four chair, which rises to the Angel Fire summit. From here you can see Wheeler Peak to the north and the snowy sweep of the Moreno Valley. With four double and two triple lifts spread across fifty-one runs, 2200 vertical feet, and 320 acres, if Angel Fire is biased toward intermediate (45 percent) and beginner terrain (36 percent), its vertical Glory Hole, Sluice Box, and the moguled Hari Kari will make most experts think twice.

Even so the majority of Angel Fire's runs are broad family cruisers cut through the evergreen and aspen forests. A fleet of groomers keeps it all scraped flat, and you can dive into the right side of Hulley Gully, cut long GS turns high against the tree line, then drop into lower Fat City, which leads back to the number 6 chair.

Along with various pro tours and family challenges, Angel Fire also sponsors the World Shovel Race Championships—a local aberration dating back to when lift operators rode their shovels down at day's end. This February event features everything from the traditional waxed snow shovels to a brass bed to the Mudshark—a converted jet belly tank that holds the record at 75 miles per hour.

As the day progresses try the Back Basin runs, the moguled Fire Escape, and the Heck No shortcut, as well as half-a-dozen others that lead back to the number six chair. Switching to the number five chair, ski Jaspers and Bodacious—long, sinuous cruisers that lead back to the base lodge.

The shadows are lengthening when I stop above Glory Hole.

Shadowed by the tall fir, the snow has kept on its moguled face, and I drop to the first bump then start to link turns. For once it all works, knees and the soft moguls, the golden light and the smell of pine, and I take a deep breath and tuck the lift line back to the base core village house.

Built in the shadow of Mt. Wheeler, Taos sits both physically and fiscally at the center of the Enchanted Circle, and the following morning I'm riding Taos Ski Valley's number five lift that follows the legendary Al's Run, a heavily bumped face that drops to the resort core.

Located 18 miles from the city of Taos and opened in 1955 by the late Ernie Blake, Taos is an American success story. In-

Staying in Taos means staying in town or on the slopes 18 miles away. At Taos Ski Valley try the **Hotel St. Bernard,** (505) 776-2251, or the **Thunderbird Lodge,** (505) 776-2280.

The Innsbruck Lodge and Condos, Taos Ski Valley, New Mexico 87525, tel. (800) 628-6139. Amenities: ski-in ski-out, group and daily rates, five- and seven-day packages complete with room, meals, lift and lesson tickets. Terms: call.

In Taos proper, stay at the **Quail Ridge Inn,** (800) 624-4448, 4 miles north of Taos and Taos Ski Valley Road. Amenities: fireplaces, cable TV, hot tubs, sauna, racquetball, tennis courts, on-site restaurant. Terms: $59–$75 double.

The **Taos Inn,** 125 Paseo Del Pueblo Norte, Taos, New Mexico 87571, tel. (800) 826–7466, half mile north of Taos Plaza on U.S. 65. Amenities: adobe fireplaces, antiques and hand-loomed Indian bedspreads, Doc Martin's restaurant, adobe bar, greenhouse, Jacuzzi, pool. Terms: $50–$95 double.

For dinner try one of Taos's many Mexican restaurants.

★

spired by the Sangre de Cristo's desert-dry powder, and filled with a veneration for hard work, Ernie, his wife Rhoda, and their three children moved to what was then known as Twining, an abandoned mining camp located at 9,207 feet. For the first eighteen years Taos ran in the red—a testimony not only to creative financing but to Ernie's native Swiss ingenuity. In the time since Taos has added seven chairs (six doubles and one triple) and 100 acres of terrain, of which a sobering 51 percent is rated advanced.

With four inches of new snow on the groomed runs, Wheeler Peak rises 13,161 feet into the bright New Mexican sky. Taos Ski Valley sits in the top of a high canyon, and in the early morning the majority of its north-facing slopes are still in shadow. From the top of number five you can ski White Feather down the bottom of number six which in turn climbs to the Highline Ridge. Aside from the 27 feet of powder it receives annually, if other resorts advertise black diamonds, Taos invented the yellow run—the same cautionary color recommended for those who make a habit of running red lights. In bold print the Taos trail map points out that Tresckow, Juares, and Fabian are for "EXPERTS ONLY, USE EXTRA CAUTION." These chutes are accessed by hiking to the Tresckow and Highline ridges and the High Traverse to the West Basin Ridge.

It's too early to risk a major beating, so follow the intermediate Honey Suckle on a long groomed traverse toward Kachina Peak. Here the snow is hard and shadowed and you can let your skis run down to Patton and the Kachina lift. Images of Kachina dolls, colored corn, and rain/sun dances eddy about in the frigid morning air as the sun rises over Kachina Ridge. Whoever thought New Mexico could be this cold? But then who could ever imagine 27 feet of snow this far south?

Off the Kachina chair, you can ski Shalako back to Patton then return to ski Hunziker Bowl to High Noon. Though none of these combinations threaten you with the death-defying steeps of the south ridges, they do offer a thorough warm-up. Because of its yellow runs, Ernie Blake took to burying glass bottles of dry martinis near ribbon-marked trees known as the "Martini Trees." A medicinal ounce of gin was reputed to do wonders for one's courage, especially when facing the West Basin Ridge.

For most skiers the ridges are rites of passage, one hundred turns to put in a portfolio. But traversing along the High Traverse, I skip Blitz because the bumps are uneven; Spitfire is no better; and in succession I find something wrong with the next three chutes until I'm standing on a single edge, a snowy wall at my elbow, staring down a narrow gully into an open bowl. This chute could be Zsdarsky . . . then again, it could be Stauffenberg. Either way, there's nothing more humiliating than studying unpronounceable names above a run I'll be lucky to survive. With the runs getting steeper, I get off the edge, jump to another, and bail out. This is steep! I kick turn away from a rock wall, link two turns, stop, link two more, and when the grade eases off find a rhythm.

So it wasn't great, but I arrive at the number two lift intact and on the ride up give some thought to attempting it again. Now that I know what to expect, I could go back and get aggressive, but I feel as if I escaped more than skied the West Basin Ridge and go off in search of easier prey.

Located above the village core, Al's Run is only one thread in a black spiderweb. Today it's closed. To the west, however, Snakedance, Showdown, and Inferno offer an alternative idea of how hard black diamonds can be. If you hate bumps, stick to the intermediate Porcupine and Powderhorn—the locals will bless you. But if you've search in vain for perfect moguls, look no further, for scattered across these tree-gladed faces are world-class rollers. Granted, much depends on conditions, but on these north-facing shadows the snow is as forgiving as a white-cake mix, and you roll your knees and extend for the next turn.

Local favorites are Spencer's Bowl, to Edelweiss, with a close variation down the steep Snakedance, and Showdown. It is now three, my legs and lower back are fried, and though the last-run rule says I should call it a day, I impulsively load the base number one lift and turn down Inferno. A Swiss downhill of the same name is run every year in Mürren, and now the Inferno recalls images of the Schilthorn, Kannonenrhor, and Maulerhubel, the precipitous drops and the high-speed traverses. Running diagonally from Al's Run to White Feather, the Taos version differs both in size and profile, for it alternates off-camber mogul faces with short traverses.

After four days this run should pull it all together. Surrounded by sunlit ridges, dark forests, and rolling moguls, I should gain a last insight into the Enchanted Circle. Perhaps the locals are right when they claim Wheeler Peak is a galactic receiver—a natural dish that amplifies cosmic energy. If the Indian dances, symbols, and Kachina dolls are an expression of this energy, then perhaps it also affects the snow. Cosmic or not, 27 feet in the desert is a phenomenon. And sensing a certain truth in all this, I drop to the next bump, feel my knees flex, and change edges.

REST AND RECUPERATION

If you take a day off, do not miss the **St. James Hotel** in Cimarron off Highway 64. Here Clay Allison, a gunfighter who reputedly killed fifteen men, danced naked on a bar and shot up the town. Other luminaries such as Buffalo Bill Cody, Annie Oakley, Bat Masterson, and Zane Grey stayed at the St. James, which today has a museum and is open seven days a week.

Then in Taos visit the thousand-year-old **Taos Pueblo,** which is located 2 miles outside the town of Taos. Cameras are not allowed on ceremonial days, but permits can be purchased for other days. Signs mark pueblo dwelling where jewelry, pottery, drums, and other arts and crafts can be purchased. Off-limits areas are marked, tel. 758-9593.

Or the **Ranchos Church** and the **Rio Grande Gorge.** Taos also has numerous museums, exhibits, and galleries. For information: Taos Chamber of Commerce, P.O. Drawer I, Taos, New Mexico 87571, tel. (800) 732-8267.

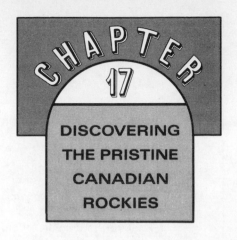

CHAPTER 17

DISCOVERING THE PRISTINE CANADIAN ROCKIES

PRIOR TO THE FIFTEENTH WINTER OLYMPICS, Americans were as likely to place Calgary in Jerusalem as in Canada. Once the flame died, however, and Calgary was grafted onto the Olympic Tree, everyone knew that white hats and cowboy boots were de rigueur attire, rock was out, country swing was in, pin trading was big business, Calgarians were a grinning Labatts Blue bunch who volunteered in lemminglike waves, and Calgary Mayor Ralph Kline was the kind of guy you'd like to invite to your Friday night poker game.

Olympics or not, few cities can match Calgary's colorful history. To stop U.S. buffalo hunters from trading whiskey for buffalo robes with the Albertan Indians, in 1875 the Northwest Mounted Police built Fort Calgary at the confluence of the Bow and Elbow rivers. Eight years later the Canadian Pacific Railroad thundered by on its mission to welcome Vancouver to the confederation, and in the time since Calgary has emerged as Western Canada's major transportation center, alternately dependent on cattle, wheat and, more recently, natural gas, oil, and tourism.

 Air Canada 800-776-3000, America West 800-247-5692, Canadian Airlines 800-426-7000, Continental 800-525-0280, Delta 800-221-1212, Northwest 800-225-2525, United (800-241-6522, and American 800-433-7300, all fly into Calgary. Rental cars are available at the airport; shuttles connect with Banff and from there to the outlying ski resorts. For information call Alberta Tours, 800-661-8888.

Though the Olympic press awarded Calgary a gold medal for its great hotels, restaurants, entertainment, and western hospitality, it went after Nakiska Ski Area with a vengeance. Today if skiers remember Nakiska at all they remember 100-mile-an-hour blizzards blowing course workers off their feet, blistering chinooks that melted the snow faster than the compressed air guns could spit it out, and punk rockers cooking weenies over Nakiska's Olympic flame. Even worse, the front-page photos of Rocky Mountain bighorns feeding next to the women's downhill course didn't exactly encourage U.S. skiers to "Fly Nakiska" once all the hoopla died down.

So informed skiers would rather focus on something famous and guaranteed; say, Paradise Bowl of Lake Louise or Sunshine Ski Area's North Divide. At the very least most reviews try to slip Nakiska in under its anglicized name of Mt. Allan.

Located an hour west of Calgary, Nakiska is Cree Indian for "to meet" and sits up a wide glaciated valley a few miles south of Trans-Canada Highway 1. Though Olympic competitors praised the technical difficulty of the downhill and giant slalom courses, realistically Nakiska's four chair lifts (a double, a triple, and two high-speed quads) service a number of long, low-angle boulevards near the base such as Homesteader and

Walking Buffalo, and a few steep faces like Bulls Head and Red Crow closer to the summit. In all honesty Nakiska is an intermediate mountain, a place the entire family can ski and probably will.

Even so, after 1988's epic three weeks of Nakiska bashing, why would anyone gamble their annual ski vacation on Alberta's sketchy snow and tropic winds? To be fair, the winter of '88 was one of the driest in history, and Nakiska does have a $3 million/75 percent coverage Delta snowmaking system. Nakiska does receive 200 inches of natural snowfall, and today there is no lack of coverage on its thirty runs and 3196 vertical feet. If television makes everyone gain ten pounds, it also flattens downhill courses. By now the miles of safety fences have been taken down and the cat track that traverses to the expert Eagle Tail is no longer guarded by course workers.

Thousands of spectators lined these runs in '88, clinging to tiny platforms stomped next to the safety netting and braving the frigid temps as Permin Zurbriggen came charging down the Bobtail face. Pointing my skis down Eagle Tail, it's obvious that imitation is not the highest form of flattery. First, the snow is too soft, the screaming spectators are missing, and there's a major discrepancy between racing for Olympic gold and hanging it out for the thrill of it all. Arcing from side to side down a groomed run is a far cry from carrying 80 miles per hour—plus down an icy face, and it doesn't take a genius to figure out what a religious Swiss ski team member the odds makers picked to win five gold medals must have been thinking. Higher speeds, tighter tucks, and no falls.

In my case, falling is an ugly option. In recent years it has gotten harder to ski away from crashes, and so I burn velocity by stepping from one edge to the next, then stop to study the Bobtail face. From here the course flattens out on Mighty Peace, dropping finally into the base area where Zurbriggen broke the finish beam to win the gold. It was a glorious moment, and standing in the deserted finish area, it's difficult not to remember the Olympic theme—that catchy tune that echoed across the opening and closing ceremonies and the laser shows at Olympic Plaza.

Combining broad runs, quad lifts, sparkling base facilities, and magnificent views, Nakiska is an hour from Calgary. No doubt Mom, Dad, and the kids will love the skiing, but with Banff less than an hour down the road and Norquay, Sunshine, and Lake Louise a short distance beyond that, Nakiska is something of a day resort. True, the Canadian Pacific Railroad's new 255-room lodge at Kananaskis is a short walk from the lifts, but even with its swimming pool, disco, and sparkling amenities, unless you get snowed in, spend your first night in Calgary and ski Nakiska on the way to Banff.

The **Lodge at Kananaskis,** Kananaskis Village, Alberta TOL OMO, Canada, (800) 828-7447. Amenities: 255 rooms, fireplace, balcony, TV, sauna, swimming pool, restaurant, lounge. Terms: double $85 midseason.

Hotel Kananaskis. Amenities: 69 rooms, same information as the Lodge, except swimming. Terms: $95.

Kananaskis Inn, Kananaskis Village, Canmore, Alberta TOL OMO, tel. (403) 591-7500. Amenities: 96 rooms, fireplace, balcony, TV, sauna, swimming pool, restaurant, lounge. Terms: double $70 midseason.

Arriving at the Inns of Banff after dark, it's hard to miss the bull elk feeding on the Inns' ornamental shrubs. This is no second season spike but a six-point royal, munching unconcernedly away as locals motor by without as much as a sideways glance. The bull is miles within the boundaries of Banff National Park—an enormous preserve that has remained basically unchanged since the Canadian Pacific Railroad blasted its tortuous roadbed through these vertical peaks.

Banff Springs Hotel, Box 960, Spray Avenue, Banff, Alberta, Canada TOL OCO, tel. (800) 828-7447. Amenities: 840 rooms, telephones, TV, sauna, whirlpool, swimming pool, restaurants, lounges. Terms: double $115–$165 midseason.

Inns of Banff Park, Box 1077, 600 Banff Avenue, Banff, Alberta, Canada, TOL OCO, tel. (800) 661-1272. Amenities: 180 rooms, telephones, TV, sauna, whirlpool, swimming pool, restaurant, lounges, centrally located. Terms: double $75 midseason.

If you ignore the local Cree Indians, Banff traces its history back to William and Tom McCardell and Frank McCabe—three Canadian Pacific Railroad surveyors who, in the spring of 1883, rafted across the Bow River to prospect for gold. Panning along a warm creek, they pushed through a stand of lodgepole pine that surrounded a rock basin bowl of steaming water. If it wasn't gold, it was nonetheless a valuable discovery, and pressing upstream they discovered further wonders. A deep, steaming grotto appeared. Using a trimmed pine as a ladder, William McCardell descended thirty feet to the floor where, in his own words, "The glistening stalactites that decorated this silent cave were like some fantastic dream from a tale of the Arabian Nights."

In 1883 McCabe and the McCardell boys were helping to implement Prime Minister John Macdonald's dream of a national railway joining the Atlantic and Pacific coasts. Isolated beyond the distant Rockies, British Columbia's admittance to the nation was by no means guaranteed. Both the time and cost of tunneling, bridging, and blasting a roadbed through the Rockies had been sorely underestimated, and as McCardell held a lighted candle up to the glistening stalactites, the CPR was staggering under enormous overruns. Even the most optimistic forecast predicted the completed line would lose money, and the CPR was searching for means to help defray costs.

For centuries the Crees had been bringing their sick and injured to the Cave and Basin. Minerals in the hot springs helped arthritis—a fact appreciated by old grizzlies, which often had to be driven from the steaming pools.

Responding to reports of the medicinal hot water and surrounding wilderness, the Canadian Parliament created the

Banff Hot Springs Reserve in 1885 for "the sanitary advantage of the public." To generate revenue on the unfinished line, the CPR envisioned a world-class spa on a par with Baden-Baden and Bath and subsequently broke ground near the Cave and Basin Springs for the Banff Springs Hotel. Five stories high, with a pavilion overlooking the Bow River, several dining rooms, a reading room, billiards, and a smoking room, all for $3.50 per day, it opened in June of 1888 and was immodestly advertised as the "Finest Hotel on the North American Continent."

More than a century later, the Banff Springs could still compete for "Finest Hotel," and Banff still feels like a small town. Located eighty miles west of Calgary, Banff serves as the southern entrance for the park. Considering three million people a year come through here, you would expect Banff Avenue to be a strip zone dedicated to T-shirts, postcards, fast foods and fast photos, blocks of motels and service stations. If tourists prefer quaint resorts they still demand a certain amount of curios, and Banff unfortunately has not completely escaped that influence. Walking past the shops on Banff Avenue, however, you're more likely to find the Hudson Bay Company, bookstores, ski shops, and fine restaurants than video game arcades and souvenir emporiums specializing in painted ashtrays.

The east end of Banff Avenue points toward Castle Peak, which the morning light strikes with soft alpenglow. Located ten minutes above Banff, Mt. Norquay Ski Area has a reputation as a local's rendezvous. Except for one detail, this 1300-foot vertical face that overlooks Banff would be a logical warm-up for the more distant Sunshine and Lake Louise. Under normal circumstances, however, you don't tackle the toughest first, and riding the Norquay double clarifies why locals love it. Along with its proximity to Banff, with two T-bars, one platter and two double chairs to service twenty runs (though Norquay claims a 50 percent break between beginner and intermediate terrain), the rest is black diamond expert.

Here you should capitalize "black diamond" to make it carry the proper impact. A prerequisite for Norquay is ten million vertical feet of experience. From the top of Lone Pine to downtown Banff looks to be one long bump run. Then there's Widowmaker, which smacks of nominal determinism. The bright spot among all these black diamonds is the Cliffhouse, where you can postpone your first turn over a contemplative cup of hot chocolate.

Since only expert skiers attempt Lone Pine, the bumps resemble the tango and rumba—rhythms that perfectly suit flexible slalom skis and fluid knees. Besides Lone Pine, the Bowl and North American (an expert trail that connects to the access road below) are serviced by the Norquay double. The gentle

Wishbone 1, 2, and 3 cruisers are accessed off the Wishbone T-bar, and with night skiing until 9 P.M. you can ski yourself to death in a day—a fact Norquay's management acknowledges with its commemorative 35,000-foot Gold Pin.

While in Banff, do not miss a soak in the recently renovated Cave and Basin Hot Springs. Also, you shouldn't miss the Hudson Bay Company on Banff Avenue. Among other things Hudson Bay is famous for yellow, black, green, and red striped blankets. Hudson Bay also sells wool jackets with the same distinct design, but if you buy one, hold off wearing it until you get home, for on Banff Avenue these wool symbols of nineteenth-century Canadiana bleat "TOURIST!" TOURIST!" to passing traffic.

If you can get reservations at the newly renovated Banff Springs Hotel, take them. If not, reserve dinner in one of its restaurants. On a Friday night the Banff Springs is given over to a convention of the Alberta beef industry—a ruddy group of meat eaters dressed in dark western sport coats, rodeo buckles, string ties, and dress cowboy boots. Try to avoid the Chinese Buffet, which is unremarkable at best. To be charitable, the Chinese cook might have had the night off, and the Banff Springs is so elegant you're willing to forgive the soggy egg rolls and questionable chow mein. There is a lesson here. When surrounded by cattle ranchers in Alberta, eat beef.

Otherwise the Banff Springs is a fine place to invest your strong Canadian dollars. With its labyrinthine hallways, period furniture, native stone exterior, eight hundred rooms, restaurants, reading alcoves, and diverse entertainments the Banff Springs harkens back to '05, when cars were banned from the park, guests arrived on the "Canadian" from Vancouver, and a walk along the Bow, a soak in the Cave and Basin, and a candlelight dinner on starched linen constituted a full day. Today there are fur shops that advertise in Japanese characters, various clothing stores, collectables, a video arcade, and a swimming pool in the basement.

Sunshine Village Inn, Box 1510, Sunshine Ski Area, Canada T0L 0C0, tel. (800) 661-1363. Amenities: 89 rooms, telephones, balconies, whirlpool, lounge, restaurants, ski-in ski-out, no TV. Terms: double $119 midseason.

Banff by night combines the best of the lower 48 ski resorts. Entertainment is balanced evenly between country swing and rock and roll. Try the Silver City for dancing or the Inns of Banff lounge for a lone guitarist playing Gordon Lightfoot's "Canadian Railroad Trilogy"—a predictable choice when you're surrounded by vertical peaks and century-old rail beds.

From Banff, Highway 93 follows the Bow River north to Sunshine Village. Elk graze through the forest beyond the snowbanks, the glaciated Rockies rise on all sides, and the sun shines through Bow mists. It takes half an hour to reach Sunshine's base parking lot and board the Bourgeau gondola. Built in 1980 and rising 1650 feet in 3 miles, the gondola replaced buses that once hauled skiers up a nailbiter of an access road. Locals recall that the ride up was more than half the fun of Sunshine—an heirloom horror story to frighten your grandkids.

Since 1932 when Jim Brewster, president of Banff's Brewster Transportation, skied into a CPR trail cabin, Sunshine has had a reputation as a snow sink. Brewster fell in love with the dry, light snow, leased the cabin, and the following year hosted ten paying skiers who had ridden Canadian Pacific Railroad's "The Canadian" from Vancouver. In the thirties Sunshine guests were required to skin up from Highway 93. The 8-mile slog turned back all but the hardiest, and it was five years before snow cats began to transport guests to the lodge. Even then skiers were required to hike for their turns. Sunshine's first rope tow was installed in 1945, and the buses started to run in '60.

Today Sunshine is owned by the Scurfields of Calgary; the old lodge is still standing and is now complemented by the Sunshine Inn. Other facilities have expanded to include restaurants, bars, a ski school and ten lifts divided among the gondola, one quad, one triple and five doubles. Dave Irwin, Sunshine's marketing manager, was one of Canada's original Crazy Canook's downhill team and as such is still one of Lookout Mountain's strongest skiers. The best way to reach Lookout's 8954-foot summit is to take the Angel Express quad and transfer to the Great Divide double chair.

Starting down the expert-rated North Divide, the snow is firm and the bumps small. Here you can carve from edge to edge back and forth across the Continental Divide and ignore the full chair. From the summit you can see Mt. Assiniboine, which resembles an 11,870-foot black spike to the south. To the north is 9200-foot Goats Eye Mountain, where three scheduled lifts will open up an enormous amount of new terrain.

No wonder early skiers slogged 8 miles in or trusted their lives to a loaded bus on icy roads, for with fresh snow and holding high pressure the views are surpassed only by the skiing. By following North Divide down to XTC to the expert Little Angel (with bumps as big as Buicks, this is no angel) to Tee Pee Town (another euphemism for bump till you crumple), you will eventually reach the Tee Pee Town double. Unloading off Tee Pee Town, turn right and start down South Divide's perfect pitch, which leads down a steep, smooth face back to the Great Divide double.

With the winter sun arcing across Sunshine's sixty-one runs, Sunshine's lopsided 20 percent beginner, 60 percent intermediate, and 20 percent advanced terrain is weighted toward groomed rollers, tilted plateaus, and moderate bump runs. On both sides of this norm beginners will find gentle grades like Rock Isle Road, which drops to the Strawberry triple chair;

while experts can take a beating on Percy's Pitch, locally known as the Oh, Shit! Pitch. The Standish double chair accesses wonderful intermediate skiing. Jerry's Run is groomed occasionally, and off the top you can ski The Virgin's big bumps.

If you're not a hardcore bump skier, Sunshine offers miles of groomed intermediate terrain with names like Red 90, Angel's First, and Boutry's Bowl. When long shadows begin to fill the gullies, take care picking your last run. A classic last ditch is the Donkey's Tail, a moderately steep, bumped pitch that drops toward the WD Saloon.

Dropping toward the faint sound of country and western, Sunshine's lifts are closing, and the social scene is gathering steam. The problem is, if you plan on returning to Banff for the night, you'd better ignore Sunshine's Trapper Bill's Lounge and WD Saloon. The party gets rolling at 3 P.M. with happy hour and continues until well past when the Bourgeau gondola has shut down for the night. The alternative to riding the gondola

---

Château Lake Louise, Lake Louise, Alberta, Canada TOL 0C0, tel. (800) 828-7447. Amenities: 520 rooms, telephones, TV, whirlpool, sauna, swimming pool, lounges, restaurants, charming history and location. Terms: double $105 midseason.

Post Hotel, Box 69, Lake Louise, Alberta, Canada TOL 0C0, tel. (800) 661-1586. Amenities: 95 rooms, telephones, TV, whirlpool, sauna, swimming pool, lounges, restaurants. Terms: double $115 midseason.

Deer Lodge, Box 100, Lake Louise, Alberta, Canada TOL 0C0, tel. (800) 661-1595. Amenities: 73 rooms, balconies, TV, sauna, restaurant, lounge. Terms: midseason double $65.

★

---

down is skiing the old bus road (Bourgeau Express) out. Officially the road run closes before dark. The gondola runs until five-thirty weekdays, ten-thirty weekends, after which Sunshine is effectively isolated. That's the way Sunshine's guests like it, for its inn offers the Rockies' only on-hill accommodations, and its ninety rooms are usually reserved months in advance.

After a dinner in the Eagle's Nest Dining Room, drift over to Trapper Bill's Lounge, where the Sunshine Ski School puts on an evening skit. What the instructors lack in polish they make up for with nonstop puns, jokes, dancing, and songs—most with a distinctly Canadian flavor. It's fast and loose, and afterward the crowd and instructors adjourn to the Sunshine Inn's Chimney Corner Lounge.

An imporant advantage to overnighting in Sunshine is its slope-side access to the lifts. If you're lucky enough to get snowed in, first light reveals empty chairs and untracked runs. Luck doesn't always run to those extremes, but staying next to the lifts gives you a jump on the crowds that arrive by gondola. At Sunshine it's easy to fall into a routine. Start by hitting the Standish chair as soon as it opens at 8:30 A.M. and take two runs before breakfast. Afterward jump on the Angel quad to the Great Divide face and ski until lunch. Linger over lunch, then ski until the lifts close. Hit the hot tub, stretch out or order a Labatts at the Saloon, catch dinner at the Inn, take a walk or read or ponder the weather report and pray for snow. After three days on Sunshine's 3500-foot vertical, you'll either drop by the personnel office and apply for a job or call the front desk and make reservations for next winter.

Built in 1890, Château Lake Louise originally served as a base for climbing expeditions into Alberta's western peaks. With the northeast face of Mt. Victoria towering above the Château's nine stories and a glacial lake stretching away from its rear veranda, the Château seems somehow out of place. At first glance its twin turrets and provincial façade rightfully belong to the French countryside. If architectural styles were the exclusive domain of the country of origin, the Château should rise in a Monet landscape of vineyards, herders' huts, and horse-drawn hay wagons. In Alberta it stands in marked contrast to the forested cliffs and hanging blue glaciers. That's not to say it isn't beautiful, for like the Greek Parthenon's skewed columns, the Château is an optical illusion, a trick of perspective that encourages busloads of tourists to expose frame after frame of Kodacolor—just to make sure they get it right.

Remodeled for the Olympics, the Château still honors the Canadian Pacific Railroad's original intent of a luxurious oasis surrounded by untracked wilderness. Though development has occurred, the Château towers above the surrounding lodges, restaurants, and shoppers' mall. If ski boots have replaced side-button shoes in the lobby and horse-drawn sleighs no longer transport guests, the Château's 510 rooms, basement steambath and swimming pool, Victoria Room Restaurant and lounges, dog sled and Nordic trails, figure skating and hockey recall an earlier age when the nation ran on rails and skiers were a mad group of adventurers who turned by dragging stout poles in the snow.

Though the Château is the most famous of Lake Louise's lodges, the village of Lake Louise has grown rapidly since '84, when the ski area invested $4 million in snowmaking. After another $60 million in local development during the past four years, today the village of Lake Louise contains eight hotels and eleven hundred rooms, eleven lounges and rock-and-roll bars and a fifteen-store shopping mall.

Summer is Banff National Park's major season but that doesn't discount Lake Louise's half-million skier days. Half a million is sufficiently major, until you factor in Louise's 11 square miles of terrain, 3250-foot vertical drop, forty-four marked runs, nine lifts (including two new high-speed quads) and 185 inches of natural snow. The point is, you can ski Louise and never stand in line. In fact, Louise is isolated enough (115 miles and two hours from Calgary and 40 miles and roughly forty-five minutes from Banff) that if you encounter crowds, it'll likely be at Christmas and Easter and then only on the most popular chairs and runs.

An absence of crowding was true before the installation of the Friendly Giant and Heaven's Above high-speed quads, but these chairs have boosted mountain capacity by an unbelievable 65 percent. Rising from the Whiskey Jack base area to midway up Whitehorn Mountain, the Friendly Giant connects with Heaven's Above to the south-face ridge. Chair time used to consume half an hour. Since the winter of '89–'90, the two quads have dropped that to ten minutes—an unbelievable rate of climb, which will focus more traffic on the south face runs of Men's Downhill, Ladies Downhill, Eagle Flight, and Juniper. Taking the speed of these lifts into account, it's easy to get burned out before noon. Thus you should warm up on the Men's and Women's Downhill courses, then cool off by crossing the ridge into the Back Bowls or the Larch Area.

The views from Louise's south face are incredible. To the west across the Bow River, the Château is dwarfed by Mt. Victoria and the Canadian Rockies. Turning down the Men's Downhill, you cannot escape the vistas, nor would you want to, for Banff National Park's mountains, lakes, and rivers have a positive affect on your skiing, make you push harder on edges, challenge bigger bumps, and risk greater speeds on the empty faces.

The Summit Platter is a concession to Louise's occasional winds and accesses the expert runs of Sunset and Outer Limits as well as the upper Back Bowl's intermediate Boomerang and the expert Brown Shirt, Ridge Run, and Whitehorn One. If this sounds confusing, it actually isn't, for Louise is composed of three separate areas. Separated from the south face area by a gentle ridge, the Back Bowls' expert-rated Paradise Bowl, East Bowl, Raven, and Ptarmigan in turn sit across the valley from Larch area's intermediate Larch, Wolverine, and Bobcat.

What this means is, as soon as the lifts open you can catch the quads to the top, ski the south face runs, then as soon as the crowds begin to form drop into Paradise Bowl, which combines a perfect fall line with alternating bumps, steep faces, and crud. Then, riding the Paradise chair back to the ridge, you can follow a tight traverse into the high and open East Bowl, which merges into Raven and Ptarmigan. Ski one or the other to the bottom, cross the valley to the Larch chair, and a few minutes later you're at the top of Larch run.

One way to get all this sorted out is to take a free guided tour with one of Lake Louise's "Friends of Louise." These local volunteer hosts and hostesses can show you the best terrain for your ability as well as give you a history of the area, what's happening with local entertainment, and generally offer an insider's view. The "Friends" is a great deal, as is Louise's learn-to-ski package, or group lesson, for $14—and if you don't learn you don't pay.

If there's a problem with Louise it's not terrain, lifts, the Whiskey Jack or Temple Lodge mountain facilities. It's snow. With an average of 185 inches, Louise can't depend on east divide dumps. Thus the south face snowmaking, which covers 80 percent of the available terrain, is expensive insurance against Alberta's periodic droughts. On a good year Louise opens by mid-November and closes May 4. February is the most dependable month, with March close behind.

If the United States tends to regard Canada as a close cousin, different in name only, the Canadians might disagree. Calgary proved that Albertans are a well-adjusted bunch who know how to organize an Olympics, but there's more to this inland province than hockey, Nordic jumping, bobsledding and figure

---

For snow report, hotel and flight information call Alberta Tourism at (800) 661-8888. To book hotels in Banff, Banff Central Reservations, for lodging (800) 661-1676 Box 1628, Banff, Alberta, Canada T0L 0C0

★

skating. Start with the Rockies, add snow, a bunch of lifts, great restaurants, clean hotels, and incredible views, and the gold medals start to pale in comparison.

REST AND RECUPERATION

If you have time, try to see Calgary's **Zoo** which is the second largest in Canada, the **Glenbow Museum for Canadiana,** the **Tyrell Museum of Paleontology,** the **Heritage Park,** and **Canada Olympic Park** with its 90-meter jump and bobsled run.

Downtown Calgary's commercial district is serviced from outlying districts by a light rail rapid transit system. The different shops are connected by enclosed elevated walkways and a downtown pedestrian mall.

Try the **Paliser, Westin Hotel,** or other downtown hotels where a car is not necessary. Lunch at the **Cadillac Cafe,** a '60s motif with a pleasant campy atmosphere. For dinner try **Reiko's Restaurant and Sushi Bar** on 11th Avenue S.W. or **DeFilippis Italian** on 12th Avenue S.W. Try to catch a **Calgary Flames** hockey game in the Saddledome as well as any training at the **Olympic Oval** or COP.

Take in **Fort Calgary** on 9th Avenue S.E., with its audiovisual history of Calgary's early pioneers, and **Heritage Park,** which features original nineteen-century buildings relocated from around western Canada. Calgary's **Chinatown** is on 3rd Avenue S.E. and its hottest nightclubs are located on 11th Avenue—the infamous Electric Avenue—and though "Abandon All Hope Ye Who Enter Here" is a bit strong for Friday and Saturday night's frantic celebrations, it's close. For information, rates, brochures and city maps call Calgary's Tourism and Convention Bureau, tel. (403) 263-8510.

When you stay in Banff do not miss the **Cave and Basin Hot Springs** on Cave Avenue across the Bow River from downtown Banff or the **Upper Hot Springs Pool** on Mountain Avenue, also across the Bow. These two springs played a major part in the formation of Banff National Park and the construction of the Banff

Springs Hotel. If you don't stay at either, the **Banff Springs Hotel** and the **Château Lake Louise** are worth walking through. Calgary, Banff, and Lake Louise all have shopping, entertainment, and fine dining. Also, since the ski areas sit in the **national park,** watch for the elk, mule deer, and bighorn sheep that frequent the roadside. The **Cave and Basin Marsh** is home to ducks, mink, and dippers.

Banff also has a wonderful city library on Bear Street with rich historical archives as well as ongoing displays; and if you want a feel for a bygone era, drift down to the **Canadian Pacific Train Station** and watch "The Canadian" arrive. Or visit the **Whyte Museum** on Bear Street (762-2291), the **Park Museum** (762-3324), or the **Natural History Museum** (762-4747).

Lake Louise offers excellent Nordic track and sleigh rides as well as the amenities of the Château. For brochures and further information contact Banff/Lake Louise Chamber of Commerce, Box 1298, Banff, Alberta TOL OCO, tel. (403) 762-3777.

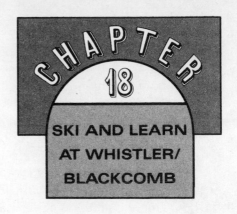

CHAPTER 18

SKI AND LEARN AT WHISTLER/ BLACKCOMB

I HAD BEEN ON THE ROAD SINCE EARLY MORNING, trying to make Whistler/Blackcomb before 10 P.M., and only intended to stop by my sister Janice's long enough to give the kids a squeeze and grab a cup of coffee. But one hour turns to three, and I had to call the Château Whistler to say I wouldn't be checking in until past midnight.

"Whistler/Blackcomb, boy are you lucky!" my sixteen-year-old nephew Justin says, shaking his head. "Did you know that Blackcomb has the highest lift-serviced vertical in North America? 5280 feet! A vertical mile!"

I admit I didn't.

"Did you know that Whistler has the second highest at 5020?"

I confess I wasn't aware of that.

"They have twenty-eight lifts and 214 marked trails, including Saudan Couloir!"

His mother once told me Justin would rather ski than eat

(and eating's right up there). Now he exclaims, "Whistler/ Blackcomb! I'd give anything to ski there!" Which is how he ends up riding shotgun to Blackcomb. Admittedly one ski trip can't make up for ten years, but it's a start.

To get to Whistler/Blackcomb from Vancouver you take Trans-Canada Highway 1 through the city to Highway 99 through Squamish and Garibaldi. British Columbia calls this the "Sea to Sky Highway," and for obvious reasons the drive is best enjoyed during the day; but with a full moon reflecting off the fjords there is an undeniable magic to the night, a promise of labyrinthine ski runs and enormous vertical and Pacific storms that thunder ashore in devastating left-right combinations.

Tonight we follow the wind-whipped shore until the road

Vancouver is the nearest major airport and is serviced by direct flights from Seattle on Canadian Air, (800) 426-7000, Air Canada, (800) 776-3000, Alaska Airlines, (800) 426-0333, United, (800) 241-6522, and Continental, (800) 231-0856; and from New York on Northwest, (800) 225-2525, Delta, (800) 453-9417, United, (800) 241-6522, and American, (800) 433-7300.

B.C. Rail leaves daily from the B.C. rail station at 7:45 and arrives at the Whistler station at 10:09; it departs Whistler at 6:05 P.M. and arrives in North Vancouver at 8:35 P.M. Cost is $11.50 one way for adults.

Maverick bus lines departs seven times daily from the Vancouver bus depot; connections from Vancouver Airport to the depot or major Vancouver hotels can be made on the Airport Express. From December 23 to April 20 Perimeter Transportation Ltd. travels from Vancouver Airport to Whistler and back. Cost is $22 one way, $11 for children. Reservations are required; tel. (800) 663-4265.

★

starts to climb away from the ocean up into the forested foot-hills. Over the years 99 has weathered rain, ice, and the abuse of a million cars, and tonight we negotiate a ragged ribbon of asphalt out of Squamish, where huge boulders record sudden thunderous releases from the cliffs above.

It is past midnight when we start up a short grade to the Château Whistler. From a distance the $50 million Château resembles a lighted tiara. With its gable roof and majestic cen-

---

Château Whistler Resort, Box 100, Whistler, British Columbia VON 1BO, tel. (800) 828-7447. Amenities: full-service hotel, 343 units, ski-in ski-out to lifts, combination baths, cable TV, minibars, health club facilities, indoor and outdoor heated pools, whirlpools, small pets okay. Terms: $195–$215 double.

Whistler Village Inns, P.O. Box 970, Whistler, British Columbia VON 1BO, tel. (800) 663-6418. Amenities: outdoor swimming pool, sauna, Jacuzzi, 2 queen-sized beds, TV and telephones, laundry facilities, Keg Restaurant upstairs, ski in. Terms: $130 double.

The Blackcomb, 4220 Gateway Drive, Box 400, Whistler, British Columbia VON 1BO, tel. (604) 932-4155. Amenities: village center, ski-in ski-out, fireplaces, queen beds, TV, restaurant and lounge, indoor pool, whirlpool, sauna, and underground parking. Terms: $105–$200.

Nancy Greene Lodge, 4154 Village Green, Box 280, Whistler, British Columbia VON 1BO, tel. (604) 932-2211. Amenities: full-service hotel, queen and king beds, studios and lofts with kitchenettes and fireplaces, satellite TV, minibars, pool, steam room, restaurants, lounge, parking. Terms: $89–$149 double.

For more information and reservations: The Whistler Resort Association, P.O. Box 1400, Whistler, B.C. VON 1BO, tel. (800) 634- 9622.

★

tral tower, it is the first grand château hotel built in Canada in more than a century and the first hotel of any kind built by Canadian Pacific Hotels in thirty-five years. Like the Château Lake Louise, the Banff Springs, and the Jasper Park Lodge, the Château Whistler is a latter-day monument to that bygone era when Canada rode on rails instead of radial tires, when the word "service" wasn't automatically followed by "station," and when white linen, chandeliers, ballrooms, fine dining, and bellmen who discreetly delivered your bags to the room were the rule rather than the exception.

For Justin's sake I try not to gawk at the Château lobby's 40-foot ceiling with its faux art leaf motifs or the supporting columns of Squamish rock or the green slate floor. Instead I feign a jaded sophistication, take in the beautiful Mennonite carpets, the lobby's hickory/pecan paneling and enormous stone fireplaces, and cross to reception.

Our third-floor room overlooks the Blackcomb resort core, where a lone couple strolls through empty pedestrian malls. With oak furniture, pastel walls, and framed art of wildflowers and Indians, the room evokes rural British Columbia. CNN is on the tube, and Justin is inspecting a packet of information the receptionist handed me. I know I should be organizing my gear, but after sixteen hours on the road, I can't keep my eyes open.

"Do you stay in places like this often?" he asks, ignoring the TV.

"As often as I can," I yawn, which is the truth. What I neglect to add is the Château Whistler is in a class by itself, and for every night I pass in its palatial splendor, I will pay penance on sagging mattresses, garish flowered bedspreads, and art that runs to velvet paintings of bugling elk.

The last thing I hear before I fall asleep is Justin talking about "343 rooms, two restaurants, a health and fitness center, and indoor outdoor pools. Uncle, what do yo think about an early morning swim? Uncle . . . ?"

The alarm goes off at 7 A.M. During the night the high pressure intensifies, the temperature plummets and the morning dawns clear and very cold. At 9 A.M. we meet Ben Tice in the office of Ski Esprit. Tice works as supervisor for Ski Esprit, stands six foot one, weighs 175 pounds, is clean-cut—in short an ex-ski bum trying to go straight as an instructor. So far the cure isn't 100 percent for he admittedly wouldn't trade a powder day on Blackcomb for an insider's stock tip.

Operated jointly by the Whistler and Blackcomb ski schools, Ski Esprit's **Directed Skiing** combines ski instruction with a guided tour of both mountains. The program features three days of skiing for $125 (price does not include lift pass) with an optional fourth day for $25. Also included are race training, a weekly race, video analysis, on-mountain brunch, awards, a photograph, and après ski activities. Programs begin each Monday; preregistration is recommended, with suggested minimum age thirteen years old. Tel. (604) 932-3400.

Now he leads us out to Blackcomb's Fitzsimmons triple where the temperature hangs at five above. Blackcomb's thirteen lifts include four express quads, five triples, and one lone double that service eighty-five runs. With roughly 20 percent expert, 55 percent intermediate, and 25 percent beginner terrain and annual snowfall of 450 inches, Blackcomb's broad fall lines and rocket quads complement Whistler's classic forest trails and double chairs. Despite a joint Whistler/Blackcomb marketing effort, these two resorts face each other across a wide valley and contest every skier day. When one throws a triple lift, the other counters with a quad. In the past decade the competition has produced new chairs, new runs, and steadily improving skier numbers.

On the chair, Tice explains that Ski Esprit complements the Whistler and Blackcomb ski schools. No matter how innovative an instructor might be, most skiers only hear the "school" in ski school. If everyone wants to improve, everyone hates the repetition, imitation, and patience it requires to stand around while someone repeatedly crosses their tips. Time is burning, lift tickets aren't cheap, and skiers know you learn to ski by skiing.

Sandy Millar, director of Ski Esprit, points out that "by combining the role of instructor and guide, you can take four days

of lessons for $150 Canadian and still get an enormous amount of skiing. When people find a run they like, they tend to yo-yo up and down it. We know destination skiers are not going to find a quarter of the available skiing. Over three days an instructor can show them a variety of terrain and, in all honesty, an hour lesson isn't enough time to focus on a problem and determine which teaching method works best."

At some point I expect Tice to diagram the beginning, middle, and end of a turn in the snow. Instead he skates down Merlin toward the Wizard express quad. I see him glance over his shoulder at us and figure we'll get his critique on the chair. I'm somewhat relieved when he zips his jacket and explains how at 7 A.M. a physical therapist was icing his lower back. It seems Tice blew the landing on a big air jump and felt something give. Even with a brace his lower back is very tender.

"Would you mind staying out of the really big bumps today?" he inquires, gently straightening in the chair.

"No, that would be no problem," Justin and I quickly agree.

The Wizard quad rises 1857 feet to the base of the Solar Coaster Express, which in turn climbs another 2044 feet to the Rendezvous Restaurant. On top the temperature is holding at eight above and Tice asks if we 'd like to warm up.

"If it's all the same to you guys," Justin interrupts, "I'd prefer to ski." Bold words for a young man who can't stop gritting his teeth. We follow Tice down the wide, groomed Springboard to a cat track, which connects to the equally flawless Snoozer and the Solar Coaster quad.

Watching Justin ski, I note his style resembles an F-15 going supersonic. Once he reaches terminal velocity he stops turning. Keeping track of him in my peripheral vision, I feel like I've strayed into a restricted airspace and Justin's been scrambled for a flyby. That doesn't excuse my own flaws. When I'm cold, stiff, and skiing for an instructor, my bad habits appear with a startling ferocity. I skid my tails, neglect to stand up tall, bend at the waist instead of the knees . . . the list is endless and embarrassing. Loading the Solar Coaster, I figure Tice is going to lower the boom. Instead he reminisces about a summer spent teaching in Queenstown, New Zealand. A few minutes later we're back at the Rendezvous Restaurant, stumbling on numb feet toward the coffee machine.

Unlike many U.S. resorts that boomed and busted on mining before discovering the alchemy in chair lifts that turns winter snow into white gold, Whistler/Blackcomb's development was far less haphazard. The Whistler Valley's earliest inhabitants were the Salish Indians, followed by cattlemen, loggers, and more recently Alex Phillip's famous Rainbow Lodge fishing camp. In response to the '60 Winter Olympics in Squaw Valley, the Canadian Olympic Committee started to look for a suitable site in B.C. for the '68 games. At that time Whistler (which was called London Mountain) showed the best potential for development. Base on that estimate, a group of Vancouver businessmen formed the Garibaldi Lift Company, which was headed by Franz Wilhelmsen, a Norwegian skier who had immigrated to Canada after World War Two. The Garibaldi Lift Company subsequently hired Willy Schaeffler, who had worked as a consultant for the Squaw Valley Olympics. After cutting trails and installing the four-person gondola, the Red chair, and two T-bars, Whistler opened for business in February of 1966.

It was almost fourteen years before Whistler's companion Blackcomb solved financial and permit restrictions to open. In the early '70s, Al Raines an ex-Canadian National Ski Team coach and his wife, Nancy Greene Raines, former Olympic and World Cup Champion, had petitioned the province to build a ski resort at nearby Powder Mountain. Though the petition was denied, the provincial government subsequently commissioned Raines to prepare a study for a future ski area in the Whistler Valley. Raines picked the site of the present-day Blackcomb and as a result was named Provincial Coordinator for Ski Resort Development. In the years that followed, Blackcomb struggled with recession and changing national governments until 1978, when Fortress Mountain Resorts Ltd. (a subsidiary of Aspen Ski Corporation) was picked to build the resort. Blackcomb officially opened in December of 1980.

In the time since, both areas have weathered major recessions. As a result, Whistler/Blackcomb lacks the sprawling multimillion dollar row houses and condominium chock-a-blocks that mar other resorts. In a nod to increased demand, the municipality recently opened up tracts in the Village North area, which will effectively double the size of the Whistler Village core. In the hope of avoiding resort sprawl, Village North will be developed under a master plan that not only specifies height, size, and location, but structure usage as well.

If Whistler has managed to resist the blandishments of quick-buck developers, the local advertising is heavy on smiling real estate agents gesturing to golf courses and prime lots—a bad sign if this resort hopes to preserve its character into the coming century.

Considering the amount of combined skiable terrain between the two resorts, Whistler/Blackcomb's 1.2 million skier days is a relatively small number. From the Rendezvous, Tice leads us along the Expressway Traverse out to the 7th Heaven Express and Blackcomb's 7494-foot summit, where the frigid air shrinks distances and peaks in the Garibaldi Provincial Park rise in our faces.

Dominating the small summit, Horstman's Hut is named after Harry Horstman, a local gold prospector who was equally famous for his scattered mining claims and tall tales. To the south, across an intervening valley, Whistler's major runs appear as alleys cut in the fir and spruce forests, restaurants are distant specks, and lifts shrink to black threads rising above vast snowfields.

Tice maintains a brisk pace, and we follow a cat track down to the groomed intermediate Cloud Nine, which leads back to the 7th Heaven quad. So far we've only seen Tice the knowledgeable guide. I'm still waiting for Tice the critical instructor to slam our technique and now wonder if we're that good or that bad. On our second trip to the top we ski off the north side down Horstman's Glacier to the Showcase T-bar. Skating away for the lift, I note that people are climbing across to a chute that enters the Blackcomb Glacier.

The Blackcomb Glacier fills an enormous bowl that lies within the ski area boundaries. Accessed off both the 7th Heaven Express and the Showcase T-bar, it gets a fair amount of traffic—especially after a powder storm, when conditions vary from breakable crust to deep powder. Losing a ski can mean trouble, whiteouts are common, and there are tricky sections on the traverse out. Tice points out that your first run should be with someone who knows the terrain.

Saudan Couloir is also accessed off the summit. At forty-five degrees this double black diamond face is reputed to be the steepest named run in North America. Even more incredible than its reputation is an annual race through its junkyard bumps to the Blackcomb base. Before you consider jumping into Saudan Couloir, or the other double black diamond runs, such as Cougar, Climax, Sylvain, and Pakalolo in Blackcomb's Secret Bowl complex, you best be as limber as Gumby and as ballsy as Rambo, for a single crossed tip here can land you in traction. Or worse.

Secret Bowl is only part of the reason moviemakers Warren Miller and Greg Stump are drawn to Whistler/Blackcomb. Besides the enormous amount of terrain offered by these two linked mountains, the annual 35 feet of snow, and breathtaking steeps, W/B skiers make excellent extras.

Skirting Saudan Couloir, we instead ski the single diamond Swiss Cheese. We're not the first nor only ones skiing this mixed crust-and-powder face. Riding his tails, Justin crashes, collects himself, then cautiously traverses from side to side. I ski it but not brilliantly, and once we reach the flats below Tice demonstrates a maneuver he promises will make us sparkle in the junk. During the last hour we ski the Jersey Cream express runs, the black bumps of Stair Case, the cruiser Hooker, followed by a last run down Springboard to Lower Gear Jammer and finally back to the château.

Justin steps into his swimsuit and bolts for the pool while I cross to the Whistler Village for a T-shirt shop. The village's stone façades, pedestrian walkways, alleys, and archways remind me of a French mountain village. With a light snow beginning to fall, I pass the Citta Bistro, where the après crowd is contemplating their cocktails. The Keg sounds full, the Longhorn is rocking, I've been told to try Buffalo Bill's, the Savage Beagle, and Tommy Africa's with its equatorial ambiance, disco light shows and go-go girls. It sounds like more adventure than I can stand, so I drift over to Buffalo Bill's basement bar for a quick beer. Back on Village Square, Japanese couples are snapping photos of each other in front of Chez Joel's sidewalk ice sculpture of a valentine's heart. A couple asks me if I'd mind and hands me a point-and-shoot Nikon.

Because of a favorable yen/dollar exchange rate and direct flights to Vancouver, Whistler/Blackcomb has been discovered by the Japanese. In 1990 their numbers grew by 50 percent, which places them just behind the Americans in terms of total destination skier visits. With the yen at the highest point in history, the Japanese arguably exert more economic clout. On the mountain they wear expensive (but tasteful) suits, ski Rossignol skis and Nordica boots and stick together. You rarely see them yodeling through deep powder or popping helicopters beneath loaded chair lifts. But then, you rarely see a Japanese beginner either.

Even with the favorable exchange rate, the Whistler/Blackcomb logo does not come cheap. I watch a Japanese couple

---

Other recommended restaurants are the **Rim Rock Cafe and Oyster Bar,** 932-5565, to which we were unable to get reservations. We did try the **Trattoria di Umberto,** 932-5858, (which took us without reservations) for its excellent Italian cuisine. **Christines,** 932-3141 (ext. 269), is a full-service restaurant at the Rendezvous on Blackcomb Mountain that serves grilled swordfish and passion fruit, halibut cheeks in light curry sauce, and spectacular views. We tried **The Keg,** 932-5151, for serviceable steak and chicken. There's the château's **La Fiesta** for Spanish hot rock cooking. Small restaurants include **Myrtles,** 932-5211 (ext. 106), **Cafe Presto,** 932-6009, **Hattro's Cafe,** 932-8345, and the **Whistler Cookie Company,** 932-2962.

★

spread a dozen sweatshirts on the counter. The total comes to $665!

"You ship?" the man politely inquires.

The shop owner quickly admits he does. Or if he doesn't, he just started to.

The ascendancy of Japanese visitors has not been lost on Whistler merchandisers. The village supports two Japanese restaurants—Sushi Village and Teppan Village—Japanese signs and Japanese interpreters.

For dinner I meet Bill and Stephani Murra at Araxis, Whistler's gourmet restaurant on Village Square. Bill works for the Whistler Resort Association, which coordinates marketing for Whistler businesses. The association's efforts must have worked: surveys show Whistler is the fastest growing resort in North America. The food at Araxis is excellent, the service is attentive without being intrusive, and as we linger over coffee the waiter asks if we'd care for dessert. When we decline, he appears disappointed and returns a short time later to politely inquire if we're positive we wouldn't like dessert. The chef's hazelnut meringue and strawberry dessert is very special and, well . . . we really should try it.

We discover it's better than simply "very special" and afterward tip his quiet persistence. Outside I bid Bill and Stephani good night and start through the falling snow. Flakes whisper across my jacket, and I stop by the Savage Beagle, a disco/video/dance bar where tanned couples boogie to a DJ's smooth exhortations while Glen Plake and Scott Schmidt leap off cliffs in "Blizzard of AAAhs." From the Beagle, after a search, I find Tommy Africa's in the basement off Village Square. Aside from myself, a bartender, and a bouncer, it's deserted. I'm told Africa's attracts a late crowd and to come back later when the disco dancers, smoke shows, and fetid jungle atmosphere are running under a full head of steam.

The following morning three inches of new snow cover the ground when we meet Tice at Whistler's Express gondola. This five-person lift climbs a whopping 3796 feet to the Round House Station, from where we take the intermediate Porcupine down to the Little Red chair. Snow is falling at half an inch an hour, and we arc beneath the gray cloud base, then ride the short double chair to a ridge above the Round House. Here we have a choice of skiing the broad, popular Green Acres down to the Green quad, or the expert Chunky's Choice or G.S. down to the Blue double chair, which also returns to the Round House.

By now we've fallen into a rhythm. Ski a little, stop and work on technique. Ski some more, work on technique, then attempt something more difficult. In two days Justin's skiing has shown marked improvement and on top of Peak chair we encounter Sandy Millar, the director of Ski Esprit, who has time for one run. The majority of terrain off Whistler Mountain's bare summit is expert and with a skiff of snow and white light we try to avoid the sheer bumps and open snowfields.

Millar is an excellent skier. Bumps, jumps, or junk, he flows with the terrain, and we traverse around the intermediate back side of the Whistler Glacier and down onto the cornice leading into Harmony Bowl. Looking over the edge, it's a 10-foot drop to the snow, which we decline. Instead we follow the ridge down to a broad snowfield that leads to Burnt Stew Bowl. Here the snow is dense and windblown, and you must jump turn to ski it. I try to hang with the two instructors but get rocked back and bail out.

Even the unflappable Tice has a little trouble, and after watching him get launched over his tips, we relax and drop down to the Burnt Stew traverse. From here we ride the Blue chair through the trees, where a lone skier on Dad's Run drops from one crunching bump to the next.

Millar checks his watch and votes for one last Franz's Run to the bottom. Named after Franz Wilhelmsen, the first president of the Garibaldi Lift Company, this serpentine run encounters a variety of terrain. From groomed faces to short flats, sweeping curves, and abrupt transitions from bumps to powder to glades along the sides, Franz's is a chameleon that never runs out of surprises. In fact it's arguably the best run on either mountain, and if it weren't for the languid pace of the Whistler Creek gondola or the slightly faster Olive chair (which are scheduled for replacement), it would be packed.

Back on top I ask about bumps. Though Tice's back is sore, he leads us down Raven. With big but tameable moguls and a fall line that leads to Ptarmigan and the Black chair, Raven is empty, and we match a rhythm next to the trees then hit Lower Whiskey Jack and the lower right and left Ego Bowls. Conditions continue to improve, and by three-thirty my legs are running on empty when Ben stops at the Whistler base.

"That's it, boys," he admits, then adds, "You guys are skiing pretty well," which may be a big lie but endears him to us anyway. And with promises to stay in touch we say good-bye and thanks. Tice shoulders his skis and starts down the Whistler Stroll as the snow drifts out of the darkening sky and the crowd closes around him.

We had planned to ski until four the following day, then head back to Seattle. The seven-hour drive would put us there after midnight, and I let Justin choose between Whistler and Blackcomb. That night over dinner at the Trattoria, he admits he likes Blackcomb's Cruiser, Choker, Springboard, and Secret Bowl. He likes the express quads and the grooming. But he also likes Whistler's Franz's Run, Burnt Stew Basin, and the myriad of runs off the Blue, Green and Black chairs. He likes the cappuccino bars at the Rendezvous and Round House, the cold snow and brilliant vistas, and, if it turns out to be a tough call, this is Whistler/Blackcomb's strength: two ski areas facing each other across the Fitzsimmons Valley—not a mirror image, but more like a dovetail joint: what one lacks the other supplies. And in a final effort to see it all and ski it all before the drive back to Seattle we decide to ski Whistler in the morning and Blackcomb in the afternoon.

The following morning, with fresh snow swirling around our boots, we ski Franz's Meadow above the Little Red chair where the bumps push beneath our edges and the powder spills past our shins. We do Raven and Seppo's beneath the Black chair. We ski without stopping, Justin often taking the easier sections but never slowing down, and it is one o'clock when we switch to Blackcomb. We make it as far as the top of the Wizard express, where a lift operator mentions that the forecast is calling for 2 feet of snow in the next twenty-four hours. "I just heard that Seattle is expecting a foot," he adds.

I scoff at the notion. Snow predictions are less accurate than tarot cards. A foot in Seattle would set a century record! At that point we're hit with a dense flurry. But if it is true, I should extend our reservations and unpack the Gore-Tex. If it is true, the next three days will be incredible. Another flurry hits us, and for once I think like an uncle. I wonder if I should expose Justin to the hedonistic joys of deep powder at the expense of more unexcused days from school. He has a final he shouldn't miss and a soccer game . . . I tell myself that forsaking one of North America's top two resorts during the biggest storm in a century take maturity, balance, and strength.

Six hours later we're down to 10 miles an hour, and the flakes are falling in an iridescent veil. It's obvious we made the wrong decision.

"I wonder what it's doing in Whistler," Justin says from the darkened right seat.

REST AND RECUPERATION

Aside from extensive opportunities for shopping, dining, swimming, and pumping iron, at Whistler you can also go heli-skiing with **Whistler Heli-skiing.** Three glacier runs for a total of 7000–10,000 vertical feet will cost $280 Canadian, which includes a heliguide, transportation to the helipad, and lunch, which is a great deal and well worth the day off the mountain. For information Whistler Heli-Skiing, Box 368, Whistler, British Columbia VON 1BO, tel. (603) 932-4105. For something different, the **Whistler Center for Business and the Arts** offers week-long seminars in management development. Running from mid-February to mid-March, the seminars cover such topics as "The Marketing Game" and "Communicating with Impact." Cost is $375 Canadian, which includes an open reception, instruction, course materials, and a continental breakfast. Course hours are 7:30 to 9:00 A.M. and 5:00 to 6:30 P.M., leaving ample time for skiing.

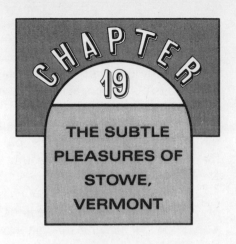

CHAPTER 19

THE SUBTLE PLEASURES OF STOWE, VERMONT

T IS JANUARY 18 AND I AM STANDING IN THE woods on Stowe's Mt. Mansfield. Below me an unmarked glade drops 400 vertical feet to a narrow exit through a brushy wall. It's obvious this secret run was not created by natural forces. Fire does not discriminate between deadfall and healthy birches. Saplings do not spontaneously wither down a perfect fall line. The careful spacing shows the hand of a conscientious gardener—someone who had a vision of this place in winter, who knew how quickly a ski turned and who counted both as sufficient reward for the silent hours spent sweating in Vermont's summer humidity.

Writer, builder, Wintermeister skier and woodsy philosopher, K.B. is more than a little responsible for Mansfield's mirror side—its hidden, hand-cut runs. K.B. is not much interested in publicity. Nor does he care to attract busloads of skiers to Stowe.

Even fifty years ago powder runs were closely guarded secrets. Skiers are instinctively drawn to natural glades—areas

either cleared by lightning or disease where the snow lies undisturbed by the wind and sun. Lightning fires, however, do
not always burn two trees and leave a third nor seek the best
north faces.

"It's volunteer forest management," K.B. admits nodding to
the mature birches. "When people hear about clearing trails,
they think of chain saws blasting 20-foot paths through the
woods. In fact nothing is further from the truth. No one uses
anything bigger than small bow saws. And then they only remove enough for two or three lines."

Even so, publicizing this glade won't make anyone happy.
Not K.B. Not Mountain Manager Rich Wiseman and certainly
not Gary Kiedaisch, Stowe's general manager, who will be
rightfully concerned about the young, dumb, and innocent
blowing it in the woods.

So why forsake the West's open bowls for Stowe's bootleg
tree runs? Blame it on an enormous high that has skiers pray-
ing for the bounty of a single, violent blizzard. During the past
two months, winter storms have been shunted into British Columbia, Alberta and Saskatchewan only to descend on the east
coast like some meteorological apocalypse. When Wall Street
gets six inches, Stowe gets bombed. Try 9 feet in December

Stowe Winter Carnival, P.O. Box 1320, Stowe, Vermont
05672, tel. (800) 24-Stowe. Known as the "King of Winter
Carnivals," this is its sixteenth consecutive year and includes such diverse competitions as sled dog races and
the Wintermeister 15k cross-country, alpine giant slalom,
and 1000-meter speed skate. Scheduled for the second
week of January, the Winter Carnival also features a community church supper, a Tyrolean Night, snowboard competition, Stowe/Sugarbush challenge race, and the Pro-am
race.

★

alone. Then add Stowe's boisterous Winter Carnival, Delta and United's direct flights into Burlington, and the fact that you can have Stowe to yourself while other East Coast skiers are still smarting from the Christmas crowds.

For skiers Vermont's Route 100 serves as something of a road to OZ. As it meanders from south to north it passes the ski resorts of Haystack, Mt. Snow, Magic Mountain, Okemo Mountain, and Killington before turning into Stowe's main street. I'd only just arrived when J.R. introduced me to K.B. in Happletons. K.B. had just won the Stowe Winter Carnival's "Wintermeister"—a three-event race that includes a giant slalom, Nordic race, and a 1000-meter speed skate. When I inquired about local history, K.B. alluded to forest trails, and that's how I find myself in this glade.

Daily flights on United (reservations: 800-241-6522). Delta (reservations: 800-221-1212) and Continental (reservations: 800-525-0280) into Burlington. Fly/ski packages through Mt. Mansfield Resort, tel. (800) 252-4SKI. Vermont Transit from Burlington to Stowe; bus terminal, tel. (802) 253-7131.

Say "Stowe" and skiers get an image of the East's most beautiful, authentic and technically demanding area. Granted, it is the oldest ski resort in the east, and driving in from Burlington on Route 100, Stowe has a certain New England style. With its high-steepled church, clapboard houses, weathered storefronts, and single stoplight, Stowe has the look and feel of a New England village. Not so odd if the main industry is antiques, maple syrup, or hardwood logging; but Stowe has been a four-season resort for more than a half century and as such should bear a few scars from the typical boom/bust resort cycle.

And, truthfully, Stowe hasn't been totally spared that impact. With a good map you can still eat at McDonald's, and there are T-shirt shops, souvenirs, and condominiums, but you have to be focused to find them. What distinguishes Stowe is its covered pedestrian bridge, the surrounding hardwood forests, logging trucks rumbling down the main street, the pyramids of maple syrup tins in store windows, the Trapp Family Lodge Nordic trails, the Top Notch Spa, the small country inns and smaller restaurants nestled in the middle of the Green Mountains.

Trapp Family Lodge, Stowe, Vermont 05672, tel. (800) 826-7000. Owned by the Austrian Trapps of *The Sound of Music*, the lodge is surrounded by miles of groomed Nordic tracks. Amenities: 93 rooms, phone, television, game room, sauna, whirlpool, pool, 6 miles from slope. Terms: $235 for two people, breakfast and dinner included.

★

Stowe is famous for its inns, restaurants, and hospitality. Little wonder it's known as the "Ski capital of the East," for skiing dates back to 1902, when locals started experimenting with hand-bent slats. With chair lifts and cleared runs still thirty-five years in the future and little to do during snowy winter days, locals used to coast down white cow pastures. Then, in 1913, the Swedish Svedin brothers moved to Stowe and began to demonstrate the bent-legged telemark turn. Stowe's famous "Toll Road" was first skied in 1914, and twenty years before Sun Valley fixed chairs to a banana conveyor Stowe locals had already left tracks on Bruce's Trail, Tear Drop, and Hellbrook.

No one knows who cut the first bootleg trails. By definition it would have to be after 1937, when the first rope tow was erected on Mt. Mansfield. If charging for a lift lent a certain legitimacy to the sport, it also put pressure on the accessible terrain. Frowned on or not, a little creative pruning mirrored the pioneering hard work that originally cleared the surrounding pastures. Removing a sapling here, some deadfall there, left space for a row of corn. Or, in Mt. Mansfield's case, two turns. Maintain the line for a decade and the result is the Glades off Nosedive, which was cut in the mid-thirties by the Civilian Conservation Corps, or The Miniboos out beyond the gondola. In '40 Mt. Mansfield Lift Inc. erected a 6,300-foot chair lift. A T-bar followed three years later, runs were cut, and skiers in search of untracked snow traversed further into the woods.

K.B. and other Stowe locals have been maintaining trails for more than a decade. Their efforts have obviously benefited the forest; by removing the weak, stunted, and dead, the strong have flourished. And if in the process glades where a ski might be turned suddenly appeared, these selfless laborers kept that secret to themselves.

"We don't get Utah or Targhee's snow . . . but who does?" K.B. admits. "We average 250 inches a season, about the same as Jackson Hole. In the forties when locals first started skiing the Nose Dive they noticed the Glades were gentle and held snow. It was natural they would clear the deadfall there and on trails off the Toll Road that runs back to Stowe. . . ."

"So how many are we talking about here?' I inquire.

"That do the work?'" he pauses. "There's a hardcore bunch that shows on Saturdays during the summer. A lot of people ski these trails. The point is you don't show it to people who can't ski and you don't deliberately confront management."

To ski these glades, first you must find them, then you must be able to pop from edge to edge around 6-inch-thick slalom poles. Stowe's woods also contain certain guarantees. First, if you hook a tip, you're going to wish you hadn't. Next, the snow is as good as you'll find.

Discounting Stowe's famous Front Four—Goat, Starr, Liftline, and National—K.B. feels Mt. Mansfield is as expansive and challenging as anything you'll find in the West. "There are big differences between the East and West," he admits as skiers pound down runs outside the forest. "In the West you get deep powder dumps on open terrain. Here, because, the powder quickly gets skied out on the main runs, if you love the untracked, you've got to ski the trees." And unable to wait any longer, he points his skis at an opening, carves around the

first tree, unweights for the next turn, establishes a rhythm, and flows downhill. I follow, but used to western glades where the trees are three feet thick and thirty feet apart, I can't relax. You've got to stay forward in the Vermont forest, but the sight of tall sentinel birches guarding a 4-foot portal rocks me onto my tails and sends me deep into the pucker brush. In contrast K.B. maintains a metronomic beat until the trunks close behind his flashing purple jacket.

How do you put the proper spin on this hidden run? So far K.B. hasn't said "off the record," but with the silver light filtering through the bare three limbs no one needs to point out that this is one of Stowe's closet skeletons. Despite the possibility of offending all and pleasing none, I wonder how you simply ignore it. How do you not make the connection between this moment and when Stowe was populated by foresters, farmers, inn owners, and a few dozen eccentrics who regularly disappeared into the woods on long hickory skis?

This lone glade is not Mt. Mansfield's only secret. Half-a-dozen others exist between the groomed runs. With cryptic titles like Angel Food, and Red Sled, they add up to a type of alpine underground. Most Stowe locals are familiar with one or two. Few, however, (K.B. included) know about them all. Most of the lower glades would be rated intermediate. Higher up the majority are capital *E* expert. And all but world-class skiers should forget the two suicidal faces near the summit.

If I wasn't sure what to expect from Stowe, I didn't expect this.

After all that's been written about Stowe's venerable past, its halcyon days when Austrian Sepp Ruschp arrived in 1936 to found a ski school with himself as sole instructor (and later to manage the Mt. Mansfield Company); when Lowell Thomas broadcast from The Lodge basement; when the Von Trapps (of *The Sound of Music* fame) settled in Stowe; when the Kennedys, Du Ponts, and Vanderbilts descended en masse for Christmas; when Billy Kidd and Tiger Shaw used the Mt. Mansfield Ski Club as a springboard to the U.S. ski team; I suspected Stowe locals would be an aloof, self-indulgent lot.

Not so General Manager Gary Kiedaisch, whom I meet in Mt. Mansfield's Toll House Restaurant. Kiedaisch was born and bred in the ski business. His parents owned a retail ski shop, he started skiing when he was three, raced in the Junior Nationals and subsequently worked his way up various repping jobs to Raichle/Tyrolia's vice president in charge of marketing. From there he moved to Waterville Valley, where within a year he was recruited to replace Stowe's departing Wayne Hoss.

With snow falling outside the Toll House, Kiedaisch says that Stowe's future lies in a return to its heritage—the lodging, racing, and European influence that once earned it the title of "Ski Capital of the East." It seems that a Boston *Globe* writer was caught in a huge snowstorm. Conditions deteriorated, Route

100 closed, farms were isolated, and power was interrupted. At that point locals contributed beds, meals, and warm clothes to aid skiers who were stranded by the storm. The kicker was that when the plows finally reached Stowe, the inn owners wouldn't accept money for the rooms or board. The *Globe* writer appeared in Boston claiming he had discovered the "Ski Capital of the East."

Forty years later Kiedaisch is still wary of turning Stowe into an alpine K mart. "With a maximum of 450,000 skier days, Stowe isn't trying to compete with Killington," he says, then admits, "when Sepp Ruschp was no longer involved with the company, Stowe lost a bit of magic."

To recapture that magic Kiedaisch believes Stowe needs to hire more Europeans and to host a World Cup race. Both would lend the place an international ambiance. With a goal of attracting a World Cup, the Mt. Mansfield Ski Club has increased its number of races by roughly one third, from forty-two to sixty-four. Besides weekly "Ski Bum" head-to-heads, during '89–'90 these races will include the NORAMS, NCSA Regionals, NCAA Nationals, and The University of Vermont Winter Carnival.

Because Vermont's restrictive covenants make it difficult to throw up tons of lifts or condominiums, Kiedaisch believes Stowe's village atmosphere is unlikely to change. "We're fortunate not to have to build condominiums to pay for lifts," he says.

You can forget finding a Motel 6 in Stowe. Here you either sleep in a country inn or your car. When he's not baking bread, brewing coffee, skiing Mt. Mansfield, or trading puns with his guests, Bud McKueon of Fiddlers Green Inn heads Stowe's Winter Carnival. And then there's Englishman Chris Francis who, during an '83 tour of America with his wife Lyn, fell in love with Stowe. Short on cash and long on the American Dream, Francis used a Visa charge card for a down payment on the old San Souci Lodge.

"Our ignorance was actually a blessing in disguise," he says, glancing around Ye Olde England Inne's immaculate interior. "The first year, when the roof leaked, we shuffled the beds around," he recalls with a laugh. "Then, when the water heater burst, flooding the kitchen, we had the guests wear ski boots to breakfast." Six years, numerous remodels, and uncounted hours of hard work later, Ye Olde England Inne is one of Stowe's finest, and Francis is understandably bullish on America.

"I could have never done this in England. Never."

Down the Mountain Road it's hard to miss the bright lights of the "Spa at Topnotch," Stowe's new four-star, four-diamond, 23,000-foot, full-service, self-sufficient fitness center. After a day spent pounding through Mt. Mansfield's black diamonds you can take a full body massage, a seaweed body treatment, a herbal wrap, or a loofah body polish.

In response to a crack I made about the seaweed wrap, Topnotch's Lynn Cantisano patiently pointed out that the treatment didn't consist of being buried in kelp with a variety of sea critters.

"In fact, you'd probably enjoy it," she said, unaware that if rumors about a body polish or seaweed wrap ever reached Idaho, I'd have to sell my four wheeler, sportarized assault rifle, and leg hold traps and move to San Jose.

Along with the various classes and exercise regimens, Topnotch promotes proper eating habits, with the emphasis on palatable cuisine. The mere mention of dry toast, a leaf of lettuce, and soft-boiled egg is sacrilege. But moderation is a key here; such things as salt, butter, mayonnaise, and Snickers bars are carefully labeled with a tiny skull and crossbones. Working under Executive Chef Louis Cabot (lately of the Four Seasons), Spa Chef Todd Weisz points out that if people are going to make a lifestyle change, they have to enjoy the food. Thus a typical dinner includes swordfish, tomato bisque, fresh salads, and sorbet for dessert.

Topnotch at Stowe, Mountain Road, P.O. Box 1458, Stowe, Vermont 05672, tel. (800) 451-8686. Topnotch is a resort within a resort offering classes in water aerobics, yoga, lower-back strengthening, fly-fishing and Tae Kwon Do. If you can still stand up after all that, there are also nutrition seminars, stress management classes featuring biofeedback and relaxation techniques, fitness assessments and risk analysis, and consultations. Amenities: 111 rooms, TV, telephones, pets accepted, and a 23,000-square-foot destination spa with indoor pool, cascading waterfalls for hydromassage, and full complement of treatment and fitness areas. One package, "Mountain Romance," includes complimentary champagne, strawberries, breakfast in bed, and après massages. Terms: $137.50 per person, per night double occupancy.

The following morning I meet Rich Wiseman in his office behind the Base Lodge. Rich does not look much like a mountain manager. Nor does he act like one. For starters he's too easy going, joking with the lift operators as we load the Mountain triple that runs from the base to the top of Lower Lord, North Slope, and Lower Standard.

"So what's this about 9 feet of snow in December?" I inquire.

Wiseman suspects that a glitch in Champlain's lake effect caused Stowe's early winter bounty. As the chair rises into a flurry of flakes he admits, "It was a fantastic start to the season successive 8-inch dumps right up until New Year's."

"So what happened after New Year's?" I persist.

"Forty-seven degrees and rain, followed by minus twenty degrees." He shakes his head.

"Tough luck," I agree, mildly depressed by this lost image of Shangri-la.

Without Mt. Mansfield's new THC tiller cats the mountain

would have glistened until spring. Using a combination of snow guns and tiller bars, Wiseman's crews brought the mountain back from the dead in three days.

"Everybody thinks Stowe only consists of the Front Four," he continues as the chair climbs between the birches. "But honestly if the Four aren't covered with deep snow, no one skis them. That's where Stowe's backup terrain, the North Slope, Lord, Standard, Nosedive, and Sterling come in." Once we unload, he leads me down North Slope's fall line rollers back to the triple.

Stowe's reputation as an experts-only mountain overlooks the intermediate terrain a resort must have if it is to survive. On the next run we are alone on Lower Lord. With the towering hardwoods casting long shadows across the wide trails, we ride from edge to edge, ignore the threatening overcast, and openly congratulate ourselves for being cagey enough to catch first tracks.

Falling away to the left of the Lookout double, Hayride combines a fine pitch, consistent snow, and regular grooming. The lowering clouds reduce visibility, and we ski down to the Forerunner quad, which rises 2300 feet in less than ten minutes to the Octagon Restaurant. Because the Forerunner crosses three of the Front Four, if you're so moved you can check out the conditions before committing. Today the Four are covered with X-rated bumps—small, hard, and fast—and Rich and I take one look and drop down Nosedive.

Prior to 1965 Nosedive had seven turns, which were subsequently reduced to three. Now at night the cats reduce the upper section to a fine crystal base. On a typical day, the snow gets skied off to the sides, the bumps build, and experts resort to skiing the chancy line next to the snow fence where the boldest of the bold dive down the final icy pitch to skier's right. From that point on Nosedive widens and the pitch decreases, giving all but beginners a chance to strut their stuff.

Between Nosedive and the gondola a new lift will create additional intermediate terrain and eliminate something of a skier's void—no lifts, no trails (unless you count those maintained by K.B. and crew). Wiseman says that because of environmental studies and Vermont's restrictive permits, the lift is still not expected until 1992 or so.

Stoweflake, Mt. Mansfield Road, Stowe, Vermont 05672, tel. (800) 782-9009. Amenities: fireplaces in rooms, TV, phones, restaurant on premises, indoor pool, 4 miles from slopes, Jacuzzi, sauna. Terms: $96 double occupancy.

Fiddlers Green Inn, Mt. Mansfield Road, Stowe, Vermont. 05672, tel. (802) 253-8124. Amenities: original structure built in 1820, traditional ski lodge, complimentary hors d'oeuvres, 2 miles to mountain, warm setting, gracious hosts. Small but comfortable rooms. Terms: $40-$60 per person, breakfast and dinner included.

Ye Olde England Inne, Mt. Mansfield Road, Stowe, Vermont. 05672, tel. (802) 253-7558. Amenities: English atmosphere, Laura Ashley decor, close to Stowe, Dickens Room restaurant, reading rooms, Jacuzzi, 6 miles from Mt. Mansfield. Terms: $68–$95 per person modified American plan, or $80–$125 per double bed and breakfast.

Green Mountain Inn, Stowe Village, Mt. Mansfield Road, Stowe, Vermont. 05672, tel. (800) 445-6629. Amenities: included in Natonal Registry of Historic Places, private baths, cable TV, phone, canopied beds and period furnishings, restaurants, library, and spa (whirlpool, steam room and Jacuzzi), 7 miles from slope. Terms: $100 double occupancy.

Mount Mansfield Resort, P.O. Box 1310, Stowe, Vermont. 05672, tel. (800) 253-4SKI. Amenities: Ski-in ski-out, Toll House Restaurant, Fireside Tavern, full health club, TV, phones, Jacuzzis. Terms: $109 double occupancy.

★

Mansfield's gondola rises to the Cliff House, the mountain's onslope gourmet restaurant. Too often onslope gourmet means a tablecloth on the Formica and French mustard on the cheeseburger. At the Cliff House, the views are spectacular and the food's worth a try.

Off the gondola, Perry Merrill offers a combination of changing pitches and fresh snow. Named after the onetime head of the Vermont Forest Service who co-opted the Civilian Conservation Corps into cutting the Bruce Trail and Nosedive, it serves as a fast cruiser back to the gondola base. The weather is starting to fall apart, and after a run down Gondolier, which follows the lift line, we catch the free shuttle over to Spruce Peak. Because it receives less pressure than Mansfield, Spruce Peak's four lefts and eleven named runs offer great soft-snow skiing off Sterling, Main Street, and Smugglers. To that end, slopes have been re-contoured and brush-cleared. Riding the Big Spruce double Wiseman tells me Stowe and Smuggler's Notch (which can be reached by a short traverse of the top of Spruce Peak) share a reciprocal one-run ticket.

A warm wind is kicking up, the snow has softened, and the intermittent flurries are a few degrees short of sleet. The chairs are banging into the standards, and on top Wiseman radios back to close the chair. We take one slow run down Sterling and call it a day.

During dinner at the Stoweflake Inn that night, owner Chuck Baraw casually mentions that he is planning to compete in a mountain bike race. Over the tournedos and cabernet he tells me, "You look in pretty good shape, and heck, someone'll probably scratch in the restaurant heat."

Baraw's image of overweight chefs puffing around on eighteen-speeds is a powerful inducement to enter, and hesitating only a second I admit, "I'd love to, but unfortunately I don't have a bike."

"A bike," Baraw smiles. "No problem."

That's how I find myself in the men's open surrounded by

twenty-two-year-old cross trainers with oak-thick thighs and icy stares. The other heats were filled, none of the chefs had scratched, and did I want to race or not? What follows isn't pretty. Even if the bike hadn't jumped out of gear, and even if I hadn't crashed twice, I wouldn't have won. If I had cheated I might have stolen third maybe, but no better.

Two days later I find myself at the Winter Carnival's pro-am calcutta, reaching for a cheese cube at the hors d'oeuvres table when Wiseman remarks that the fourth member of Gary Kiedaisch's team has dislocated his shoulder in the bicycle race and am I any good at running gates?

"Terrible," I reply and the next I know I am signing on.

Stowe Winter Carnival's Celebrity pro-am benefits the Copley Hospital in Morrisville, and waiting for my second and last run I watch how the pros skate for the first gate. During our team's first run, Gary Kiedaisch's time is up with the pros. Rich Wiseman is solid, and I am something less than brilliant. You can lie to your friends, but you can't lie to the clock. I skidded, I slid and forgot to skate.

On the next run Kiedaisch is wearing his race face. If Kiedaisch and Wiseman trim a second off their times and I cut two seconds off mine, we might hold on to second. Forget about first. With an eight-second lead and Olympian Moose Barrows as their celebrity, the two University of Vermont racers have a virtual lock on first place.

Kiedaisch's flawless second run cuts a half second off his time, which places him in with the pros. Wiseman goes for broke but stays even, and though I feel like I'm also a second quicker I actually slow down two-tenths. In the end we're grateful for second.

Winter Carnival officially closes at Stowe's Las Vegas Night, where the subdued New Englanders kick off their hiking boots and do up their hair. The women arrive in elegant evening gowns, the men in tuxedos, crowding into the Spruce Base Lodge to play blackjack, roulette, and craps for charity. The object is to win Stowe Dough, which can be used to buy raffle tickets for the grand prize trip to the Bahamas. I see Chuck Baraw and Bud McKueon. K.B. is dapper in a jacket and tie. Gary Kiedaisch gives a short speech of thanks to the participants, organizers, and sponsors. Lynn Cantisano is stunning in a blue evening gown and, standing at the blackjack table hitting thirteen, for a moment I wonder if those seaweed wraps really work.

The dealer gives me a queen. Six, seven, queen . . . 23. I slap $500 in Monopoly money on the felt and wait for cards. So what are my chances of winning the trip to the Bahamas? Not nearly as good as finding powdery skeletons on Mt. Mansfield.

Mr. **Pickwicks Pub Grub,** sandwiches, steaks and English fare, and world-class assortment of beers, 253-7064. **Trattoria La Festa,** Italian specialties and desserts, 253-8480. **Stoweaway Inn and Restaurant,** Mexican cuisine, 253-7574. **Partridge Inn,** seafood and steak, 253-8000. **Stubb's Restaurant,** difficult to describe but interesting, 253-7110. **Isle de France,** classical French, 253-7751. **Ten Acres Lodge,** fresh seafood, lamb and fowl, reservations, 253-7638. **Trapp Family Lodge,** Austrian specialties, dinner reservations required, 253-8511.

★

REST AND RECUPERATION

Though ice cream may seem out of place in the middle of winter, try **Ben and Jerry's Ice Cream** tours on Route 100 just north of Waterbury, Vermont. Starting in 1978 with five gallons of rock salt and an ice freezer, Ben and Jerry's has grown to thirty-four flavors of what *Time* magazine called the best ice cream in the world. Costs $1 for adults, children under twelve free.

If you come to Stowe, don't ignore its network of Nordic trails. Mt. Mansfield's Nordic system interconnects with those of the Trapp Family Lodge, Edson Hill, and Topnotch Ski Touring centers for over 150 kilometers of wooded trails. Beginning in January, races are held each Wednesday evening for diagonal stride and skating. For information call (800) 253-6617.

Because free buses run between Stowe and Mt. Mansfield, transportation is no problem, and shopping for New England antiques, maple syrup, and local crafts can consume a day in itself. During the **Winter Carnival (usually the third week in January),** there is ice skating, costume parades, the Wintermeister Race, Dogsled Races, and Snow Golf. If you need your skis tuned try **Bed Side Tuners** (253-7222), which offers free pickup and delivery, complete ski tuning, and a fresh blueberry muffin for $20.

Finally, dont' forget to take the traverse over to **Smuggler's Notch.** With four lifts, fifty-three trails, and 2610 vertical feet, it complements Mt. Mansfield.

CHAPTER 20

MOZART AND MOGULS NEAR SALZBURG, AUSTRIA

THE BEAUTIFUL THING ABOUT MOZART IS HE'S been dead so long that the copyrights to his music have all expired. Thus, anyone who needs a classical score to sell cars, cosmetics, deodorant, or pizza pie can pillage his collected works. This is not a complaint. For the majority of baby boomers who were weaned on top 40, a classy commercial might be their only exposure to Mozart. And if a teenager thinks the *Jupiter* Symphony was composed as background music for a red sports coupe blowing through fall leaves, it's far better than his not hearing it at all.

That's one extreme. The other is Mozart Week in Salzburg, Austria. During this late-January series of symphonies and operas, if you even intimate a relationship between Mozart and, say, a gourmet chicken pot pie, the crowd assembled in the Mozarteum's Landestheater will hoist your head on a lance. Do Salzburgians take Mozart seriously? Glancing around the sea of black tuxedos, sequined evening gowns, diamonds, and opera glasses, I would say that is something of an understatement.

The Landestheater is one of three concert halls in Salzburg's Mozarteum, an institution dedicated to her most famous son. With its baroque ceiling, crystal chandeliers, and muted strains of the orchestra, the Landestheater may seem a bit far afield from skiing, but Mozart week coincides with midseason at the surrounding ski resorts of St. Gilgen, Saalbach-Hinterglemm, and Badgastein. Running for nine days in late January, this music festival offers a rare chance to nurture both body and soul. Using Salzburg as a base, it's possible to ski until the lifts close and still make it back in time for the St. Martin's of the Fields presentation of *Il Re Pastore*.

Lufthansa, (800) 645-3880, offers nonstop flights from New York to Munich as well as early morning Frankfurt/ Munich connections from New York, Chicago, Boston, Atlanta, Miami, and six other U.S. gateways. Lufthansa's reservation system allows hotels and cars to be booked at the same time as the flight. A car is a must to make this adventure work, and the major car rental companies have offices in the Munich airport.

Salzburg is one of Europe's most beautiful cities. At night, with Hohensalzburg Fortress, St. Peter's Church, the Archbishop's Palace, the University of Salzburg, and all the squares and fountains illuminated in its Old City, it is little wonder they call Salzburg the "Rome of the North."

Excavations have revealed that this city of 140,000 was built on a Stone Age settlement. The Romans used the site as an administrative center, but it was St. Rupert the Bishop who reestablished a monastery in the seventh century and thus created a foundation for an archbishopric with authority over the dioceses of Bavaria. The descendent bishops of Salzburg were responsible for Salzburg's sovereignty in the thirteenth century and its later growth to an independent imperial principality.

Salt built Salzburg. Called "White Gold," it allowed Archbishops Wolf Dietrich von Raitenau, Markus Sitticus, and Pâris Lodron to underwrite the seventeenth- and eighteenth-century architectural revival that characterizes the city today. Following the Napoleonic Wars, Salzburg lost its independence and was annexed by Austria in 1816.

Sitting in the Landestheater, I've been told I am lucky to get tickets to *Il Re Pastore,* even though, when compared to *Don Giovanni* or *The Magic Flute,* it is one of Mozart's lesser-known works. Written when he was only nineteen, the story concerns Aminta, a young shepherd who is picked to succeed the Emperor. To become Emperor, Aminta must leave his beloved Elisa. The story addresses issues of duty to state, duty to self, and the power of love. If it lives up to even two of the three, I suspect that *Il Re Pastore* will be somewhat frothy for my tastes.

One thing about this opera, however, does intrigue me. After writing the United States off as bastion of hard rock, country rock, rap, and heavy metal, I discover that three of the leading roles are sung by Americans. Born, bred, and educated in the U.S.A., it takes guts to tackle Mozart in Salzburg. Imagine Japanese rockers doing Springsteen in New Jersey!

Angela Maria Blasi, who was born in New York and educated at Loyola University in Los Angeles, plays Aminta. Sylvia McNair, who received a master's in music from Indiana University, sings Elisa. And Jerry Hadley of Bradley University in Illinois plays Alessandro. Once I discover they are Americans, simple patriotism forces me to take sides. Seated in the Landestheater and surrounded by Salzburg's bejeweled first families, I truly hope Maria, Sylvia, and Jerry are brilliant.

The lights dim, conductor Neville Marriner enters to polite applause, the curtains come up, and the first incandescent

notes descend upon the audience. In that first brilliant passage, though I am neither given to public displays of emotion
nor fluent in Italian, tears spring from my eyes.

For the next two hours I forget that the leads are sung by
Americans, the conductor is British and I haven't slept in thirty-
six hours. All that exists is the music, alternately soaring to the
baroque ceiling and whispering down the aisles, touching the
audience with its simplicity and its power. And when the curtain finally falls, I'm one of the first on my feet, applauding
until my hands grow numb.

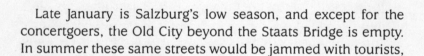

Brochures with concert schedules and artists are printed
almost a year in advance and along with tickets can be
obtained from the International Stiftung Mozarteum,
A-5024 Salzburg, Schwarzstrasse 26, Postfach 34 Salzburg, Austria.

Late January is Salzburg's low season, and except for the
concertgoers, the Old City beyond the Staats Bridge is empty.
In summer these same streets would be jammed with tourists,

but now the venerable Stiftskeller St. Peter Restaurant, Mozart's birth house, Salzburg's museums, and the numerous shops on Getreidegasse near the main Staats Bridge belong to the locals. The gilded shop signs seem to demonstrate that the city has changed little since the small Kapellmeister walked these same streets.

(Salzburg is also known for *The Sound of Music*. In the U.S. there's no doubt about whether Mozart's piano concertos or "Edelweiss," "I Am Sixteen," and "Doe a Deer," put Salzburg on the map. Tours can be booked through the local tourist office, but be prepared for a bus full of your fellow countrymen, exclaiming, "Honey, get a shot of me standing where Maria kissed the Baron.")

Following her marriage, Mozart's sister Nannerl moved to St. Gilgen, located 20 miles from Salzburg on the forested north end of Lake St. Wolfgang. When you dream of small Austrian ski resorts, you probably see St. Gilgen. Driving down the narrow cobblestone streets, I park in the town square—which is dominated by a statue of Mozart—and grab my skis.

At the tourist office, I am introduced to Hilde Pfeffer, who has been persuaded to show me the Zwölferhorn. Along with her husband Norbert, Hilde was born and raised in St. Gilgen and now owns Sport Noppi—a local ski/clothing shop. We shoulder our skis and walk to the Seilban gondola, which climbs to the Zwölferhorn's 5000-foot summit. Hilde tells me that torrential Christmas rains were followed by a snap freeze. Bad enough that the rains washed out the Zwölferhorn's flanks, she continues, but since then the temperatures have stayed below freezing, and now the upper slopes are boilerplate.

"It is very very hard," she says, shaking her head in apology. With the tram, a single chair, a T-bar and two rope tows, the Zwölferhorn's uphill capacity is not large. "It is a shame there is no new snow," she adds, stepping into her bindings. "Because St. Gilgen doesn't have crowds, it lasts for days."

Except for a broad sugary lane the cats have tilled down to

the single chair, the Zwölferhorn is glazed blue steel. Still, the vistas remind me that I am skiing in Austria, and by rolling my knees and accentuating my edge sets, the conditions are not that bad; not packed powder but still skiable. Hilde used to race, and for most of the day we alternate runs on the shadowed north faces down toward Lake St. Wolfgang with runs into a sunlit west bowl, from where we can see the distant 9840-foot Hoher Dachstein and the 8000-foot Bleikogel. In spite of the hard snow, she shows me gladed meadows until the lifts close. Then we ride the gondola back down.

"Now we must have a pastry at Nannerl's," she tells me. "Mozart's sister once made this her home," she adds as we climb the stairs to the front door. Inside, antiques, sepia photos, and portraits of Mozart and Nannerl fill the room. For the next half hour we relax in the cafe's welcome warmth before I return to Salzburg for a performance by Salzburg's Marionette Theater.

Created by Herman Aicher, who directed the company for more than half a century, and now run by his daughter Gretl, tonight the Salzburg Marionette Theater is presenting *The Magic Flute*. Composed in Vienna for Emanuel Schikaneder's Theater auf der Wieden during the late eighteenth century, *The Magic Flute* offered a radical mix of freemasonry and fairy tale that would eventually become a cornerstone of German opera. If the plot is at best complex, before the first act is over the marionettes' strings have disappeared, their fixed expressions are now animated, and the opera's small scale is no longer noticeable. The marionettes project an element of magic, and when the curtain comes down and the players take their bows, the applause swells for Tamino the prince, Pamina the princess, and especially for Papageno the bird catcher.

At 11:30 A.M. the following morning I am seated in Mozarteum's Grand Hall, waiting for the Mozarteum Orchestra to enter. The atmosphere is more relaxed than the opening night at the opera—blazers and ties, skirts and sweaters are acceptable for this matinee featuring Mozart's Concert for Piano and Orchestra (KV 271). Conductor Hans Graf strides quickly to the podium and holds his hand out to soloist Maria Tipo, who enters stage left, bows to the audience's applause, and takes her seat. A pause and the music lifts gloriously into the hall.

Maria Tipo curtsies to the enthusiastic applause, and after a short intermission the concert continues with the ballet from the opera *Idomeneo* (KV 367). Why Mozart? How did the son of a Salzburg musician come to serve as a synonym for musical genius?

Wolfgang Amadeus Mozart was born in January of 1756 in a three-story house on Getreidegasse in Salzburg's Old City. His father Leopold was an assistant conductor to the court of Archbishop Sigismund of Salzburg. A superb musician and composer in his own right, Leopold had already begun to instruct his seven-year-old daughter Nannerl on the piano. What he did not anticipate was that three-year-old Wolfgang would began to imitate her at the keyboard. One afternoon, when Wolfgang was barely four, he penned his first concerto for the clavier, and the following year, at one of his father's afternoon rehearsals, he insisted on playing second violin—an extremely difficult part that he carried off without a flaw, all without having had a single lesson. If this sounds like fiction, it was confirmed by the court violinist Wentzl and the trumpeter Schachter, two eyewitnesses who also played in the trio.

A deeply religious man, Leopold regarded Wolfgang's extraordinary precocity as a gift from God, a trust to be received and nurtured. If the world owes a debt to providence, it is equally indebted to Leopold for directing and encouraging that talent. Leopold understood that in order for Wolfgang to succeed, to find a position and to help defray the bills, of which there would be many, he needed exposure. When Wolfgang was six Leopold took both children to Munich, where they played for the Elector Maximilian Joseph III

The children delighted Maximilian, and in years afterward

they performed for royalty throughout England, Italy, Poland, and France. If Mozart's childhood was filled with triumph, his twenties were marked by defeat and frustration. Though he continued to tour and compose, he failed to secure a position worthy of his talent. Under increasing pressure from his father to return to Salzburg, he accepted an appointment to the court of the Archbishop Sigismund of Salzburg. The archbishop, however, treated Mozart like an indentured servant, and the young composer soon departed for Vienna.

The movie *Amadeus* did much to familiarize America with Mozart's life in Vienna. He had been there only a short time before he married Constanze Weber, who would bear him two sons.

Though chronically short of funds, during his years in Vienna Mozart created some of his most brilliant work—*The Marriage of Figaro, Don Giovanni, The Magic Flute,* and the Jupiter Symphony. And yet, even as his genius flourished his health declined, and while working on his famous Requiem he died in 1791. He was buried in an unmarked grave by a drunken laborer who two days later could not even remember where the body was. As is often the case, it was only after his death that the world realized what it had lost.

The doorman at the Hotel Pitter tells me that Saalbach-Hinterglemm is 86 kilometers (53 miles) through Germany. I never confirm the mileage, because early the following morning I make a wrong turn at Lofer and am halfway to Kitzbühel before I realize my mistake. Kitzbühel is also within 50 miles of Salzburg, which makes it a reasonable option, but I'm expected in Saalbach. Returning along the winding mountain road through Weissbach and Saalfelden, it is 10 A.M. before I reach the end of this steep canyon, where I am met by Wolfgang, who taught skiing for eighteen years and now works for the local tourist office.

"So, how many days will you stay?" he asks.

"Only until the lifts close," I reply.

With 175 hotels spread around Salzburg's city center, the trick is finding one within walking distance of the Mozarteum. Rooms generally get cheaper the further you go from the center, and if you're comfortable with local buses and don't mind a bathroom down the hall, you can save a significant percentage on accommodations. Postal codes are all A-5020 Salzburg, Austria.

Pension Wolf, Kaigasse 7, tel. 84-34-53. Amenities: private showers and baths, telephones, central heat, parking. In the Old City a half block from Mozart Platz. Terms: room and breakfast $51–$70.

Pension Am Dom, Goldgasse 17, tel. 84-27-65. Amenities: shower and bath, telephones, elevator, central heating, on the corner near Residenz Plazt. Terms: room and breakfast $63–$75.

Hotel Pitter, Rainerstrasse 6, tel. 84-78-571. Amenities: telephones, radios, elevator, restaurant on premises, garage, near Mozarteum. Terms: room and breakfast $44–$55.

Osterreichishcer Hof, Schwarzstrasse 5-7, tel. 72-5-41. Amenities: showers and bath in room, telephone, restaurant on premises, elevator, parking, cots for children on the Salz River facing the Old City. Terms: room and breakfast $75–$110.

The Salzburg Tourist Office also offers a package that includes four nights, three Mozart performances, city tours, an excursion to Berchtesgaden, as well as various welcome and good-bye gifts for $424 per person in a double room. Prices, options, telephone, addresses, tours and maps can be obtained through Stadtverkehrsburo Salzburg, Auerspergrstrasse 7, A-5024 Salzburg, reservations: 72-34-52 or 34-67, or the Austrian National Tourist Office, 500 Fifth Avenue, New York, New York 10110, tel. (800) 223-0284.

★

"Just that long?! Surely that is not nearly enough. . . ."

Taking a triple chair out of Saalbach, I begin to understand his concern. Spread between the mountain towns of Saalbach and Hinterglemm, the ski area is enormous. With thirteen distinct peaks serviced by sixty lifts capable of handling 57,000 skiers per hour, Saalbach-Hinterglemm calls itself the Ski Circus and is slated to host the '91 world championships. On the chair Wolfgang says that if we hurry, we'll be able to ski one run in each area.

Wolfgang weighs over 200 pounds and uses that size to advantage. To warm up we follow the wide, groomed Bernkogel run down to Bernalm, where we catch the triple to the summit. From there we follow a short run through the trees down to the Reiterkogel double and for the next half hour we yo-yo up and down this sunlit face. The conditions range from packed powder in the shadows to corn in the sun, and I let my 207s run, swing away from the piste and dive through bump fields until Wolfgang cautions me against the rocks.

"It has been a bad year for snow," he explains. No less than prophecy, for as we drop toward Hinterglemm the snow thins, the sun cancers spread, and toward the end we are forced to jump a fence and ski through a backyard in order to reach the street. "You wish to eat now?" Wolfgang inquires.

"*Nein,* I wish to ski now."

"*Sehr gut,*" he nods and leads me to the base lift. With so little time, we take two double chairs to the summit of Schattberg West (Shadow Mountain) and from there follow an intermediate run through open snowfields to Schattberg East to a rolling traverse through the trees that drops 4.5 miles to the Vorderglemm valley floor. From there we cross to the 5900-foot Kolmaiskopf tram. On this sunny south face we make two runs before Wolfgang suggests we stop for one beer.

One beer turns into a full lunch, after which we traverse between the alms—Maisalm, Panoramaalm Asteralm, and Turneralm—perfectly groomed runs that swing toward the valley floor.

On the final run Wolfgang stops above Saalbach, where he pulls out a trail map and points to the runs we've skied. The trail map is twenty pages long with three double-page fold-outs. "Now, is all this clear?" he inquires. "Yes? Good, now I buy you a hunter's tea before your return to Salzburg."

I never find out exactly what a Jäger tea contains. Some potent mix of 80-proofs, hot water, and cinnamon that hits me like a semi in the oncoming lane. By heading south on Highway 311 through Zell Am See (another Salzburg ski area) to Werfen and Highway 159, I manage to cut an hour off the drive. Even so I barely make it back in time for an evening's concert by the Vienna Philharmonic.

Held in the Festspielhaus, which was originally the Archbishop's stable, tonight's concert has been sold out for weeks. Rows of seats rise steeply from a broad center stage. This is not the time or place to make a definitive fashion statement: dress runs to black dresses, pearls, shawls, black suits, tuxedos, and dark ties. Around me conversation is subdued as members of the audience discreetly study the program notes and copies of the score.

Minutes later the orchestra enters, followed by conductor Leopold Hager, who bows to the applause, raises his baton, and begins the Symphony in G Major (KV 318). It is a fantastic performance, and within the swirl of strings, woodwinds, and horns, Mozart once again lays claim to Salzburg's heart. To my right a young man follows the score on sheet music, while two rows in front another man tentatively draws an invisible violin bow. When the orchestra rises for intermission, the usually subdued Austrians shake the rafters with their applause.

A grand piano is wheeled to center stage and soloist Yasuko Matsuda appears to prolonged applause. Squaring herself to the Steinway, she begins the Concert in C-Major for Piano and Orchestra (KV 467). Watching her fingers move across the keyboard, I realize that even though Mozart was born in Salzburg, performed throughout Europe, and worked and died in Vienna, there is a universal miracle in his music. Japanese, Chinese, Russian, African, or American, it touches a chord in us all. For that reason the symphony seems brief, and I exit through the massive doors and wander along Gstättengasse next to the cliffs below the Spielcasino, where a line of discos and night clubs blare New Wave into the street.

Salzburg is known for excellent restaurants, coffee houses, and beer halls. Try **Zwettler's**, 84-00-44, on Kaigasse for Salzburger and Austrian specialties. **Zipfer Bierhaus**, 84-31-01, on 12 Sigmund-Haffner-Gasse for Salzburger/Austrian.

Midrange are the **Eulenspiegel** and the **Stadtkrug**, 78-2-44, on 20 Linzer Gasse, for Salzburger/Austrian specialties. The **Pitter** of Rainerstrasse, 78-5-71, for Austrian specialties. The **Winkler Hotel**, 73-5-13, on Franz-Josef Strasse, offers a terrace and Salzburg and Austrian specialties.

More expensive are the **Monchstein Schlosshotel**, 84-85-55, Salzburger/Austrian/Music, and **Zum Mohren**, 84-23-87, on 9 Judengasse, offers typical Salzburg and Austrian menus. The **K and K**, 84-21-56, Waagplatz 2, offers fresh fish along with a spectacular view of the city.

Disco? I don't think so. And so I continue along until I reach the Old Grenadier. I have been told the Grenadier is one of Salzburg's hot nightspots, but the door is closed, and through a window I see young Austrian MBAs in three-piece suits trying to hold the attention of statuesque blondes. Though it might provide an insight into Salzburg's nightlife, I've seen it before and cross the Salz to the shadowy Mirabell Gardens where locals stroll arm in arm, their conversations muted by mists that eddy among the bare winter trees.

Sixty-two miles south of Salzburg, Badgastein was a ski resort before it was a spa. Radon gas and hot water were the big draws here. Seeping into old gold mines, it's the same stuff you put those cardboard testing kits in the basement for. In Badgastein they take a somewhat different view of radon, spread cots in the shafts, and treat everything from rheumatoid arthritis to bronchial asthma.

Taking the treatment is supposed to expose you to a year's worth of normal background radiation, but if radon's contra-indications are still making front-page news, Badgastein, with its five-star and five-story hotels clinging to the steep eastern flanks of the Stubnerkogel, has evolved into a major ski area. People still flock to Badgastein to take the cure, some floating in the radon thermal waters, far more arcing down the steep, sunlit faces above the village.

I like Badgastein. There is a grandeur about its Victorian hotel façades rising beneath the 8800-foot Kreuzkogel, a sense of the Grand Tour in its shops. It is past 10 A.M. when I board the Stubnerkogelbahn (gondola) that climbs to the 7366-foot Stubnerkogel summit. Seated in the gondola is a Stubnerkogel ski school instructor named Werner who spent six months restoring furniture in San Francisco and now speaks nearly unaccented English. With a few hours between clients, he is out freeskiing and suggests I come along.

Like the rest of Europe, Badgastein is showing the effects of drought. Rocks have surfaced in the centers of heavily trafficked runs, and so we ski the sides—first down the sunlit Glackfeld toward the town below, where we skirt the small moguls that appear whenever the trail narrows. Born in Badgastein, Werner has skied the Stubnerkogel for twenty years and now threads the open lanes between the pistes. Like St. Gilgen and Saalbach-Hinterglemm, its seven lifts access an enormous amount of open terrain, and though the snow is hard, images of knee-deep fluff and low visibility keep flashing in front of me. It's obvious that with new snow the Stubnerkogel would offer world-class powder skiing.

Badgastein is a part of Ski Gasteinertal, an enormous ski interconnect that links four villages, six major peaks, fifty lifts, and 155 miles of groomed pistes. Here you can travel 6 miles down the Gastein valley without ever taking your skis off. Werner and I follow the wide, groomed Angertal for 7 miles down to the Angertal triple lift. One run, seven miles! Dozens of others drop toward the valley, and we ride back to the summit then jump on the Jungeralm, a broad solar bowl where short mogul fields are connected by groomed pistes. Here we can let our skis run, let the wind wrap around our glasses as we bank off frozen drifts and carry air off deceptive transitions. At the bottom Werner must hurry to catch a class and tells me, "Well, I enjoyed this. For an American you do not ski badly. . . ."

"And for an Austrian, you don't counter rotate." I return his compliment and watch while he tucks off the summit.

With little time to spare and the base area devoid of snow, I take the tram down and connect with a cab across the valley to the 8100-foot Graukogel. With its north-facing runs cut through the trees, two chairs, and T-bar, the Graukogel is the smallest of the five surrounding areas, but it also offers some of the most challenging terrain. American Buddy Werner nearly won the Graukogel's FIS downhill. He was well ahead but carried too much speed into the final compression and fell within sight of the finish.

I only have a couple of hours left until the lifts close and ski the intermediate Standard to the base, return to the summit, and ski Standard again to the T-bar. And then, feeling something akin to the courage needed to sing Mozart in Salzburg, I point my skis down the FIS Rennstrecke course, carry my speed over a transition onto a steep face, and am suddenly carrying far too much speed. I try to bleed some of it off, but the snow is hard and I hit the compression, feel my skis squirm, and almost go down.

So the courage ebbs as quickly as it comes, and as I link precise round turns down the final face I remember when I was twelve and advertisers used Mozart to sell peanut butter. Back then the music made the sandwich taste that much better and now, looking across the valley at Badgastein and the late-afternoon light on the Stubnerkogel, I think the same can be said about skiing.

Travel light. Fly into Salzburg, use the late morning and afternoon to tour the city and book a performance the first night. Days 2 through 3 stay and ski in Saalbach. Back to Salzburg that night for a performance, then out to Badgastein for days 4 and 5. Return to Salzburg that night for a performance, ski St. Gilgen day 6, and return to Salzburg for a performance that night. Also tour Salzburg that night. Catch the morning flight out on day 7.

REST AND RECUPERATION

The problem with Salzburg is it tempts you to forget skiing entirely. There is so much to do, so many museums, gardens, parks, the cathedral and university: it simply overwhelms you. For that reason I would suggest a tour of the city with an expert on Mozart who can point out sites that were important to his life and work. These include the house where he was born and the Festival halls. With prior arrangements it is possible to go backstage with the marionette masters. For information: Salzburg Tourist Center, Auerspergstrasse 7, A5024 Salzburg, (0662) 8072-0.

There is superb shopping on Getreidegasse, and don't miss **St. Peter's Cemetery,** the **Meribel Gardens** (even if they are subdued by winter), the **Hellbrunn Castle,** or the **Hohensalzburg Fortress**.

If you have time, try **Badgastein's** thermal curative springs, the **Felsenbad** (swimming pool) and, depending on your feelings about radon, the **Böckstein** healing gallery.

With the university located near St. Peter's, the Festspielhaus, and Mozart's Birth House, much of Salzburg's nightlife occurs in the **Old City**. Nightclubs on Gstättengasse are built into the cliff face: the **Spielcasino** offers gambling and magnificent city views, while other clubs are back across the Staats Bridge on Linzergasse. **"Sound of Music"** and city tours can be booked through the tourist office. Try **The Old Grenadier,** 84-37-18, Ursulinienplatz 2, for an upscale Salzburg watering hole. Also the **Montevideo,** 73-6-62, on Steingasse 3, the Bazillus, 71-6-31, on Imbergstrasse 2A, and the **Saitensprung,** 71-06-82, on Steingasse 11.

★　　　★　　　★　　　★　　　★

ABOUT THE AUTHOR

ANDY SLOUGH STARTED SKIING AT SIXTEEN AND *has quested after perfect snow on spectacular mountains ever since. He has been writing about skiing and other sports for fourteen years for such publications as the* Washington Post, *the* Miami Herald, Sports Illustrated, Outdoor Life, Outside, Powder, Cross-Country Skier, *and* Condá Nast Traveler. *Working as a Contributing Editor for* Ski *magazine affords him frequent trips to the slopes of Canada, South America, New Zealand, Europe, Russia, and much of the United States. He lives in Sun Valley, Idaho, with his wife and two sons.*